International Institutions
at Work

International Institutions at Work

Edited by
Paul Taylor and A.J.R. Groom

St. Martin's Press, New York

© Paul Taylor and A.J.R. Groom, 1988

All rights reserved. For information, write:
Scholarly & Reference Division,
St. Martin's Press Inc, 175 Fifth Avenue,
New York, NY 10010.

First published in the United States of America in
1988

Printed in Great Britain

Library of Congress Cataloging in Publication Data

ISBN 0-312-02096-1

Contents

*Chapters based on lectures delivered at the NALGO international conference 1981.

Introduction

This volume is intended to introduce those who are relatively unfamiliar with the work of international institutions to this aspect of relations between states. Hence it gives less attention to theoretical aspects of the subject and rather more to practical matters. In particular it describes the role that is played by international institutions in a number of specific areas of activity chosen because they seem, in the late 1980s, to be both important and interesting.

Indeed the activities discussed in the central part of the book are a comprehensive range of those which are now fundamental to the security and survival of individuals. Everyone depends ultimately in some way upon the maintenance of orderly economic relations between states, upon the attainment of a satisfactory range of human rights — be they in the workplace or more generally defined — upon the provision of effective relief in the event of natural or man-made disasters, upon responsible defence policies, upon the maintenance of effective global communication, and, indeed, upon a wider recognition that there is a real and common heritage of mankind. In all of these crucial areas international institutions have an important role to play, and we have attempted to describe and explain this.

The book is not, however, a progress report about the development of global welfare. The stress is upon the way in which international organisation has been arranged to respond to the various problems, to take advantage of opportunities, and upon the approach which has been followed by specific institutions. Of course, quite often the arrangements have not been well conceived, or have become inappropriate, and the approach has sometimes been clumsy and ineffective. These issues are considered. Nevertheless, the volume is about organisation rather than policy.

In the first part of the book the pattern of development of international institutions is considered, and an attempt is made to indicate the capacity of international institutions to formulate distinctive international positions. Their staffs develop viewpoints of their own and they do not in their day-to-day activities simply follow the instructions of national governments. There are, of course, arguments about whether the state remains the primary actor in international society, or whether in contrast there is now a 'world society', which are not considered here. The point needs to be conveyed at the outset, though, that institutions can indeed make a difference: they need to be studied.

In the concluding section of the book are chapters on the reform of the system. The editors are grateful to Maurice Bertrand for his help in summarising his excellent 1985 report, *Some Reflections on Reform of the United Nations*, which he prepared for the Joint Inspection Unit, and for agreeing to its inclusion. Not only does it include a number of insightful proposals for reform, but also a penetrating account of the problems in the system and the way in which it now works. The most recent — in 1987 — developments in the attempt to reform the system, particularly those resulting from the financial crisis brought about by the withholding of funds by the United States, are discussed in a concluding chapter. The sense is conveyed that, after a period of resistance to change, a new phase of adjustment has begun. It remains to be seen whether this will be as far-reaching in its implications for relations between states as that which saw the initial creation of international organisation in the nineteenth century.

The editors wish to thank the members of the team for their excellent contributions. The volume has its origins in the proceedings of a conference which was organized by NALGO at Trinity Hall, Cambridge in 1981, which were edited by Paul Taylor and published in 1982. Versions of several of the chapters included in that volume are included in what follows and the editors are grateful to NALGO for their permission to use this work, and to the contributors for updating and, in some cases, extensively rewriting their earlier efforts. A number of chapters were, however, especially written for the present volume, and the editors have indicated where this is the case. We are sure, however, that our colleagues would agree that extensive rewriting is often as arduous a task as creating anew, and we are equally grateful to all contributors.

If this volume succeeds it will have introduced the reader to the work of international institutions and demonstrated both their value, their potential and their deficiencies. It will also have generated a curiosity about some of the less straightforward theoretical and philosophical aspects of the subject. These are considered in a companion volume, *Frameworks for International Cooperation*, to be published shortly by Pinter Publishers. Indeed, ideally the present book and its companion should be read together.

In both volumes, however, there are bibliographies which it is hoped will guide the interested student through this considerable literature. The editors and the contributors will be content if this has been an encouraging start.

Finally, we are, as ever, in the debt of our secretaries Elizabeth Dorling in Canterbury and Elizabeth Leslie in London.

Paul Taylor
A.J.R. Groom
Canterbury and London, October 1987

Part I

The emergence and capacity of international institutions

1 The advent of international organisation

A.J.R. Groom

The purpose of this book is to focus upon international organisations at work. It cannot, of course, be comprehensive, but it can throw light upon a remarkable new and growing phenomenon — the work of international organisations. It is a new world in that only a century ago there were relatively few international organisations and any conception of a system or network was at best embryonic. Now international organisations touch upon the daily life of all but a few of the world's population to the extent sometimes of making a difference between life and death. There have been many theories to categorise and explain the different modes of organisation but this volume contents itself with a selective description of some aspects of international organisations at work and an analysis of such phenomena.[1] But contemporary international organisations cannot be fully understood without some reference to their philosophical and historical background. Hence the need to touch upon attempts to organise European and, later, world society and the bodies to which such attempts have given rise. It concentrates more on the embryonic period of organisation rather than its maturity since that, after all, is the subject of the rest of the volume.

The study of international organisation

Why should international organisation be studied? Students of social science are committed to the quest for an empirical theory of behaviour. They assume that behaviour is patterned and that hypotheses can be formulated and tested against the data in such a way that behavioural regularities can be identified. Probabilities can be assigned to the regularities and the propositions can then be offered as grist to the decision-maker's mill — whether for good or for ill. However, social scientists are, at present, far from being able to offer the sort of empirical theory of behaviour to which they aspire. Any avenue of research towards such a theory is, therefore, worthy of consideration and the study of international organisation has, prima facie, much to recommend it.

Any patterned interaction between actors is likely to give rise to some form or degree of organisation. The organisational form is thus the indicator of a system of transactions. Of course, the institutional form may be very incomplete in its reflection of what actually happens and of what is important; nevertheless, it is a starting point. It is a signpost to activity. But an organisational form may be more than this. It can also be the forum for decision-making and thus a nodal point in a network of transactions. Since the study of decision-making — that is, the process by which demands are made, goals are determined, roles are allocated, means are devised and feedback is assessed — is crucial in any attempt to describe and explain behaviour, the institutional aspects of organisation become of great interest and relevance. While a patterned interaction between actors or a set of transactions can be analysed on the basis of the actions of its constituent parts, the whole may be greater than the sum of the parts. There may be a systemic input arising from the interaction of the parts over time in an organisational framework which can best be captured through study of the activities taking place in and about its institutional form.

In this volume there is a special interest in institutions as well as in the general problems of organisation. Organisation in a general sense refers to the fact that there is a system, that behaviour is not random and that it has an element of repetition which creates additional systemic inputs, while institutions or, in our case, international organisations are the structures within, by and through which the systemic functions are performed. The structural functionalists have suggested usefully that all organisations are alike in that if they are to survive they must perform four functions at least to a minimal level. Of course, whether a particular organisation is to survive, be it the Ford Motor Company, the International Olympic Committee or the United States is, in essence, a value question. It is, however, dependent upon the organisation's ability to maintain an effective channel of communication internally and externally with its social and physical environment, its ability to integrate its sub-units, its engendering of loyalty, that is of 'we feeling', and its capacity to generate enough self-knowledge to enable it to steer in the sense of being able to set goals reflecting preferred values. These functions remain constant although the structures or institutions through which they are performed vary widely according to circumstances. Consider, for example, the differences between the structures for governing the village of Blean in Kent and those for governing a village in the highlands of Papua New Guinea, but the same functions have to be fulfilled, albeit in very different ways. The four functions are a useful conceptual framework as institutional forms can be related to each of them, but they are not the only way of relating organisation to institutions. Institutions are a framework within which transactions may be facilitated, coordinated and even stimulated. In none of these roles is the influence of the institutional framework entirely absent. Structural variables always have some influence on behaviour. Thus institutions are both evidence of, and actors in, systems of transactions.

These reasons for the study of organisation and institutions apply at any systems level or in any functional dimensions. The concern of this volume is with world society and in particular with 'international' organisation and institutions. The academic study of International Relations has been characterised by the use of the state as the basic unit of analysis and the dominant school of thought for the last three decades or more has been the power or 'realist' school. However, this paradigm has been under challenge for some time in both its principal aspects — the state as unit of analysis and power as the dominant characteristic of relationships. The use of systems analysis and a greater emphasis given to legitimised relationships do not imply that state actors and power politics are unimportant, but merely that they are not axiomatic. Nevertheless, the choice of unit of analysis is crucial, since it influences the questions asked, the organisation of data and the findings. There is a need, therefore, to know what unit of analysis is appropriate for which cases. The tremendous range of international institutions which taps the real world in so many of its facets may provide evidence that will help to clarify the appropriateness of competing paradigms. These, then, are some of the reasons why international organisations and institutions should be studied. Are they also the reasons why they are in fact studied?

Presumably even if international institutions and organisation were of no conceivable interest to social scientists there would still be a statistical distribution of people who would be interested in them for their own sake in the same way that there are people who collect milk-bottle tops. Their interest would be relatively pure, idiosyncratic and unsullied by notions of general utility. The second reason why scholars study international organisation and institutions is rather more important: the study of international relations grew in part out of the study of international organisation and institutions and has been greatly influenced by it. Along with the diplomatic historian, the international lawyer, with a penchant for institutions, and the progressive rationalist social engineer and institution-builder of the late nineteenth and early twentieth centuries were the progenitors of International Relations as it emerged as an academic subject after the First World War. Courses on 'international institutions' or 'international organisations' have been the staple diet of students ever since — often to their chagrin. However, the study of international organisation has changed. While old-style legal and historical analyses still exist and do, indeed, have their place, the study of international organisation has entered the main stream of International Relations. Evidence of this can be found in the changing type, subject matter and methodology of articles in *International Organisation*, the leading journal in the field.

It is a sad fact that the study of international organisation and institutions is in a serious imbalance. There is very little to be found in the (Western) literature on the notion of organisation *per se* as applied to world society. Yet anthropologists and sociologists (not to mention social anthropologists!) have for long been active in this area. While their findings may not be automatically transferable to a different systems framework, their paradigms are, to say the least, of great heuristic value. The literature on bureaucracy is burgeoning, and it could make a greater impact on the study of secretariats. A central concern of social science as a whole is decision-making, but the functional elements in the decision-making process such as the articulation of demands, recognition of demands and so on have not been used often as a framework for comparative analysis. Instead there is a plethora of general works of a descriptive, historical or legal bent on the United Nations or the League of Nations and a growing body of case studies of aspects of those bodies and certain alliances and efforts at regional integration, often of considerable methodological sophistication. To this can be added a monograph or two on each of the major Specialised Agencies but very little on non-governmental organisations with the exceptions of the International Committee of the Red Cross and the League of Red Cross Societies. This, of course, is to be expected in that the state-centric power paradigm of International Relations has been the dominant one, but if the pluralist model or multi-centric transactions model of world society is to be fully assessed then the focus will have to shift somewhat to transnational NGOs. Here is a fertile area for aspirant doctoral candidates (and others) and their labours might add greatly to the choice of appropriate paradigms and the posing of relevant questions.

If what has been studied is but a part of the whole, has there been an equal degree of complacency in research methods? The response to this questions is somewhat more encouraging. The greater epistemological awareness, the increasing sophistication in research techniques, the growing meticulousness in the observation, collection and analysis of data which have characterised the study of international relations generally in the last three decades have not been without their effect on research on international organisation and institutions. Again, the empirical evidence for this can be found in the pages of *International Organisation*, *World Politics* and the *Journal of Common Market Studies*. For example, the analysis of records is no longer confined to a historical interpretation of resolutions and speeches. Analyses of voting behaviour that would have been virtually unthinkable by hand can now be undertaken using a computer. But voting and speech-making may tell little, or even be misleading, about who was the principal lobbyist for a resolution and the intensity of commitment to it, so techniques of field investigation and participant observation have been developed. Moreover, simulation offers the possibility of experiment through manipulation and replication and, while problems of validation of findings with the real world are considerable, such research has proved useful. The thousands of international institutions also provide scope for aggregate data analysis.

There is no empirical evidence to suggest that there is any methodological 'royal road' in the study of international organisation and institutions and it would therefore be wise, in its absence, to adopt an open-minded attitude. Just as research using traditional methods can be second-rate, misconceived or badly executed, so can research using more scientific methods. The study of international organisations and institutions is, therefore, useful but fraught with difficulties as well as being too frequently devoted to areas which do not always reflect developments in the real world. But what do we mean by an international organisation or institution?

International organisations: definition and type

There is no universally accepted definition of what constitutes an international organisation although we are within sight of a working consensus among both practitioners and academics. There is agreement, for instance, to exclude non-Western types of organisation, such as Chinese secret societies, or the transnational networks associated with Islam, such as those between fundamentalists, notwithstanding their important impact upon behaviour at many levels, including globally. That an organisation is an international institution if its membership, its finance and its field of operation involves three or more countries is a minimal description that would command a good deal of support.[2] If its membership is based on states as in the case of states members of the United

Nations then it is properly international, whereas if its membership is not based on states or territories then it is transnational. This is the case of the Association of Commonwealth Universities which is made up not of national branches from India, Britain or New Zealand but of individual universities wherever they might be located.

There are many ways of categorising international organisations. The more conventional distinctions are between governmental, non-governmental and business; universal, regional and selective; general and specialised; and between forum and service functions. Intergovernmental organisations (IGOs) are generally considered to be those established by treaty, while international non-governmental organisations (INGOs) are those not so established unless they are profit-making whereupon they qualify for the delightful acronym of BINGO (Business International Non-Governmental Organisation). The number of such organisations is rising rapidly and so is the membership of each organisation, although that of IGOs is likely to be finite since the number of states is not likely to pass the 200 mark in the foreseeable future. There are at present some 400 IGOs and ten times as many each of INGOs and BINGOs. But many of these organisations are hybrids. Membership of the International Labour Organisation (ILO) is formed of states, but they are each represented by three separate delegations of government, management and labour reflecting the predominant mode of capitalist organisation at the time of the ILO's foundation after the First World War. IATA (International Air Transport Association) is the principal body of the world's airlines, but many of these are state-owned, and supposedly profit-making, which blurs IATA's categorisation as an INGO.

The distinction between universal, regional and selective also presents anomalies. A universal organisation presumably contains all members of the set, but even the United Nations has not quite achieved that goal. The Swiss people, despite their government's urging to the contrary, have reaffirmed their wish not to be a full member; nor is the Korean peninsula represented in part or as a whole. Regional bodies have as a basis some notion of a geographical area be it Africa, the North Atlantic or Europe, but they are often far from complete. The OAU (Organisation of African Unity) does not include South Africa, nor NATO (North Atlantic Treaty Organisation) Ireland, and 'Europe' frequently means no more than a truncated part of Western Europe. Selective member organisations, as such, are fewer in number and tend to be transregional. The Commonwealth, the Non-Aligned Movement and various Islamic bodies are of this nature, whereas many BINGOs are transnational.

Organisations which are termed 'general' have a competence in a wide range of topics — political, economic, social, cultural, security — such as the UN at the universal level or the OAU at the regional. Specialised Agencies may also be universal, regional or selective in their membership but they share the characteristic of specialising in one function as in the UN family of Specialised Agencies such as FAO (Food and Agriculture Organisation), WHO (World Health Organisation) or WMO (World Meteorological Organisation). Such agencies may be predominantly forum or service organisations. In the case of forum activities the principal purpose is to serve as a meeting place for a discussion of principles but not to negotiate the detailed design and undertake the execution of programmes. That is the service function, although many institutions serve both purposes. But the balance is important for it is likely to have consequences on the budget, size and style of the secretariat and the characteristics of the decision-making process. Service organisations tend to have larger budgets and secretariats than forum organisations and their decision-making processes are more likely to emphasise problem-solving by experts than bargaining by diplomats.

These categories of international institutions are among those commonly used. But they are of themselves of little interest. A typology is only useful for a purpose and that purpose has to be reflected in a particular question. It is therefore for each student to formulate his own typology as a function of his interests and needs. But the world of international organisation is both vast and important. It is, moreover, in urgent need of greater exploration especially in its non-governmental aspects both in the Western mode of organisation and, tantalisingly, beyond. The Western mode of organisation normally includes a constitution, although a body as large (some fifty states) and as important as the Commonwealth manages very well without one — or, at least, not a written one. The constitution sets out the rights and duties of the members, both individually and collectively, and specifies the constituent parts of the institution. The normal pattern is to have a general assembly of all members which meets annually, or at some other regular interval, between which a smaller body acts on behalf of the assembly. This role is supplemented frequently by a secretariat whose potential may be great or restricted to mundane administrative tasks. Finally, there is a budget since some collective costs will be incurred inevitably and they must be covered — usually by some system of assessment of the members. The variations in this theme of constitution, assembly, council, secretariat and budget are many, but it remains the normal basis of a Western-style international institution.

The emergence of international institutions

International institutions are a recent phenomenon. If we restrict ourselves to the modern period and to 'Western' types of international organisation and institutions then our period of interest begins in 1815 and comes to maturity in another great burst of 'peacemaking' and systems organisation a little over a century later. Since then there has been almost continuous expansion in variety, numbers and functional dimension of institutions with the exception of the period of the Second World War. This tremendous growth is the outcome of two major events which left their mark on nineteenth-century Europe — which, with the Americas, is the birthplace and still the centre of the international institutions world — and, more recently, on much of the rest of the world. These two events were the Industrial Revolution and the French Revolution.

Prior to the industrial revolution trade had been relatively limited in Europe, since there was no mass production, exceedingly bad and dangerous communications, and small markets. The agrarian and industrial revolutions changed all that. The flow of goods, services and people increased many-fold both within Europe and between Europe and other continents. The world became a more integrated place as a Euro-centric, but quasi-global, economy came into being. Of course, it was not an equal development and much of it took place within the boundaries of particular political units which sometimes defended themselves against transnational systems with devices such as tariffs, yet the contrast with the previous state of affairs was clear enough. However, the French Revolution and the activities of Napoleon accentuated a trend in the opposite direction.

The French Revolution was many things, but not least it was a great harbinger of nationalism in Europe. The emerging middle class in France, seeking to carve out for themselves a place in a society which was dominated by a dynastic regime presiding over a 'feudal' structure of aristocrat and peasant, helped to create a revolutionary situation which boiled over in 1789. No longer would a family, such as the Bourbons, define the political unit; rather it would be defined by the nation under the aegis of, and in many ways thanks to, the middle class. In the nineteenth century the middle class waged a nationalistic struggle against both aristocratic universalism and proletarian internationalism and won. In this they were given a good start by the French Revolutionary and Napoleonic armies which, while often welcomed as liberators, outstayed their welcome by becoming imperial reorganisers. They evoked a nationalist response from Spain to Russia and their institutional reorganisation gave a fillip to nationalism in Italy and elsewhere. Whereas in the war at the beginning of the nineteenth century it was possible for a group of gentlemen-scholars from London to travel to Paris to confer with their counterparts there, in the war at the beginning of the twentieth century it would have been inconceivable for them to have travelled between London and Berlin. State boundaries were no longer permeable and loyalty to nation displaced loyalty to class or to interest in the event of a clash of loyalties.

While the Industrial Revolution tended to promote transnational integration on a largely anational and aterritorial basis, the growth of nationalism and the creation of nation-states served to give state authorities a gatekeeper function in the movement of goods, services, people and ideas. Both freedom of movement and control were desired: were they incompatible? In absolute terms they were, but in practical terms international institutions provided a means by which an acceptable balance could be achieved. The purpose of international organisation was to promote freedom of movement under a set of rules which were negotiated by governments, governmental bodies or national branches. The effects of the French and Industrial Revolutions were reconciled by the development of international institutions to bring about controlled integration. As the Euro-centric world became both more integrated and more nationalistic international organisation became more evident. The development of international institutions was slow, with only a handful of IGOs and INGOs in the first half of the nineteenth century, but by the last quarter of the century it was gathering momentum. It has grown apace since both in numbers, in variety of form and in functional dimensions.

The philosophical spirit of the times

International organisation and institutions are also an indicator of modernity. Both the French and Industrial Revolutions — and subsequent events — were powerful indicators that men were not prepared to accept either their social or physical environments as given. Such environments were manipulable, albeit clumsily and with little effective control. The possibility of change conceived and initiated by man was evident and in many instances it required some form of international organisation. It is no coincidence that the 'take-off' period for international institutions was also marked by a great flowering of rationalist and progressive thought. Western European elites were, as the nineteenth century progressed, growing increasingly confident of their ability to control their physical environment through the application of science. The rational, scientific approach which appeared to be vindicating itself in science might, therefore, also be applied to social problems: hence the original 'functional' institutions.

There also developed among the major powers a self-confidence in their ability to define, elaborate and impose upon international society a code of acceptable behaviour. Such a code was, of course, primarily designed to facilitate great power relations and to promote their interests. A general spirit of optimism can also be seen in the procedural innovations in international institutions, in attempts to civilise the conduct of war, in the opprobrium poured on secret alliances and in the efforts to improve standards in such areas as conditions of work or the control of the traffic of drugs or of women.

The general atmosphere of exhilaration, achievement and the prospect of further success gave rise to a belief in progress. Progress was to be based on reason and its achievement would lead mankind to unity. It was assumed that what was reasonable was self-evident to any fair-minded man or group, given full information, and that such values were shared values, at least in the civilised world. To the extent that reasonable behaviour was not forthcoming, it was due to a lack of civilisation, an autocratic system of government or to deviancy. If the cause was lack of civilisation the British were prepared to shoulder the 'white man's burden', the Americans to accept their 'manifest destiny' and the French to embark upon a *mission civilisatrice*. There was no room for pluralism: rationality was defined by white, Christian, imperialist capitalists who sought to impose their conception of it upon the rest of the world. The imposition of European rationality and civilisation provided an ideology for colonialism even if it was not its only motive. Should the 'cause' of non-rational behaviour, so defined, be an undemocratic form of government then the situation was more delicate. The notions of liberty, equality and fraternity were far from being universally accepted throughout Europe. Indeed, it was not until the Western democracies had defeated the more autocratic central powers and lost their Eastern ally in 1918 that Woodrow Wilson was able to state his ideas at full force. Even then he was constrained by foot-dragging on the part of Clemenceau and Lloyd George, among others. The argument ran that man would behave rationally if he was allowed to do so and that he would pursue his individual interests in a reasonable manner from the point of view of the collectivity. A democratic structure would therefore allow public opinion to influence governments and to ensure their good behaviour. But democracy could only flourish in homogeneous nation-states so that in order to make the world safe for democracy it was necessary to make it national. In the event that the government of a democratic, national state transgressed the norms of reasonable behaviour then it would be rightfully treated like the autocratic, revolutionary and colonial states and be subjected to sanctions until it reverted to non-deviant behaviour.

The doctrine of nationalism was the reason why no great desire was evinced for a universal state. Sanctions were to be the preserve of a league of separate nation-states, a specifically international institution, not of a world Leviathan. Schiffer points to a further reason why this was so from the progressive point of view as

Unity achieved among free peoples by the community of natural interest and by the general recognition of common standards of reason and justice seemed to be superior in dignity to unity effected by a powerful world government. The ideal situation which progress was expected to bring about could satisfy men's desire for living in separate independent groups, as well as their longing for a sphere of reason, liberty and justice beyond the states.[3]

It is in man's insistence upon the state and yet his anxiety about adjusting the circumstances of its existence in international society that we find a further reason for growth of international organisation and institutions. How, in fact, did they set about trying to achieve this?

A hundred years of organisation

The modern state system is often said to have finally crystallised about the time of the Congress of Westphalia in 1648. By then it was evident beyond repair that the notion of Christendom had evolved into a secular Europe of separate sovereign powers increasingly willing to claim, and able to command, the loyalty of their 'subjects' who were soon to become 'citizens'. Unity had become diversity and thenceforth international organisation was one of the ways in which a new integration was sought in diversity. However, it was not until an equally famous post-war Congress, that of Vienna in 1815, that international institutions of a modern type emerged. The institutions of the next century can be categorised as either political or functional institutions. The main political system was the Congress and, later, the Concert system, as subsequently modified by the Hague Conferences. At the same time a network of functional institutions began to spread. The trends begun then are still with us.

The meetings of the Congress and the Concert system were relatively frequent with only thirty-six years of the century ending without meetings.[4] But the system remained relatively unorganised and there was in no sense a legal obligation to hold meetings or to attend them. Nor was there a set pattern to the form of the meetings or to the types of decisions taken and their execution. It was an extremely pragmatic system, but the great powers certainly regarded it as an institutional mechanism and it was used as such. It was hierarchically organised, being conceived by and for the benefit of the great powers as a class, for the discussion of matters of general interest for the European system. It was the forum within which they could regulate their own problems and impose their will upon the small powers. In so doing the great powers tacitly acknowledged that each would submit its own policy to the scrutiny of its peers and respond to their judgement in a satisfactory manner. This was particularly the case until the Congress of Paris which ended the Crimean War when major changes were legitimated by the collectivity of great powers. Thereafter changes occurred outside of a great power consensus and were made to stick through the operation of self-help in the context of the balance of power. But if the balance of coercive forces which underpinned a particular settlement changed, it was a powerful incentive for the beneficiaries of change to attempt to capitalise upon their new-found power. The absence of legitimacy therefore made the system more prone to violent upheaval.

In general the process was a reactive one: a Congress or Conference would be called if one or more powers held their interests or that of the system as a whole to be threatened by the policy of another power or by internal developments within a state. The power invoking it could not claim any special advantage for itself. But the whole process was effective only when the plaintiff was upheld by the other members. In such a case there was an overwhelming alliance in face of which it was deemed prudent by the offending power to back down. Smaller powers were invited to play a role if the great powers thought that the matter at hand warranted it, but for the most part the small powers were the objects of the Congress and Concert system rather than participants in it. More generally so far as politics was concerned, the Congress and Concert system was, in Sir Alfred Zimmern's words, 'the medicine of Europe rather than its daily bread'.[5]

Thus, in the latter half of the century, worked a classical balance of power system. It was founded upon the inability of any one actor to overthrow the system and a clear recognition on the part of all that submission to rules that were far from onerous was better than the risk of attempts at hegemony or anarchy. Power politics were the mores of the system, both between the great powers individually and between them collectively and other actors. And within that conflictual framework there was a limited degree of cooperation. It worked because there existed a certain common rationality, trusted information, common perceptions and, until towards the end of the period, a high degree of tactical flexibility. It was also firmly rooted in an environment — political, social, economic and physical — which changed rather slowly. When the change became sufficiently great — particularly in regard to nationalism in the multi-national empires of Eastern and Southern Europe and industrialisation in the United States and Japan — no amount of tactical flexibility could do more than stave off collapse. A balance of power system frequently has no notion of systemic adaption other than collapse: there is no creative path to an open future. The collapse of 1914–18, in the progressive–rationalist climate of the early twentieth century, gave an added impetus to other notions which had already surfaced in the Hague system.

The Hague system was an attempt to modify and potentially to transform the Concert system. The power politics basis of the Concert system could not be abolished overnight but, given the progressive–rationalist assumptions of the time, the balance of power system to which it had given rise could be made safer. In fact, the Hague Conferences of 1899 and 1907 were exercises in arms control, that is, they sought to make a system of power politics safer in the context of the developing technology of war. Some, at least, had a conception of changing the nature of war through incremental reforms. The means used in the Hague system to achieve this end involved measures to contain the arms race, the codification and amelioration of the law and conduct of war (along with the Red Cross) and procedures for the consideration of political questions. In contrast to the Congress system, the Hague Conferences included the small powers not only of Europe but also of Latin America as a matter of right.[6] Thus, substantively, the Conferences initiated a concern — arms control broadly defined — that has remained with us to this day as well as establishing an institutional form, since the Conferences may be taken as the beginning of a general assembly of the world to consider political questions of mutual concern — a function continued in the Assembly of the League of Nations and the General Assembly of the United Nations. Moreover, they were the setting in which parliamentary diplomacy first began to emerge both in its procedural and tactical aspects. If the Congress and Concert system was, with its successors, the Leagues's Council (and Conference of Ambassadors) and the UN's Security Council, the institution of the great powers, the Hague Conferences, and its successors, were that of the small powers. The relationship between the two was not, and is not, always easy.

The successor institutions to the Hague Conference developed a general competence for all matters of political interest and are not merely bodies which respond to political crises as and when they arise. Such a competence was first mooted in the Hague meetings and in the Americas. They gave rise to the expression of an embryonic will to provide a permanent order for the rational promotion of good relations between states as well as the peaceful settlement of disputes. The social engineers and the lawyers set about drafting an institutional framework and code to enshrine the liberal–progressive–rational principles to which all reasonable men would adhere. They did not progress far in the two Hague Conferences, but they started the foundations on which, to no small degree, the League of Nations was built. In this work the growing network of functional institutions was an inspiration, example and guide.

The functional institutions of the nineteenth century have been classified into three categories by Paul Reuter:[7] International River Commissions, temporary quasi-colonial organisations and administrative unions. Moreover, they existed both in Europe and the Americas. The Central Commission of the Navigation of the Rhine is one of the oldest international bodies in continuous existence.[8] It is an example of Reuter's first category which was envisioned in Article 5 of the Treaty of Paris (30.iv.1814) and Articles 108–16 of the Final Act of the Treaty of Vienna of 1815. It is a classic example of a functional institution in that the convenience of all demanded that the great multinational rivers of Europe be given a single regime. The second category contained arrangements

whereby a group of European states undertook jointly to provide or supervise
services that non-European authorities were unwilling or unable to provide, such
as in public health or finance, in areas such as the Ottoman Empire, its successor
states and China. They were on the whole short-lived, although in part they seem
to be the precursors of the League's mandates and the UN's trust territories and
temporary administrations such as in West Iran and *de facto* in the ex-Belgian
Congo. Of far greater importance are the administrative unions dealing with
such matters as telegraph, posts, rail transport, and economic, scientific and
social affairs. Many of these bodies still exist, after a suitable metamorphosis
to take account of the changing environment. Their significance is collective,
cumulative and continuous. Moreover, they were and are supplemented by an
even greater network of international non-governmental organisations.

A similar process is evident in Latin America where the first rather abortive
efforts at international organisation occurred at the Congress of Panama in 1826.
However, while in Europe no single power had a preponderant role in the
process of organisation, the United States aspired to such a role in the Americas
to the chagrin of some Latin American governments. From 1889 Conferences
of American States were held regularly, which gave rise to numerous conventions, not all of which were implemented. By 1901 a Commercial Bureau had
emerged which, in 1910, became the Panamerican Union, dealing with cultural,
administrative, technical and political matters. With the Monroe Doctrine
concerned with high politics, the Panamerican system combined elements of the
Hague system with administrative unions. Of particular note is the participation
of most of the American states, including the smaller ones, even in political
questions. Moreover, the institutions were permanent and sought to anticipate
and to resolve difficulties and not merely to act as a conduit through which the
major powers could impose their will. It was thereby a direct forerunner of the
League and Americans, both North and Latin, had a major role to play in the
philosophy behind and in the actual drafting of the Covenant. The extent to
which non-governmental organisation grew in the Americas is more difficult to
discern.

By the time of the First World War a recognisable system of organisation and
its attendant institutions had emerged. It encompassed both Europe and the
Americas, political and functional questions, governmental and non-
governmental activity. As Claude summed it up:

The Concert stood for compromise; the Hague stood for regulation; the public international unions stood for cooperation. The cooperative concept is not essentially idealistic
or altruistic. Its focus is on the satisfaction of needs, which demands not so much the
sacrifice of sovereignty as the utilization of the resources of sovereignty to create institutions and methods capable of supplementing the functional activity of national governments. The creation of public international unions was indicative of the recognition of,
and of a groping after compensation for, the functional inadequacy of sovereignty.[9]

In terms of need, ideological conviction and experience the prerequisites for
expansion were present and the building of a new world after the Great War was
the pretext.

The beginning of twentieth-century institutions

The First World War resulted in a marked decrease in the Eurocentricity of the international organisation and institutions system. The effect was not felt immediately due to the isolation of the United States, the exclusion of the Soviet Union and the slow growth of nationalism in the colonial world. The mondial nature of the new system was not predicated upon the First World War, since the growth of the United States and the decline of colonialism were independent factors leading to the decrease in Euro-centricity. Nevertheless, there was a new globalisation in intent and, to a lesser extent, in activity. The institutions of the League were universal in aspiration and centralised in structure (unlike the UN which stresses coordination, decentralisation and regionalism). The League mechanisms strove to promote economic and social welfare throughout the world and to provide a means to settle disputes. Indeed, as it failed in the latter it endeavoured, through the Bruce reform proposals, to strengthen the former in a vain attempt both to find a new role and to stave off the Second World War.

The collapse of the European system in the First World War was interpreted by the rationalist–progressives as a vindication of their analysis. While their belief in the automaticity of progress could not be other than shaken by the carnage of 1914–18, they argued that the war was due to the failure to apply rationalist principles to political problems. Autocratic polities pursuing their private interest were to blame. Democracy, national self-determination and institutional mechanisms for the peaceful resolution of disputes based on procedures acceptable to all men of reason and goodwill were the remedy. War no longer served a social purpose at an acceptable cost: the mechanisms of the League were both to obviate it and to act as its functional equivalent. They would obviate it by replacing power politics with the development of economic and social programmes designed to increase the welfare of all through cooperation. A network of cooperative relationships would thus give rise first to interests in common and, eventually, to common interests, so that power politics — the pursuance of selfish interest with no regard for and to the detriment of the interests of others — would become a thing of the past and democractic world opinion would ensure that this would so remain. The mechanisms of the League would also act as the functional equivalent of war in that there were elaborate procedures to handle disputes in a manner any reasonable man would accept as satisfactory — and sanctions to endorse them in cases of non-compliance.

The rationalist–progressive belief in the essentially cooperative nature of human relations is well founded theoretically in that objective conflict exists only in cases in which an actor has a single value or goal.[10] In practice, however, parties to a conflict may see their relationship in objective terms, and experience has shown that it may take much more than institutional tinkering to induce them to accept the subjective and erroneous nature of their view. Institutionalised mechanisms for the settlement and resolution of disputes are, of course, important, but only if they are legitimised by the actors in the system. The dreams of the well-meaning international lawyer and the hopes of the progressive–rationalists gave rise to the League of Nations Covenant in which such dreams and hopes were tempered, both in the drafting and in later practice, by the wiles and ways of old-style political practitioners. In short, the League system was too out of touch with political reality seriously to be able to influence it in the peaceful processing of demands for change. It was seen too frequently as the instrument of the victors and it sought to preserve their values against any potential threat from the defeated or revolutionary states. The institution of colonialism was woven into its very fabric, although the mandate system brought a notion of international responsibility in such matters. Nevertheless, it was an instrument within which conflict could be waged rather than resolved; it was a weapon of the victors and the status quo powers, yet outside the sphere of political disputes it met a felt need and its social and economic activities thrived and prospered.

The League of Nations

The League of Nations nevertheless provides a benchmark in the evolution of international organisation. Moreover, it should not be seen merely as the idealistic outcome of the dreams of utopians. President Wilson of the United States was a practical politician who had struggled to the top of two greasy poles — the presidencies of Princeton University and the United States — and he had a clear idea of what the world required, which reflects an intellectual heritage that may be out of fashion, but that is not dead.

Wilson, like many others, proceeded from the assumption that the people were essentially peace-loving since it was they, not the military, economic, political and social elites, who bore the greatest burden in war. Men lived for years in trenches in the most ghastly conditions, prior to slaughter, while Paris, Berlin or St. Petersburg danced. World public opinion needed therefore to be allowed to play its full role as a buttress for peace. This could be done in several ways, the first of which was to make states democratic in the sense of being government of the people, for the people and by the people. But it was recognised that nationalism was an important social and political force that had been one of the root causes, as well as the trigger, of the First World War. It was therefore necessary to make nations into states. Democracy and nationalism were seen as preconditions for peace, particularly if the secret diplomacy of Europe's chancelleries and royal families gave way to 'open covenants, openly arrived at'. Democracy and nationalism would also allow the fundamental harmony of interest to be revealed as the reasonable and rational voice of the people was heard. In international society, then, just as in national society, there was likely to be a high degrees of consensus. In the new conditions international politics would be like national politics, but writ large. However, even within national societies there were a small number of deviants who, if they threatened the well-being of that society, had to be restrained forcibly if they refused to accept the judgement of the democratic courts safeguarding the people's will. And so it was at the international level with the League of Nations.

The League of Nations was given a range of functions which collectively would militate in favour of a peaceful world. It embraced the notion of collective security rather than the balance of power which had been found wanting in 1914. In 1914 the rigid system of alliances, and the attendant military preparations together with the autocratic systems of government of Austria–Hungary, Germany and Russia, combined to give an inexorable quality to the unfolding tragedy as other statesmen observed, seemingly helplessly, as the lights went out over Europe. The system had lost its tactical flexibility: it was also doomed in its 1914 configuration because no amount of tactical diplomatic manipulation could cope with the decisive impact that the growth of nationalism was likely to have upon the long-term viability of most of the major actors of the system — Austria–Hungary, Russia and the Ottoman Empire in the short run and the colonial multinational empires of Britain and France in the future. Only the United States, Italy, Germany and Japan of the major powers were likely to remain unscathed. In short, a balance of power system was unlikely to be able to cope with systemic change. Collective security, which was less adversarial in nature and was not directed against a third party not a member of the system, became the central plank of the security platform.

Collective security is based on the idea that a number of states (in the League the ambition, but not the practice, was universality) came together freely, and in full knowledge, to elaborate a set of rules which henceforth will govern their behaviour (including rules on how to change the rules). They do so in the belief that there is a basic consensus on fundamental values among them which, when they have been articulated in the code of behaviour, will thereafter be defended, if necessary by collective action eventually of an overtly coercive nature. Once the pact is made each member will be constrained to keep it by all of the others. Any deviance from the rules creates an automatic alliance against the male-factor. Security is therefore collective.

In the case of the League, although the aspiration and rhetoric were evident, the practice was not. Neither Germany nor the USSR were allowed initially to join the League, nor were they allowed to participate in forming the consensus. They were both treated as pariah states and acted accordingly with a due sense of grievance. Germany was demilitarised and stripped of its colonies and suffered the humiliation (as it saw it) of territorial adjustments to its disadvantage in Europe not to mention crushing economic reparations. Russia, in the course of its metamorphosis to the USSR, was the target of military intervention by fourteen states and vilified in an intoxicating mixture of shock, horror and fear. The United States participated fully with France and Britain in what was not a collective consensus but that of the victors. However, then it withdrew into isolation forsaking the League, although its policy was such so as not seriously to embarrass or undermine the League. Japan and Italy, although victors, did not enjoy the full fruits of their victory. Japan, in particular, was the victim of a rankling humiliation when it was refused a racial equality clause in the League's Covenant, whereas Italy felt aggrieved because Britain and France were well served with the spoils of victory and Italy did not have its territorial ambitions fulfilled. Collective security, therefore, did not fail in the context of the League; it never started. But the institutional framework of collective security was created and, in part, it established some useful precedents.

The architects of the League were not under the illusion that the harmony of interests was automatic in practice. Even within a broad framework of value consensus, disputes could arise. Such disputes were meat either for judicial or political settlement and the League had an elaborate set of dispute-handling procedures. These procedures had some modest successes in the 1920s, but these merely masked the absence of that basic consensus which alone would permit their long-term efficacy. Thus, when the value dissensus gave rise to fundamental disputes in the 1930s, the institutional arrangements proved to be irrelevant, an embarrassing encumbrance or mere propaganda weapons since the conditions for their proper management had never been established. But at the same time ideas of collective security were thereby brought into derision. It is therefore worth stressing again that collective security did not fail; it was never tried. The founders of the League never addressed the fundamental issue which was not the institutional form but how to elicit that value consensus without which all else was futile. The people, democracies, nation-states were not invariably, or at least immediately, peace-loving. That social relations are in essence non zero sum is a proposition that can be defended at the level of basic needs, if not at that of wants, but the ways in which practically to explore this notion in the real world are only now being addressed in international politics.[11] However, no matter how much anguished, bitter or derisive comment the essential failure of the League's dispute-handling mechanisms incurred after the Manchurian crisis, the framework conceived by the architects of the League had other fundamental aspects.

The League's founders were practical politicians. They were well aware that the world did not stand still and so a consensus once achieved had constantly to be renewed as circumstances changed. Indeed, stability required change of an adaptive sort to an ever different environment. This change would be of two sorts: not only was it a question of dealing with difficulties, problems and disputes as they arose — the negative side of peaceful change — but also, more positively, of taking advantage of opportunities as they presented themselves more effectively through joint action or even of collective measures to engender such opportunities. Peaceful change was as prominent a maxim as any in the League's repertoire. The prime organ through which this would be achieved was the League's Assembly which, for this purpose, especially aspired to and required that universality it was denied. It was a role that was also taken up with gusto by some of Europe's brightest young men in the League's Secretariat. Although the Secretary-General of the League had seen his powers whittled down in successive drafts of the Covenant — at one point he was to have been Chancellor in the continental sense — and the first incumbent, Sir Eric Drummond, was imbued with the ideas of neutrality supposedly second nature to the British civil service, nevertheless the League idea drew young men of vigour, talent and enthusiasm into its services in its early years in a remarkable camaraderie united to make the world a safer and better place. As the Secretariat expanded, as elements of it become more politicised, for example Italian nationals being pressured by Mussolini, as the initial *élan* was dissipated in a necessary bureaucratisation, some, but by no means all, of this was lost.

Secretariats were also important in developing the third element of the League framework — that of functional cooperation or a working peace system.

Administrative unions set about further developing such functional ties either directly under their own auspices or by example and encouragement elsewhere. Although the League was conceived as the coordinating agency for such bodies, those that preceded the League were jealous of their independence and others, such as the International Labour Organisation, quickly asserted their autonomy. Coordination, to be effective, had to be voluntary and since the will was absent a *modus vivendi* emerged. There were advantages to this in that there was less of a risk that the fledgeling League would be overwhelmed by a wide range of demanding tasks, and later when the League was in difficulties in political matters, functional cooperation was able to develop, to a certain degree, outside this context. Nevertheless, in narcotics, refugees, technical assistance, intellectual cooperation and the like the League developed a significant role. Its success was commented upon favourably by the Bruce Report at the end of the 1930s and its expansion was recommended. This expansion occurred in the context of the UN, but it is worth remembering that the League laid the foundations of a working peace system which, while not always without conflict and certainly not a panacea for conflict resolution, nevertheless has a potentiality for security by association and which has some properties as a conflict prophylactic.[12]

The management of disputes together with the promotion of positive peaceful change and functional cooperation were the major practical aspirations and partial reality of the League's work. The object of this was not to achieve a world state for which the League as then constituted was an embryonic world government. Cooperation rather than integration was the goal — a cooperation which brought peoples and governments together fructuously while not denying their diversity, their individuality and, above all, their sovereignty. The goal was to be the fostering of fraternity and community at a global level — it was after all a *league* of nations that was being called into being. And it was on the League's chequered experience that the founders of the United Nations had good cause to reflect.

Notes

1. For a more conceptual survey, see A.J.R. Groom and Paul Taylor (eds), 1989, *Frameworks for International Cooperation*, London, Pinter Publishers, which is a companion volume to this.
2. For a discussion of various definitions, see Clive Archer, 1983, *International Organisations*, London, Allen and Unwin, pp. 32–5.
3. W. Schiffer, 1954, *The Legal Community of Mankind*, New York, Columbia University Press, p. 155.
4. See Stanley Hoffmann, 1954, *Organisations Internationales et Pouvoirs Politiques des Etats*, Paris, Collin.
5. Sir Alfred Zimmern, 1936, *The League of Nations and the Rule of Law, 1918–1935*, London, Macmillan, p.78.
6. Inis L. Claude, 1964, *Swords into Plowshares*, New York, Random House, 3rd ed. rev., pp. 25 ff.
7. Paul Reuter: *International Institutions*, 1958, London, George Allen and Unwin, pp. 207 ff.

8. However, it was reduced to two members while Alsace-Lorraine was under German control from 1871 to 1918 and therefore does not qualify under the Union of International Association Yearbooks' coding rules.
9. Claude, op.cit., p. 40.
10. See A.J.R. Groom in Edward E. Azar and John W. Burton (eds), 1986, *International Conflict Resolution*, Brighton, Wheatsheaf.
11. See Azar and Burton, op.cit.
12. For an expansion of the theory of functionalism, see David Mitrany, 1966, *A Working Peace System*, Chicago, Quadrangle, and A.J.R. Groom and Paul Taylor (eds), 1975, *Functionalism*, London, University of London Press.

Recommended reading

Clive Archer, 1983, *International Organisation*, London, George and Unwin.

Inis L. Claude, 1971, *Swords into Plowshares*, New York, Random House.

David Armstrong, 1982, *The Rise of the International Organisation*, London, Macmillan.

F.S. Northedge, 1986, *The League of Nations*, Leicester, University of Leicester Press.

2 The United Nations as a political system

Peter Willetts

Consideration of the politics of international organisations fits into a wider theoretical debate about the nature of the international system.[1] This chapter will take sides in that debate and argue the case for analysing the United Nations as a distinct political system. Traditional questions, about the legal status and the power of the member countries in relation to the UN, do not lead to an understanding of what really happens. Both the formal legal description of the status of delegates to international organisations and the theoretical assumptions of most academic analysts tend to place the United Nations on the fringes of world politics. The legal view of international organisations is that foreign policy is made in the capital cities of the world and that the foreign ministries send out formal instructions which the UN delegates follow. This may be legally accurate, but does not correspond to the actual processes of communication between delegates and their foreign ministries. Similarly, in Realist academic theorising, the United Nations is seen as having little or no 'power' and is only a mirror of inter-state relations in the outside world. F.S. Northedge has put forward clearly this point of view:

The effectiveness of the United Nations. . .does not rest on any intrinsic power within that organisation to effect events on its own account, but on the readiness of member-states. . .to work together for the common good. . .what we conventionally call its will is in fact none other than the joint wills of the states which make up its voting majorities. . . International organisations, in other words, reflect state initiatives rather than determine them.[2]

However, discussion with foreign ministry officials and delegates to international organisations quickly reveals that such a description does not match up to the complexities of the UN system. Not only does traditional theorising deny the role of governmental delegations as distinct actors; it also ignores the presence and the impact of the representatives from non-governmental organisations (NGOs) and secretariats of inter-governmental organisations.

In the academic study of international relations, an alternative to Realism, which may be called the Global Politics approach, has been developing in the last ten to fifteen years. The literature on transnational relations and on bureaucratic politics has disaggregated the state,[3] to the extent that it should no longer be considered a useful concept except in a strictly legal context. The literature on human rights, the environment, population, food supplies, baby-feeding, North–South relations and theorising about political economy has

---

The author wishes to express his thanks to R.J. Vincent for his comments on an earlier draft of this chapter.

raised new issues for study. The literature on regimes[4] and on interdependence[5] has provided new ways of conceptualising global systemic structures. The literature on conflict analysis allows one to study the psychological, social and political dynamics of conflict, bargaining and negotiation, without being bound by relatively static, *ex post facto* power explanations and without being bound to a single level of analysis.[6] Most important of all has been the path-breaking work by Mansbach and Vasquez seeking to base the study of global politics not upon a supposed struggle for power but on contention over issues.[7] This wide range of literature can all contribute to and be reinforced by a different perspective on the United Nations and other international organisations. The concept of interdependence has been used mainly to analyse economic exchanges. It can also be extended to cover political communications. If the images of political actors and the content of political issues are shaped by a global debate, then the United Nations is clearly central to that debate. It affects what images of governments are formed and how issues are put on the public agenda.[8] The impact of the UN has been significant in the transformation of the inter-state legal system in five major ways: the decolonisation process has extended statehood to cover virtually the whole globe; empires are no longer accepted as legitimate units; very many small territories are now recognised as states; UN membership has become an essential political attribute of statehood; and there has been a decline in the use of force in inter-state (rather than intra-state) relations.[9] This chapter will now be devoted to the concepts which are necessary to understanding the political process *within* the United Nations system. The UN is an arena for governments, IGOs and NGOs to engage in contention over proposals for the resolution of global issues.

The impact of working with the United Nations system

The plainest way to modify the traditional view is to examine the implications of calling the UN a system. In the everyday use of the word, 'system' has the loose meaning of an organisational structure. The technical meaning of the term is more precise. A system is a group of elements which engage in a higher volume and/or intensity of interactions with each other than with elements outside the boundary of the system. Elements cannot be both part of the system and part of its environment. Therefore, if the UN is seen as being a system, the legal conceptualisation of states as members of the UN falls down. One has to distinguish between the delegations within the UN system and the other bureaucracies of the governments outside it, in the capital cities. Putting a boundary around the delegations implies that they are engaging in more interactions with people in the UN than they are with those outside, i.e. that the delegates relate more to the other delegates, the NGOs and the secretariats in New York (or wherever the meeting is taking place) than they do to their home ministries. We may then expect such patterns of interaction to have an impact on the delegates' own attitudes and actions. In other words, to describe the UN as a system carries the presumption that the delegates' role is considerably more complex than suggested by the traditional emphasis on delegates receiving and following instructions. The statement 'the UN is a system' is only tenable within the Global Politics approach.[10] We must choose between the two approaches by examining what actually happens at the UN.

What can we expect to be the effects of working and having a social life within the New York diplomatic corps? Firstly, patterns of friendship with and loyalty to other delegates develop at the personal level and influence outcomes. Secondly, past patterns of behaviour will affect the current issue. This may be due to the necessity of maintaining a general consistency of one's arguments across different issues. Alternatively, it may be the result of 'log-rolling', that is, one delegation supporting another on one issue in return for receiving support for their position on a different issue. A third hypothesis is that the longer delegates stay in New York the more loyalties will develop to the institution as a whole and to its goals. Fourthly, the delegate who gains respect within the United Nations may come to see himself/herself as having better career prospects within the institution than within the home diplomatic service. Some prestigious positions, such as elections to the Security Council, to the President of the General Assembly or to the chair of a major committee, are only achieved by remaining an official delegate. Other positions, such as election to be Secretary-General or a judge at the International Court or being chosen as an Assistant Secretary-General, will require leaving the diplomatic service of one's own country and becoming an international civil servant.

All these effects (except the desire to remain consistent with previous arguments, on occasions when one has been in the minority) will promote convergence towards an international consensus rather than the continuation of conflict. Of course these effects may well assist rather than hinder a delegate's attempt to follow instructions. For most delegates, most of the time, success in the UN and success at home will be judged by the same criterion: obtaining the largest possible majority for a resolution they support. However, a delegate's life will not always be free from conflicts of interest and differences with the home government can arise. In addition we must consider more subtle processes by which delegates have influence that does not produce a conflict with their ministries but equally their actions are not devised by their home governments.

Acting without instructions

This perspective opens up the local possibility of loyalties in New York and loyalties to the home government pulling in opposite directions. If one asks delegates directly whether they would disobey instructions, one receives a shocked response that it is out of the question. That is not to say that direct disobedience does not occur, but information on it is not going to be readily available. One sophisticated and rich study devoted solely to the relations between the US delegation and the State Department records:

Washington had decided that the United States vote on a resolution during the Korean debate should be 'Yes'. Secretary Dulles approved the decision. Instructions went off to USUN to vote 'Yes' the next day. The next day, Murphy read in the newspaper that Lodge had voted 'No'. When he remonstrated with Lodge over the telephone about failure to follow instructions, he was told, 'Instructions? I am not bound by instructions from the State Department. I am a member of the President's Cabinet and accept instructions only from him.'[11]

More recently, *The Guardian* reported:

The Foreign Minister, Mr Bill Hayden, said yesterday that the Australian delegation to the UN apparently ignored instructions from Canberra and voted for a General Assembly resolution that deplored the invasion of Grenada.[12]

Such events are obviously rare, but the fact that they occur at all encourages one to believe that a range of more subtle actions can and do occur more frequently.

Delegates can obey instructions, but let other delegates know they are doing so against their personal wishes. An interesting example occurred when the US delegate, Gross, supported discussion of Tunisia's independence by the Security Council in April 1950 and the State Department issued instructions to abstain. Gross was also under instructions to read a prepared speech. He started, 'I express the following views of my government on this subject'.

After I read that opening sentence, from that point on it didn't matter what I said. The blunt tone of that sentence was enough. On the record nothing could be held against me by Washington because I had said what I was supposed to say. But when the Security Council recessed, I was surrounded in the Delegate's Lounge by a group of Asians and the small number of Africans then in the UN. They shook my hand and they were so pleased. What I had done was to make it possible to continue the dialogue.[13]

Delegates can take initiatives, which they suspect would not be approved at home, by failing to inform the foreign office in advance. This was the case in November 1975, when a remarkable public attack on the chief US delegate was made, without approval from London, by the head of the British delegation. Ivor Richard publicly rebuked Patrick Moynihan for his aggressive ideological style:

I do not see [the UN] as a confrontational arena in which to 'take on' those countries whose political systems and ideology are different from mine. I spend a lot of time preventing rows at the UN — not looking for them. Whatever else the place is, it is not the OK Corral and I am hardly Wyatt Earp.[14]

Not surprisingly, Patrick Moynihan did not survive in post to serve for a second session as the head of the US delegation to the General Assembly. Another example of unauthorised behaviour arose when a subsequent US delegation leader, Andy Young, was sacked for meeting the PLO representative at the UN. This was merely the last in a long line of unauthorised initiatives by Andy Young. (He was sacked not so much for the formal misbehaviour as for it becoming public and because there was an intensive Israeli lobby against his action.)

One point that must be remembered about the UN is that, like all debating forums, the debate can move in unanticipated directions. Delegates then have to decide whether or not they should report home to ask for instructions. If they fail to do so and as a result act contrary to what the instructions would have been, then the effect is logically the same as if instructions have been received and disobeyed. Policy has been made by the delegate. In practical terms it is impossible for most delegates to obtain instructions rapidly. Until the late 1960s a reply from home might take a couple of days at the best. With the advent of direct international telephone dialling this problem has eased and a considered reply may be available in hours. Some delegations do now make frequent use of the telephone. Nevertheless communications cannot always be rapid enough.

Because the United States has vast oceans to both its east and its west, the sessions of United Nations organs in New York from late morning to early evening, local time, do not coincide with office hours in Europe, Africa or Asia. Notwithstanding the speed of global telephone communications, only the Canadian, Latin American and Caribbean delegates can attempt to obtain instructions on unanticipated questions while the debate is still in progress. Even the United States delegation can at times be caught unprepared for a snap decision.[15] Such problems most obviously arise when procedural votes are sprung as a tactic in parliamentary diplomacy. They also arise when amendments to resolutions are tabled very near the end of the debate or orally in a delegate's speech.

The problem of communications is far greater than the simple practicalities of working across the world's time zones. It cannot be assumed that governments at home always act coherently. The processes of bureaucratic politics may produce a significant delay before an authoritative decision arrives out of the foreign ministry. If that process has not been completed by the time the delegate has to respond to the UN's own timetable for decision-making, then again the delegate must use some judgement to arrive at a decision. Even the government with the most sophisticated communications system in the world, the United States, faces this problem. In June 1982 after some days of debate within the administration of policy towards the Falklands War, the United States representative, Jean Kirkpatrick, joined Britain in vetoing a Security Council cease fire resolution. Three minutes later Kirkpatrick announced to the Council that she had received instructions to abstain and would have wished to change her vote.[16]

Delegates may have broad instructions which are so clearly specified that they can unambiguously apply them to the new development in the debate. They may feel able to make an intelligent guess as to what their instructions would be. They may decide to vote in line with the other members of their regional group. They may decide to cast an 'Abstain' vote or not to vote at all. Only when the general instructions cover a wide range of situations does the traditional model apply. If the delegate guesses or votes as a group member or abstains, then political processes internal to the UN can be part of the explanation for the outcome.

Who writes instructions?

We must now move on from considering situations where delegates take their own decisions independently to more 'normal' situations where delegates have been in effective communication with the home ministry. Still there are many reasons why the traditional model is unlikely to apply.

First of all, one may note that the heads of delegations are usually far senior in status to those officials who issue them with instructions. Many countries appoint senior politicians to the UN or its agencies. Inconvenient potential opposition leaders can be removed to New York without offending their constituents at home. Alternatively, former foreign ministers or even occasionally former prime ministers can be given an honourable retirement. Most important of all, personal appointments can be made by the head of government as a means of impressing political activists that foreign policy is in ideologically reliable hands. The latter has been the norm for British heads of UN missions under recent Labour prime ministers and for United States heads of missions under both Democrat and Republican presidents. Figures of experience and political weight are not going to be given instructions as if they were some junior official. They are not going to accept that a diplomat within the foreign ministry is their superior and they will only take instructions emanating from the minister or head of government.

Even when the main delegate is a career diplomat, he/she will be of high seniority. The post in New York is often considered to be either the most prestigious appointment or second only to Washington. Even for the British government, which in the mid-1980s did not look too favourably upon the UN, the permanent representative to the UN, Sir John Thomson, was high in the Senior Grade, that is among the top half-dozen posts in the whole diplomatic service.[17] By contrast the head of the foreign ministry department at home will be of much lower standing; a high-flyer perhaps but in the early stages of a career that is just taking off. In Britain the head of the United Nations Department in the mid-1980s was of Grade 4 rank, that is among the top 400 posts in the service.[18] A promising young man is going to show deference towards, not exercise authority over, a man so plainly his senior.[19] Again, only the foreign minister or the head of government is really in a position to be able to issue instructions which are unwelcome.

There is another purely practical problem about the relationship between UN missions and foreign ministries. There are far more delegates in New York than there are people at home monitoring their activities. The ratios seem to be in the range of 5:1 to 10:1. A normal assumption would be, other things being equal, that larger bureaucracies have more impact than smaller ones. It just is not credible that all politically significant interactions in New York are recorded, reported home, assessed, fed into policy formation and given their due weight in subsequent instructions. Much of the assessment and policy modification can only be done in New York. One head of delegation told me that he tried as much as possible to avoid sending the text of draft resolutions home, though he took more care if he anticipated casting a veto.[20] If that was true for resolutions, how much more must discretion have been exercised in reporting back information on formal and informal diplomatic interactions.

A third factor producing imbalance between New York and the capital cities is the complexity of the United Nations system. This has two aspects to it: a great deal of information has to be acquired before one knows how to go about putting proposals forward and getting them through; and a significant amount of experience is needed before one has the judgement and the skills to do it successfully. Neither the information nor the experience is likely to be acquired by the desk officer at home. (This depends partly on how long the desk officer remains in the same post.) Delegates generally seem to think that they only have a chance to be effective from their second session onwards. By this logic a new delegate might be at a disadvantage in relation to an experienced desk officer, but it will be rare for the whole delegation to be changed at the same point in time.) Overwhelmingly the understanding and the expertise lie in New York. Again the relationship between mission and home is biased in the delegation's favour.

Thus the traditional hierarchical model, which portrays delegates as receiving instructions and reporting back on their actions and the resulting effects, must be replaced by a model of a two-way, non-hierarchical communication process. Information is flowing from the delegates to the ministries as much as it is the other way round. They can exercise mutual influence upon each other, with all the political factors (except the ultimate authority to appoint and dismiss) being balanced more in a delegate's favour. The result is that the instructions might formally come from the capital city but their content has already been substantially influenced by the delegates themselves. Indeed it is sometimes alleged by Western delegates that Third World delegates 'write their own instructions'. While this may occasionally be literally true, there will be some element of truth in it for all delegations.

Once high-level politicians at home are involved in disagreements with delegates the balance changes. The lack of time to respond to fast-moving events in New York and the complexity of understanding required still work in the delegate's favour. But seniority definitely lies with the politicians, even if only marginally so when the head of delegation is also a politician. Whether or not the home politicians will effectively exercise their authority depends upon the salience of the issue to the politicians and/or their constituents. Mrs Thatcher may at times be concerned with withdrawal from UNESCO or the future of the Falklands or some of the major issues, but she is indifferent to and unaware of much else that happens at the United Nations. Politicians can only afford to devote time and effort to issues that they regard as being of the highest priority. Therefore the important research question is 'How do foreign policy questions become salient to actors in the domestic political system?'. When policy at the UN is salient to the foreign minister or the head of government, it is highly likely to be salient to other political leaders and pressure groups. If there is contention between the delegate and the government, there is almost certain to be contention at home, with other actors supporting the delegate's position. Government leaders do not automatically pursue the policy which they most prefer.

Initiation of issues at the United Nations

The clearest way in which delegates can influence policy is when a totally new issue, or new aspect of an old issue, first arises by its inscription on the UN's agenda. The most outstanding example in modern times is the initiation of the whole complex process of revision of the law of the sea. One speech by the delegate of Malta led to all other governments having to devise a foreign policy on a range of new issues. Throughout the process interactions within UNCLOS dominated the way questions were put. Reporting back by delegates would have been the first time the questions were raised at home. And every bureaucrat knows that those who put the first papers in circulation have the highest chance of influencing the policy debate. We will consider below other specific issues where debate in the UN system has changed policy for most governments.

In more general terms one may ask why do small and medium-sized countries which appear only to have regional 'interests' actually have foreign policies which are wide-ranging in their scope? Why do African countries have a policy towards Kampuchea? Why do Asian countries have a policy towards the Falklands/Malvinas dispute? The answer in each case is primarily because they are called upon to vote on these questions in the United Nations General Assembly. In such a context the issues are perceived differently, because they arise in a multilateral forum, from how they would otherwise be perceived, were the issues to arise bilaterally. Caucus group pressures promote solidarity with the group majority and debating arguments promote comparison and alignment with positions taken on other questions on the agenda.[21]

As an illustration of the idea of considering the UN as a system, let us consider a very brief case study. In early 1980 when the Lancaster House agreement for the decolonisation of Zimbabwe was being implemented there was controversy about various decisions being taken by the Governor, Lord Soames. In particular Lord Carrington had committed Britain at Lancaster House to the complete withdrawal of South African troops from Zimbabwe. First of all this was delayed as a move to bolster the confidence of the whites and then when the troops were withdrawn from the southern part of the country a company was retained on the border at Beitbridge. Despite pressure from the Patriotic Front, from the Southern African Front-Line States, and from the opposition in parliament, Lord Soames and the British government were adamant that the troops need not be withdrawn. The Tanzanian Foreign Minister visited Cuba on behalf of the five 'Front-Line States'. President Castro, as Chairman of the Non-Aligned Movement, sent an appeal to all the Movement's members to put pressure on Britain and the Movement's Coordinating Bureau supported the African Group's call for a meeting of the Security Council. British policy then changed and the South Africans were ordered to withdraw their troops. The Security Council passed a resolution by fourteen votes to none, with Britain 'not participating', emphasising the need to comply with the Lancaster House agreement and specifying measuring to be taken including the troop withdrawal.[22]

Although Britain did not vote in favour of the resolution the government was just as legally bound by it as if they had voted in favour. The politically significant point is that they failed to oppose a resolution, which went directly counter to existing policy, and instead they complied with its requirements. The change in policy was brought about not just by the range of bilateral pressures on the government, but also by their coalescence in the multilateral forum. Clearly, if one were trying to explain events outside the UN, we would have to give more emphasis to all the domestic and foreign pressures on governments in their capital cities. The model required to explain the Security Council resolution is not the same as the model required to explain obedience to it, by the actual withdrawal of the troops from Beitbridge.

To summarise, delegates may disobey instructions; they may follow instructions unenthusiastically; they may deliberately initiate action without instructions; there may be communication problems in obtaining instructions; and it may be necessary to interpret instructions, which are broadly cast in general terms or no longer suitable in changed circumstances. The heads of delegations are of high status, with their own back-up staff and operating within a complex system, so they can have a substantial impact on the nature of the instructions they receive, particularly when an issue first arises in the UN. The evidence seems to be overwhelming that UN missions can be regarded as distinct bureaucracies within the bureaucratic politics process of policy formation. They do provide inputs to policy. In straight disagreement with home officials the delegates may be expected to have their way more often than not. In disagreements with ministers the outcome is a more open question. A two-way communications model is more appropriate than the traditional model for understanding the role of delegates to the United Nations.

Transnational actors at the United Nations

So far the discussion has only examined the activities of governments at the UN, but it must be remembered that other actors also take part in the system. More than 600 non-governmental organisations are recognised as having formal consultative status with the Economic and Social Council. A larger number are accredited to the secretariat's Department of Public Information. Officially this only gives them respectively the right to take part in the work of ECOSOC and its subsidiary bodies or the right to receive information. In practice the groups can follow all UN debates, study UN documents and gain access to the delegates. We take it for granted that with such facilities in national parliaments pressure groups will be effective at times in influencing legislation and other aspects of government policy. Yet we seem to be strangely reluctant to accept that the same process occurs in multilateral diplomatic forums.

NGOs can adopt a variety of roles. With the exception of a few of the more recent Special Sessions, NGOs have not had rights of public participation in the General Assembly. However, on most economic and social questions below the plenary level in the UN and its specialised agencies, the NGOs participate on an equal footing with government delegations, except for having the right to vote. They sit in their own labelled places in the conference chamber and they can put items on the agenda, table reports, make speeches and intervene in debates.

One particularly important way they can use these rights is by mobilising information which monitors the way in which governments live up to the formal commitments they have made. Examples range from Amnesty International's work in the Commission on Human Rights[23] and the Anti-Apartheid Movement's reporting to the Security Council committee on the arms embargo against South Africa,[24] to the impact of the International Chamber of Shipping on pollution at sea by its review of the provision at ports of oily-water discharge reception facilities.[25] It can be argued that such monitoring work does not change policy, as the governments are usually committed to the policy already. This would be a naïve view of politics. Obtaining implementation of agreed measures can often be highly difficult, particularly if significant economic costs are involved. NGOs can embarrass governments into action and IGOs into new decisions on implementation. The international secretariats and government delegations are often unwilling or feel unable to adopt this role, but may welcome and support the monitoring done by NGOs.

Although NGOs usually cannot table resolutions and in the UN cannot vote at all, that does not mean that NGOs are unable to promote resolutions successfully. Often government delegations which want to promote a specific position on an issue will seek advice and assistance from NGOs, but also NGOs themselves can take the initiative. In the general shift in attitudes which has taken place, the International Planned Parenthood Federation and its member associations are responsible for the UN and its agencies being involved in population planning, while Oxfam and the other development NGOs promoted the shift from 'trickle-down' ideas of development to the 'basic needs' approach. Individual, specific decisions of the UN can also be attributed to NGOs. International legal instruments on torture are the result of Amnesty International's campaigning;[26] the Additional Protocols to the Geneva Conventions were initiated by the International Commission of Jurists and the International Committee of the Red Cross;[27] the International Baby Foods Action Network is responsible for the WHO Code of Marketing of Breastmilk Substitutes.[28] It should be emphasised that what we are talking about in the latter examples is the NGOs actually promoting specific texts, having them tabled on their behalf and then adopted by the government delegations.

The international secretariats as political actors

The third major category of actors within the United Nations system covers the officials from international secretariats. In both the General Assembly and the Security Council, the Secretary-General of the UN sits next to the President of the meeting. In the General Assembly he may be flanked by the Under-Secretary-General for Political and General Assembly Affairs and/or the Legal Counsel. These officials can and do on occasion take part in debates. The Secretary-General of course has the special right under Article 99 to convene the Security Council and the similar right under Rule 13(g) of the Rules of Procedure to put items on the agenda of the General Assembly. Although these rights have nominally been used only a few times, they legitimise the wider comments in speeches and press conferences which can indirectly lead to items being on the agenda.

The Secretary-General attempts to set the tone of a General Assembly session with his Annual Report published just before the session opens. On many agenda items one of the formal points for debate is a report by the Secretary-General or some other secretariat official. While these reports may appear to be relatively straightforward presentation of information, the skill and extent of coverage of the topic can make a difference to the amount of attention afforded it by the delegates. The reports can go further and be partial towards particular political positions. Bias against apartheid, in favour of development or for the rights of the Palestinians is so taken for granted that it would hardly be a matter of comment. It also occurs on other issues on which there is less consensus. For example, the Secretary-General's reports (and his other actions) on the Contadora process have been clearly supporting the work of the group.[29]

Less often noted is the large number of officials from other intergovernmental organisations (IGOs) who attend UN meetings. They come from the specialised agencies and regional organisations. In the General Assembly they are accorded permanent Observer status and have officially listed delegations, seated with the members. The regional organisations have missions in New York and some have special relations with the governmental delegations. The Executive Secretary of the OAU office services the work of the African Group,[30] while the Commonwealth Secretariat actually services a single office for use as the diplomatic missions of four small countries, the Maldives, the Solomon Islands, Vanuatu and Western Samoa.[31]

In general the international officials have all the facilities open to the NGOs, plus they are much more likely to be invited to the diplomatic receptions (where business can be done informally) and they will usually have a higher status. Although they are supposed to be 'neutral' in that 'the staff shall not seek or receive instructions from any government or from any other authority external to the Organisation',[32] they are not neutral about the work of international organisations. They will seek to promote, as they see it, the status and the interests of their own organisation and their operational programmes.

Other participants in the UN system

In addition to the delegations from UN member governments, the NGOs and the international secretariats, a variety of other actors play some part in the system, and on some issues that part may be crucial. Firstly, along with North and South Korea, Switzerland and the Vatican, a group of micro-states (three from Europe and four from the Pacific Ocean) are members of UN specialised agencies without being members of the UN. Another body established by the General Assembly, the UN Council for Namibia has the same status. All these twelve 'states' may be represented as Observers at the UN and as full participants, with voting rights, at all conferences convened by the UN and in some subsidiary bodies of the UN itself, such as UNCTAD. Secondly, four liberation movements have similar rights, except the right to vote. The PLO since 1974 and SWAPO since 1976 have had Permanent Observer status, while the ANC and the PAC since 1974 have had observer status for all debates on issues involving South Africa. When they are active, the delegations from observer countries or from observer liberation movements behave in much the same way and have much the same significance as the delegations from UN members. Although for historical reasons the Vatican (officially called 'the Holy See' in the world of diplomacy) has the legal status of a state, the transnational Catholic Church is acting as a specially privileged NGO.

Thirdly, as the UN has grown bigger, the governmental delegations have increasingly found it convenient to work together in caucus groups. In the UN's diplomatic language they are known as regional groups. The main groups are now as follows:

— the Latin American Group (including the Caribbean delegations);
— the African Group (members of the OAU);
— the Arab Group (members of the Arab League);
— the Non-Aligned Movement;
— the Group of 77 (only handling development questions);
— the Islamic Group (members of the Islamic Conference Organisation);
— the Commonwealth;
— the European Community;
— the Western European and Others Group (including Australia, Canada and New Zealand, but excluding the United States); and
— the Eastern Europeans or Socialist States (both cover communist governments, excluding Yugoslavia and China: the wider group includes Third World delegations, such as the Cubans, as well as Eastern Europeans).

There is also an Asian Group, but it appears to function for little more than deciding which candidates to support in UN elections. Other groups such as the Nordic Group, the Gulf Cooperation Council, the South Pacific Forum or ASEAN may be important at times, though usually their impact will be effective by aggregation of support in one of the larger groupings. On some particular issues there are also *ad hoc* coalitions such as the Land-Locked States or the Like Minded States (a group of Western countries which are more sympathetic than the British and the United States governments to the Group of 77 on development questions).

The main groups provide a strong political dynamic to promote common positions among their member delegations. On some issues they dominate the attention of delegates and the overall decision-making at the UN is the result of negotiations between representatives of the groups. Analytically they must be seen as subsystems of the UN political system. Inasmuch as they do promote a consensus which did not previously exist within the group, their work provides another process within the UN whereby the position adopted by delegates cannot be explained simply in terms of following instructions from home. In particular when one delegate has to expound the group's position, either in negotiations with other groups or before the whole UN membership, then that person is explicitly adopting the role of being the representative of the group and not of his/her own government.

Fourthly, the UN, its specialised agencies and its conferences usually work with a complex structure of standing committees, procedural committees and subsidiary debating committees. The standing committees may work at any time during the year, with their members developing a special expertise on particular issues and preparing reports which dominate the discussions of the main bodies. UN examples would include the Special Committee Against Apartheid or the International Law Commission. The subsidiary debating committees often may devolve down into Working Groups of half a dozen to a dozen key delegates, who prepare detailed texts of consensus resolutions. As with the caucus groups, the various committees may be seen as subsystems of the overall UN system. Again, when their chairpersons or rapporteurs come before the main body, governmental delegates adopt a role which is explicitly that of representing a position other than their own government's.

Fifthly, upon election as President of the General Assembly or to the chair in other large organs, delegates are expected to abandon their position as government representatives and take on a neutral role, to serve the body as a whole, with responsibility for the smooth running of its proceedings. (In the Security Council and some other small organs, one delegate has to alternate between the roles of government delegate and neutral chairperson.) Again, to the extent that the neutral role is adopted, and generally it *is* adopted because only individuals who are widely trusted are chosen, government delegates cease to represent their governments.

Finally, there is an additional complication that not all the official delegates are actually government representatives. The practice varies from country to country and in accord with the type of meeting. Independent experts with legal or scientific knowledge may act as advisers; members of the legislature, including members of opposition parties, may come as observers; and leaders of industry, trade unions or other important social and economic groups may also be present. Although they are all included in the official delegation lists, they should still be seen by the political analyst as being NGO representatives. They have the special advantage of 'insider' access for pressing their views upon governments and the disadvantage of being more constrained than other NGOs in the manner by which they may exert pressure.

In our discussion, which has mainly been developed with the UN General Assembly in mind, we have moved from seeing the UN as composed of its member states, as in Figures 2.1 and 2.2, to a categorisation of eight types of actors, as in Figure 2.3. In the latter, while all the actors can relate to all the others, only what are believed to be the main interactions have been shown. Caucus groups and subsidiary committees have been described as subsystems, but it is difficult to represent this diagrammatically. As both types of groups have their impact upon others through their officers acting as their collective voice, just the officers have been drawn as being within the main system. Figure 2.3 is sufficiently general to show the structure of the General Assembly or of any other debating organ of the United Nations or its conferences or its specialised agencies.

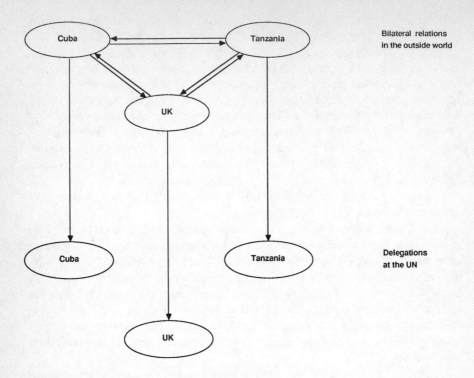

Figure 2.1 The United Nations through realist eyes

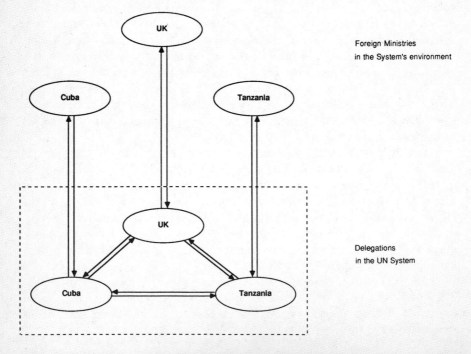

Figure 2.2 The full structure of a United Nations debating organ

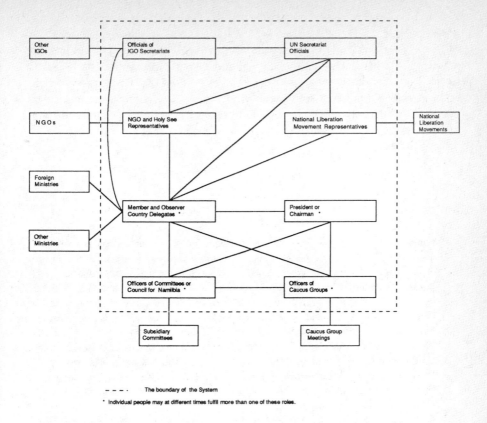

Figure 2.3 'Parliamentary diplomacy' of the United Nations

Conclusion

The application of a bureaucratic politics approach to the UN shows that states cannot be considered to be coherent actors in the system. The consideration of how delegates work shows that there are many pressures upon them, in addition to those from their home country. Recognition of the activities of transnational NGOs, of international secretariats, of observer countries and national liberation movements shows that member governments are not the only actors in the system. The fact that these other participants, who do not have a formal right to take part in decisions by voting, have a substantial impact on outcomes within the system shows that power processes are not of adequate explanatory value. The consideration of regional groups and formal UN committees shows what governmental delegates at times acknowledge publicly that they are not acting on behalf of their governments: they may engage in a variety of different types of interactions and adopt different roles at different times.

The simple legal interpretation that delegates follow instructions from their foreign offices neglects much of what happens in the UN. International relations is not reducible to the struggle for power between states. The Realist approach is wrong in asserting that United Nations' decisions are predominately determined outside the UN. Global politics is the contention between diverse types of actors over proposals for the resolution of issues. Such activity defines the nature of 'parliamentary diplomacy' in the General Assembly, the Security Council and the other organs and committees of the UN. The United Nations is an identifiable political subsystem within the global political system. International organisations should be studied in terms of the flow of communications and the mobilisation of support by political actors for their own position on current issues.

Notes

1. For ways of categorising the debate between the different approaches to International Relations, see C. Archer, 1983, *International Organisations*, *Key Concepts in International Relations Vol.1*, London, George Allen and Unwin, Ch. 3; M.H. Banks, 'Ways of analyzing the world society', in A.J.R. Groom and C.R. Mitchell (eds), 1978, *International Relations Theory: A Bibliography*, London, Frances Pinter; R. Maghroori and B. Ramberg (eds), 1982, *Globalism Versus Realism: International Relations' Third Debate*, Boulder, Colo., Westview Press; M. Smith, R. Little and M. Shackleton (eds), 1981, *Perspectives on World Politics*, London, Croom Helm; J.N. Rosenau, 'Order and disorder in the study of world politics: ten essays in search of perspective', in Maghroori and Ramberg (eds), op.cit.
2. F.S. Northedge, 1976, *The International Political System*, London, Faber and Faber, pp. 138–9.
3. R.O. Keohane and J.S. Nye (eds), 1972, *Transnational Relations and World Politics*, Cambridge, Mass., Harvard University Press; P. Willetts (ed.), 1982, *Pressure Groups in the Global System*, London, Frances Pinter; M.H. Halperin, 1974, *Bureaucratic Politics and Foreign Policy*, Washington, DC, The Brookings Institution.
4. S.D. Krasner (ed.), 1983, *International Regimes*, Ithaca, Cornell University Press.
5. R.O. Keohane and J.S. Nye, 1977, *Power and Interdependence: World Politics in Transition*, Boston, Little Brown; J.N. Rosenau, 1980, *The Study of Global Interdependence*, London, Frances Pinter; R.J.B. Jones and P. Willetts (eds), 1984, *Interdependence on Trial*, London, Frances Pinter.
6. C.R. Mitchell, 1981, *The Structure of International Conflict*, London, Macmillan.
7. R. Mansbach and J. Vasquez, 1981, *In Search of Theory: A New Paradigm for World Politics*, New York, Columbia University Press.
8. P. Willetts, 'The politics of global issues: cognitive actor dependence and issue linkage;, in R.J.B. Jones and P. Willetts (eds), op.cit.
9. P. Willetts, 'The United Nations and the transformation of the inter-state system', in B. Buzan and R.J.B. Jones (eds), 1981, *Change and the Study of International Relations: The Evaded Dimension*, London, Frances Pinter.
10. Use of the concept of a system in international relations is not unique to the Globalist paradigm. Waltz uses it within the Realist paradigm; Burton uses it within the World Society paradigm; and Wallerstein uses it within the Marxist paradigm. However, none of these authors would accept its applicability to conceptualisation of intergovernmental organisations.
11. A. Beichman, 1968, *The 'Other' State Department*, *The United States Mission to*

the United Nations: *Its Role in the Making of Foreign Policy*, New York, Basic Books, p. 107.

12. 'Big majority to condemn invasion', *The Guardian*, London, 4 November 1983.

13. A. Beichman, op.cit, pp. 178–9.

14. D.P. Moynihan with S. Weaver, 1979, *A Dangerous Place*, London, Secker and Warburg, p. 213. Moynihan asserts that 'Callaghan evidently did not know it [the speech] was coming, and was infuriated by it' (p. 221). It has been confirmed to me by an authoritative British source that the speech was made without any approval from London.

15. For example, this occurred on 29 July 1982 in the Security Council and on 1 October 1982 in the General Assembly. On both these occasions the US did not vote, the delegates citing lack of time to obtain instructions as the reasons. Presumably therefore the delegates of other countries, unless they had secret prior notice of the decision to call a vote, all voted without having any *specific* instructions to do so.

16. The vote on 4 June 1982 on the draft resolution, S/15156/Rev.2, submitted by Panama and Spain was 9 in favour to 2 against, with 4 abstentions. The confusion in US government communications was reported in 'Maggie fury over Haig's UN mix-up', *The Observer*, London, 6 June 1982.

17. The British Foreign and Commonwealth Office has now merged its Grades 1, 2 and 3 into a single Senior Grade, to give greater flexibility in moving staff around between postings and greater confidentiality on salaries. The News Department was prepared to say on the record that Sir John would certainly be in the top twenty of the Senior Grade; another official said off the record that Sir John would be in the top half-dozen.

18. In December 1985 the British FCO had the following staffing: 154 at Senior Grade; 288 at Grade 4; 439 at Grade 5; 294 at Grade 6; 553 at Grade 7 and 1,368 giving support at lower grades (making 3,096 people in total).

19. This account is a simplification for two reasons. Firstly, departments other than the United Nations Department can deal directly with New York on issues within their own area of responsibility. However, the status relationships would be similar and this complication merely increases the possibility of bureaucratic politics having an effect. Secondly, heads of departments can appeal to higher officials to back them up in their relationship with New York, though this tactic cannot be used too frequently.

20. The fact that a delegate felt he had to be more careful casting a veto than voting for a Security Council resolution turns the whole idea of sovereignty upside down. If 'states' are concerned to protect their sovereignty, the safe course is to prevent action by a veto, while much more attention must be given to the dangers of allowing a resolution to be passed. The political reality is that vetoes can cause a great deal of damage to the prestige of those who cast them.

21. Pressures for caucus group solidarity can be conceptualised as cognitive dependence and comparison with other agenda questions can be conceptualised as cognitive linkage. See P. Willetts, 'The politics of global issues', op.cit.

22. UN Security Council Resolution 463 (1980) passed on 2 February 1980.

23. E.V. Perkins, 1977, *Comparative Pressure Group Politics and Transnational Relations*: *The Case of Non-Governmental Organisations at the United Nations*, unpublished Ph.D. dissertation, Texas Tech University, May, pp. 219–35.

24. A.S. Minty, 'The Anti-Apartheid Movement and racism in Southern Africa' (p. 40), in P. Willetts, (ed.), *Pressure Groups*, op.cit.

25. International Maritime Organisation, Marine Environment Protection Committee document MEPC 22/8/2, debated by the MEPC on 3 December 1985.

26. M. Ennals, 'Amnesty International and human rights', in P. Willetts (ed.), *Pressure Groups*, op.cit.
27. K. Suter, 1984, *An International Law of Guerrilla Warfare: The Global Politics of Law Making*, London, Frances Pinter.
28. A. Chetley, 1986, *The Politics of Baby Foods: Successful Challenges to an International Marketing Strategy*, London, Frances Pinter.
29. See United Nations documents A/40/737-S/17549 of 9 October 1985, paragraph 5, and A/40/1136-S/18184 of 2 July 1986, paragraph 5.
30. C.O.C. Amate, 1986, 'The African group at the United Nations', Ch. 7 in *Inside the OAU: Pan-Africanism in Practice*, London, Macmillan.
31. *Report of the Commonwealth Secretary-General, 1985*, London Commonwealth Secretariat, 1985, p. 7.
32. This quote only directly covers the work of the UN's own Secretariat, as it comes from Article 100 of the United Nations Charter. However, all international secretariats come under similar provisions. For example, in the case of the OAU Charter there is a virtually identical wording in Article XVIII.

Recommended reading

A. Beichman, 1968, *The 'Other' State Department: The United States Mission to the United Nations: Its Role in the Making of Foreign Policy*, New York, Basic Books. (A detailed study of the relationship between delegations and their foreign ministry.)

G.R. Berridge and A. Jennings, 1985, *Diplomacy at the UN*, London, Macmillan. (An edited collection by fifteen authors, predominantly in the state-centric tradition, and therefore not compatible with the analysis in this chapter of the UN as a complex political system.)

S.M. Finger, 1980, *Your Man at the UN: People, Politics and Bureaucracy in the Making of Foreign Policy*, New York and London, New York University Press. (Accounts of the work of US delegation leaders.)

J. Kaufmann, 1980, *United Nations Decision Making*, Althen an den Rijn, Sijthoff and Noordhoff. (The best general textbook on the politics of the UN.)

D.P. Moynihan with S. Weaver, 1979, *A Dangerous Place*, London, Secker and Warburg. (The memoirs of the head of the United States delegation to the UN, giving a useful impression of how a delegate works.)

D. Nicol, 1981, *Paths to Peace: The UN Security Council and Its Presidency*, New York and Oxford, Pergamon Press. (A large number of short accounts by Presidents of the Security Council on their work and some basic information on the Council.)

UN, *United Nations Yearbooks* are published for each year by the Secretariat in New York. (They give a bland official account of events, but are very useful for basic information.)

3 The role of the secretariats of international institutions

*Anthony Mango, OBE**

The United Nations 'family' of organizations[1] today employs over 73,000 men and women, not counting the troop contingents serving with the various United Nations peace-keeping forces: while these wear the blue berets of the United Nations, the officers and men belong to the armed forces of their respective countries. Out of this total of over 73,000, some 54,000 may be regarded as international civil servants (though many of them serve in their own countries) and have the status of staff members[2]; some 17,000–18,000 are locally recruited, so-called 'area staff' of the United Nations Relief and Works Agency for Palestine Refugees in the Middle East (UNRWA)[3]; and the balance work as consultants, contractual employees and in other, mostly short-term, capacities.

The 54,000 staff members are scattered throughout the world. While the largest concentrations of them are to be found in the 'headquarters' cities of the various organizations, such as Geneva or New York, thousands work in the regional offices and the so-called field offices. Approximately two-thirds of the 54,000 perform support functions — which cover the gamut from highly paid bilingual secretaries and accounting clerks in Geneva, to cleaners and messengers in small offices in countries such as Burkina Faso or Burundi. The overwhelming majority of these staff are locally recruited and are not required to serve outside their countries. Their remuneration is based on the best prevailing conditions of employment in the locality.

The remaining one-third — or approximately 18,000 staff — are internationally recruited and belong to the 'Professional and higher categories'. These categories are divided into nine levels: five 'Professional' levels (P-1 to P-5), two 'Director' levels (D-1 and D-2) and two ungraded levels (Assistant Secretary-General and Under-Secretary-General); in the organizations whose executive heads are called Director-General, the corresponding levels are designated Assistant Director-General and Deputy Director-General. The largest numbers of Professional staff are in levels P-3 to P-5. Of the two entry levels, P-1 is virtually extinct, and P-2 may soon qualify as an endangered species. The reason for this phenomenon is that the United Nations and its sister organizations tend to recruit Professional staff in mid-career (at ages 40–45). At the senior end of the scale, by contrast, numbers have increased much faster than the overall increase in staff; this is particularly true of the United Nations itself and its related programmes, where Assistant Secretaries-General now

---

* The views expressed herein are those of the author and do not necessarily reflect the views of the United Nations.

sometimes perform functions that used to be discharged at the D-2 or even D-1 level. The main cause of this explosion in the numbers of the most senior officials is to be found in the political pressures exerted by member states for representation at those levels. In the United Nations most of those posts tend to be associated with particular countries. As the size of the membership of the United Nations increased, it was politically very much easier for the Secretary-General to satisfy the pressures by proposing to create new senior posts, than by rotating existing posts among nationals of different member states.

Some 5,000–6,000 Professional and senior staff work on technical assistance projects in the Third World: as plant-breeding specialists, medical doctors, engineers, experts in geothermal energy or the construction of dams, trainers of air-traffic controllers, port specialists, etc. The remaining 12,000–13,000 serve in the headquarters and other established offices of the organizations.[4] It is the qualifications and performance of these 12,000–13,000 men and women that determine the *input* of the secretariats of the organizations in the United Nations system. But before one proceeds to analyse those qualifications, it may be worthwhile to ask oneself whether the input should be deemed to be synonymous with the *role* of the secretariats.

The Charter of the United Nations lists the Secretariat among the principal organs of the United Nations (Article 7, para. 1). But whereas the role and functions of the other organs (the General Assembly, the Security Council, the Economic and Social Council, the Trusteeship Council and the International Court of Justice) are treated in detail, the role of the Secretariat is not defined. The Charter states that the Secretary-General 'shall be the chief administrative officer of the Organization' (Article 97), and it allows him to bring to the attention of the Security Council any matter which in his opinion may threaten the maintenance of international peace and security (Article 99). But the role of the Secretariat is left vague. The Secretariat is supposed to comprise 'such staff as the Organization may require' (Article 97), and appropriate staff are to be permanently assigned to the Economic and Social Council, the Trusteeship Council and, as required, to other organs of the United Nations (Article 101, para. 2). The staff are told what they may do (namely, seek or receive instructions from any government or from any other authority external to the Organization, or engage in any action which might reflect on their position as international officials, in the words of Article 100, para. 1, but not what they are supposed to do.

In the circumstances, the question whether the role of the Secretariat should be wholly supportive of and reactive to the mandates of intergovernmental organs, or whether it should also include a more activist approach, has never been resolved. While some states (notably the USSR) have consistently adhered to the former point of view, other states were prepared to tolerate — or even encourage — initiatives by the Secretariat, provided those initiatives coincided with what those states perceived as their national policies at the time.

Secretary-General Dag Hammarskjöld, in his address on Staff Day in September 1961 — a few days before he died in an air accident in the Congo (now Zaïre) — referred to what he described as 'a basic question of principle', namely:

Is the Secretariat to develop as an international secretariat, with the full independence contemplated in Article 100 of the Charter, or is it to be looked upon as an intergovernmental — not international — secretariat providing merely the necessary administrative services for a conference machinery?

Hammarskjöld followed the former approach, but his successors, in particular Kurt Waldheim and Xavier Perez de Cuellar, chose to avoid all initiatives which might arouse the displeasure of member states, especially the more powerful ones.

The passivity of the recent Secretaries-General of the United Nations has not meant that the entire United Nations Secretariat subsided into a state of lethargy. Individual senior officials, often working through like-minded delegations, sometimes succeeded in expanding the role of the United Nations: the emergence of the United Nations Conference on Trade and Development (UNCTAD) and the Conference on the Law of the Sea, or United Nations interest in renewable sources of energy owe much to the work of individual staff members. Furthermore, the executive heads of the specialised agencies have continued to take the initiative within their fields of competence, which are often less politicized than those of the Secretary-General of the United Nations.

Another factor which influences the role of the secretariats of the organizations in the United Nations system is that those secretariats are often highly fragmented. In the case of the United Nations this fragmentation can be said to go back to the requirements of Article 101, para. 2 of the Charter that appropriate staff are to be *permanently* assigned to the various organs of the Organization. The expansion of the economic and social activities of the United Nations has also led to a functional fragmentation, because the skills and qualifications required for work in one area are not necessarily relevant to activities being carried out in another part of the Organization. Similarly, in the Food and Agriculture Organization, for example, fisheries specialists are not interchangeable with experts in, say, animal husbandry or forestry. Even a small organization like the International Telecommunication Union, has distinct secretariats assigned to the Frequency Registration Board, to the consultative Committee for telegraph and telephones and the Consultative Committee for radio communication. One consequence of this fragmentation has been that staff often view their role in a departmental, or even divisional, rather than organization-wide context.

The functional fragmentation of the Professional staff in the United Nations system serving at the headquarters and other established offices emerges very clearly from a recent study carried out under the auspices of the International Civil Service Commission (ICSC).[5] After excluding persons in senior policy-making posts (executive heads, Under-Secretaries-General, Assistant Secretaries-General and their equivalents), and also individuals with highly specialised qualifications, the Commission identified and analysed 9,375 Professional posts (i.e. 75 per cent of the total number of 12,000–13,000 Professional and higher posts in headquarters and other established offices). These data are summarized as in Table 3.1.

Reference should also be made to the organizational fragmentation of the

Table 3.1 Professional staff at the UN

Servicing staff	3,785
of whom — translators, interpreters, editors	1,617
administration, personnel, budget	1,641
data processing, librarians	527
Technical cooperation administrators	1,576
Social scientists	2,073
of whom — economists	1,600
statisticians	241
sociologists	232
Other scientists	1,061
(medical, agricultural, biological, electrical, etc.)	
Public information specialists	516
Jurists	228
Political scientists	136

Table 3.2 Organisational breakdown of Professional staff

Organisation	Per cent of total
United Nations	34.3
Major technical assistance programmes (UNDP, UNICEF)	16.1
FAO	11.5
WHO	8.2
UNESCO	8.1
ILO	6.0
IAEA	4.8
UNIDO	3.1
ICAO, UPU, ITU, WMO, IMO, WIPO, IFAD	7.9
	100.0

Professional staff in the United Nations family of organizations. Half the staff work for the United Nations and its associated programmes (ten of which enjoy a large measure of autonomy); the other half are divided among thirteen wholly independent agencies. The organizational breakdown of the Professional staff may be summarized as shown in Table 3.2. As can be seen from the functional breakdown in Table 3.2, 57 per cent of Professional staff perform servicing and support functions: they provide language services for the various meetings and conferences; they maintain the buildings and other facilities; they recruit and pay the staff or back-stop technical cooperation projects. Their ability to influence the policies of the organizations is either non-existent or, at best, very limited.

The very large number of language staff is attributable to the linguistic chauvinism of the member states. By far the largest employer of language staff is the United Nations itself — because of the enormous volume of servicing required by the conferences and meetings of the various United Nations intergovernmental and expert bodies, a high proportion of which have six working languages (Arabic, Chinese, English, French, Russian and Spanish). Although the need to streamline the annual programme of meetings has long been recognized, all attempts at reform have so far foundered on the rocks of political differences among member states, since each meeting tends to be regarded as important by one group of states or another. The number of meetings also has a direct bearing on the volume of documentation (which, of course, has to be translated into the various working languages). United Nations documentation may be divided into three broad categories: meeting records (verbatim records for 'important' bodies such as the General Assembly or the Security Council; summary records for most of the Main Committees of the General Assembly and other subordinate organs; and reports by subordinate bodies to their parent bodies); reports and notes by the Secretary-General (i.e. documents drafted and originating in the Secretariat); and communications from governments or groups of governments. The number and length of these communications from governments have tended to increase because some governments apparently believe that circulation of a paper as an 'official document' of, say, the General Assembly invests it with extra prestige. As most of these communications tend to be polemical, the government or governments attacked feel compelled to request the circulation of rebuttals. Lengthy communiqués of meetings of regional groupings, such as the League of Arab States, the Islamic Conference or the Non-Aligned Movement, are also circulated as official documents. Recently, the Secretary-General has made a timid appeal to member states to exercise restraint in this area, but with no apparent success.

The truly 'substantive' Professional staff of all the organizations in the United Nations system included in the ICSC survey referred to above barely exceed 4,000 in all. And yet these 4,000 men and women are supposed to provide substantive support to international cooperation in all areas of human endeavour from peace and disarmament, to health, nutrition, industry, communications, the environment, etc. These professional resources are often so thinly spread that it is not surprising that their opportunities for creative thinking and initiative are very limited. Most of their time and energy must be devoted perforce to responding to the numerous requests addressed to them by the intergovernmental organs of the various organizations.

For example, at its fortieth anniversary session in 1985, the United Nations General Assembly adopted a total of twenty-seven resolutions on various aspects of disarmament. These resolutions contained over thirty requests to the Secretary-General to prepare reports and studies and to render various kinds of assistance to a number of committees; they also contained numerous requests addressed to subsidiary organs which, in their turn, would necessitate reports and studies by the Secretariat. Faced with such a plethora of requests and having also to attend the meetings of the numerous intergovernmental organs dealing with disarmament, the Secretariat would have found it difficult — even if it wished (which is sometimes doubtful, given the political pitfalls involved) — to provide a proper response, let alone perform think-tank services, were it not for the fact that some of these reports tend to be mere compilations rather than original pieces of research.

A somewhat similar situation often prevails also in the economic and social fields. Here, however, a distinction must be drawn between the smaller organizations which are often involved with standard-setting (such as ITU or UPU), whose activities are more clearly defined and circumscribed, and which, on the whole, are provided with the necessary resources, and others, such as the United Nations itself, where the staffing resources that are made available by member states are often not commensurate with the scope of the mandates.

The 'substantive' functions of the Secretariat may take a variety of forms. Perhaps potentially the most important function — though one that is very seldom performed in practice — is that of the 'good offices' of the Secretary-General, namely the availability of the Secretary-General to act as an honest broker or go-between in conflicts or potential conflict situations. By definition, an honest broker must be impartial if he is to be trusted by both sides. This creates a dilemma in situations where an organ of the United Nations has already considered the matter and adopted a resolution. Unless such a resolution is absolutely even-handed, the Secretary-General may be torn between the impartiality needed to exercise his 'good offices' and the requests addressed to him in a resolution which may be perceived by one party to the dispute as favouring the opposite side. The fact that his good offices may be sought at some time in the future also tends to inhibit the Secretary-General from speaking out on points of concern to him. The Secretary-General is in a position to exercise his 'good offices' successfully only when the parties to the dispute are genuinely interested in a settlement and are looking for ways of attaining it without loss of face. Where such predisposition is lacking (as in the dispute involving Turkey, Greece and the Greek and Turkish communities in Cyprus), 'good offices' by the Secretary-General are unlikely to be successful. As has already been said, the ability of the Secretary-General to act as honest broker is reduced or may even be eliminated when a United Nations intergovernmental organ has already adopted a resolution critical of one of the parties to the dispute — for that party would then naturally tend to regard the Organization and its servants as being biased against it.

The reason why the 'good offices' function can be successfully performed so rarely is that most of the items on the agendas of the various United Nations bodies tend to be 'perennials' on which the positions of the governments had hardened through being repeated many times. On such items the substantive role of the Secretariat becomes largely reactive. Every time the item is debated a resolution is adopted which, *inter alia*, takes note of the report of the Secretary-General that was before the particular session and requests him to submit a further report to the next session — normally a bare twelve months away. Very often in such cases everybody concerned — both the representatives of member states who have voted on the draft resolution and the Secretariat who will have to prepare the report — does not expect the report to contain any new insights into the problem. The real purpose of the report is to provide the pretext for keeping the item on the agenda. The reports themselves then become highly stylized and may consist largely of a summary of past resolutions on the subject. The new information may consist of a couple of paragraphs to the effect, perhaps, that the Secretary-General had brought the latest resolution to the attention of the member state or states concerned, and that replies had (or had not) been received. Where replies are received, they are reproduced virtually verbatim, as governments have resisted attempts by the Secretariat to summarize or synthesize the replies.

The unwillingness of member states to permit the Secretariat to express opinions on sensitive issues on which states are at odds, and the parallel unwillingness of the Secretariat to venture any opinions so as not to be criticized by one side or the other has led to a practice where the reports are requested not of the Secretary-General but of groups of outside experts or consultants, who, though often nominally independent, tend to be selected by their respective governments and reflect their views; in such cases the role of the Secretariat is limited to servicing the groups of experts.

Another role which the Secretariat is sometimes asked to play is that of 'catalyst' who would identify a need and coordinate efforts by third parties to deal with that need. A case in point is the Office of the United Nations Disaster Relief Coordinator (UNDRO) which, under its statute, is precluded from furnishing actual assistance on any large scale. The Office has been largely unsuccessful because the government of the disaster-stricken country itself is usually in a better position to identify the needs and has more direct relations with the country or countries which, for historical reasons, are likely to be in the forefront of the relief effort.

Broadly speaking, the substantive input of the Secretariats has proved to be more important in rather technical areas, especially in areas in which both the Secretariat staff and the government representatives sitting on the competent intergovernmental body belong to the same discipline and thus 'speak the same language'. The success of so many endeavours of WHO, the broad areas of agreement in the allocation of frequencies under the auspices of the Frequency Registration Board of ITU, the safeguards work of IAEA, the compilation of useful statistical handbooks by the Statistical Division of the United Nations, the conclusion under the auspices of the United Nations Economic Commission for Europe (ECE) of agreements on the intermodal transport of goods, are cases in point.

Although the United Nations was initially set up primarily as a political organization, today economists greatly outnumber the political scientists on its staff. Several causes have contributed to this result: the stalemate brought about by the Cold War and subsequent East–West confrontations; the process of decolonization and the emergence of 'technical cooperation' activities, are among the main ones. The dissolution of the colonial empires of Britain and France has internationalized what used to be bilateral relationships between metropolis and colony, and gave birth to two parallel developments: 'technical assistance', later renamed 'technical cooperation' in deference to the susceptibilities of the new states, and a call for a reordering of the economic relationships between rich and poor countries, the so-called 'new international economic order'. The impetus and the bulk of resources for the former came from the rich market-economy countries; the motive force behind the latter were the new countries themselves. Both led to a rapid growth of the international secretariats in the 1960s and 1970s, following the setting up of new organizations and programmes (among them the United Nations Development Programme (UNDP), the United Nations Fund for Population Activities (UNFPA), the World Food Programme (WFP), the United Nations Conference for Trade and Development (UNCTAD), and the United Nations Industrial Development Organization (UNIDO)).

The career prospects and, indeed, livelihood of numerous international civil servants depend on the growth, or at least survival, of multilateral technical cooperation. In this area the role of the Secretariats is threefold. The first consists in fund-raising, in persuading governments to assign greater resources to the technical cooperation programmes (which are funded largely by voluntary contributions, as against the compulsory assessments for the regular budgets of the United Nations and the specialized agencies). The second involves coordinating multilateral assistance at the country level; and the third in identifying and getting under way the individual projects themselves.

As the overall supply of voluntary funds is limited, and has indeed been shrinking in recent years, competition for funds among the various organizations in the United Nations system has been intense. Each organization lobbies donors for its own voluntary programmes, in competition with all other organizations and also with UNDP which was meant to be the umbrella funding organization. Each organization also lobbies the governments of the receiving countries to include its particular project (a model farm, for example, as against a shoe factory, or vice versa) in the country's Indicative Planning Figure (IPF). In some organizations one division will lobby against another division, in support of its own pet project.

Once the choice has been made, and a particular project has been selected and funded, the role of the Secretariat includes various aspects of 'back-stopping' — from designing the project, to recruiting and supporting the experts who will be running it, to evaluating the results achieved. A frequent criticism in intergovernmental bodies in recent years is that project design is often not thorough enough and that the evaluation is too lenient.

From the point of view of the 'Third World' countries, multilateral aid has the advantage that it comes with fewer strings attached than bilateral aid. But multilateral aid has accounted for only a small proportion of all assistance to the Third World. In recent years its nature has tended to change — away from the provision of experts and more towards the procurement of equipment (which must be purchased for foreign currency). Inevitably, therefore, the 'operational' role of the Secretariats of the United Nations and the specialized agencies will tend to decline as the 'Third World' countries develop and train their national cadres of technicians and administrators. Third World countries are already clamouring for block grants, to be spent by them, rather than for experts or equipment, and this emphasis on the provision of finance is likely to grow.

If the Secretariat has tended to tread warily in the political areas of United Nations activities (which include human rights), it has been more outspoken when it came to the relationships between the rich countries of the Northern Hemisphere and the poor countries of the South — the so-called North–South dialogue or the new international economic order. The impetus to this more activist policy was provided by the charismatic Argentinian economist Raul Prebisch, the first Secretary-General of UNCTAD. Under his guidance the Secretariat of UNCTAD came forward with numerous position papers and proposals on how to stabilize primary commodity prices through agreements and buffer stocks, how to transfer resources to the poor countries with the help of preferential tariffs, etc. These various ideas — perhaps because of the insistence and intransigence with which they were being pushed by the spokesmen for the South — aroused opposition in the rich countries, especially in the aftermath of the emergence of OPEC and the oil shocks of the 1960s and 1970s. With the North–South dialogue at a standstill, the role of UNCTAD and its Secretariat has declined.

In the early years of the United Nations an important activity of the Secretariat was the preparation of an annual economic survey which served as the focus for a general debate in the Economic and Social Council (ECOSOC) on the world economic situation. The world survey owed much to the vision of the French economist Philippe de Seynes. The emergence of UNCTAD, with its different focus on the economic fundamentals in the world, the increasing unwillingness of member states to see their economic policies analysed, or worse, questioned, in United Nations publications, has reduced the value of the world economic survey. Besides, all analyses and forecasts derived from them run the risk of being proved wrong by subsequent developments (as witness some of the more alarmist reports of the 'Club of Rome'), and that is a risk the average bureaucrat prefers not to run.

The initial success of UNCTAD encouraged the Third World countries to push for the creation of a parallel organization dealing with industrial development (UNIDO). The industrialized countries were reluctant to go along. After several years as an autonomous organization within the United Nations, UNIDO achieved the status of a specialized agency only in 1986. In the meantime, partly because of the absence of leadership such as had been exercised by Prebisch in UNCTAD, the performance of UNIDO has been generally lack-lustre.

Although, as was stated at the outset, the United Nations Charter views the Secretariat as a principal organ, in practice it has operated largely as a support institution. Just as at the national level new ideas, new initiatives tend to come from the party in power, from government and parliament, while the role of the civil service is to apply those ideas and initiatives in practice, so also at the international level, the Secretariat has tended to react rather than to initiate. Where international differences among states prevent action at the intergovernmental level, the Secretariat remains passive, fearful that any suggestion for action might be criticized by one side or another. This is regrettable, because history teaches that in most conflicts neither side has been 100 per cent right or 100 per cent wrong. In theory, therefore, it should have been possible for the Secretariat to come forward with compromise proposals; in practice, however, such an initiative would have been criticised by both sides.

There still remains the area of forward-looking analysis, of making the international community aware of potential problems and potential challenges. But this area, too, is a minefield; any mention of the dangers of over-population, for instance, will run into strongly held religious or political beliefs; environmental concerns encounter entrenched economic interests or the desire for 'development'. To identify and formulate new concerns of regional or global importance calls for a combination of vision and political awareness. This combination, always rare, is not very much in evidence in the United Nations today.

The qualities which member states, and particularly the major powers, value most in the Secretary-General are pliability and discretion; they do not want a Secretary-General who will ask awkward questions, and they have chosen accordingly. The Secretary-General's most senior assistants — the Under-Secretaries-General and Assistant Secretaries-General — are selected primarily because of their nationality; not much attention is paid to their technical competence or managerial ability. Most of them come from their respective countries' diplomatic service, and not infrequently they have served as their countries' permanent representatives or deputy permanent representatives to the United Nations. But the main quality of a successful diplomat is to be able to project and defend his government's policies. Few diplomats have had experience of managing resources, of supervising and motivating scores or even hundreds of people of different nationalities. Few of them have a vision of the world, as opposed to a national viewpoint. Few diplomats are trained to seek out and confront problems. But above and beyond that is the fact that member states tend to view the United Nations as a propaganda forum, as a tool to be used whenever possible to advance their national policies, to give respectability to their viewpoint, and not as a place for reconciling differences or searching for common solutions. As long as this attitude persists (and there are no signs that it is about to change), governments will discourage initiatives by the Secretariat. In these circumstances, the main role of the Secretariat will continue to be to service conferences and meetings, a role which it has played with great efficiency. The question asked by Secretary-General Dag Hammarskjöld a quarter of a century ago remains unanswered. But it is not too late to hope that member sates will realize that a policy of accommodation is more advantageous in the long run than a policy of confrontation; when that happens the Secretariat of the United Nations will be able to realize its full potential as a principal organ of the United Nations.

Notes

1.   The United Nations family of organizations consists of the United Nations Organiza-
      tion and its associated programmes, the largest of which are the United Nations
      Relief and Works Agency for Palestine Refugees in the Middle East (UNRWA), the
      United Nations Development Programme (UNDP), the United Nations Children's
      Fund (UNICEF) and the United Nations Fund for Population Activities (UNFPA);
      the 'specialized agencies', namely the Food and Agriculture Organization of the
      United Nations (FAO), the International Civil Aviation Organization (ICAO), the

International Fund for Agricultural Development (IFAD), the International Labour Organisation (ILO), the International Maritime Organization (IMO), the International Telecommunication Union (ITU), the United Nations Educational, Scientific and Cultural Organization (UNESCO), the United Nations Industrial Development Organization (UNIDO), the Universal Postal Union (UPU), the World Health Organization (WHO), the World Intellectual Property Organization (WIPO), and the World Meteorological Organization (WMO); and also the International Atomic Energy Agency (IAEA), which does not have the status of a specialized agency of the United Nations.

2. Official Records of the General Assembly, Forty-first Session, Supplement No. 9 (Document A/41/9), para. 9.

3. UNRWA's local area staff consist of teachers (approximately 10,000), health workers (approximately 4,000) and persons who provide administrative and social services in refugee camps. Their work is in many respects similar to that of national civil servants, except that they provide services to a people without a state of their own.

4. While there is a wealth of personnel statistics covering the various organizations, the data are often not comparable. For example, while in some documents the term 'staff' is applied only to persons appointed for a period of one year or more, other statistics (e.g. those of the United Nations Joint Staff Pension Fund) cover all persons who have served for or hold appointments for six months or more. Furthermore, for a variety of reasons, the number of persons employed by the organizations nearly always exceed the totals shown in the staffing tables in the budget documents.

5. Document ICSC/24/R,5. Annex V, dated 26 June 1986.

Recommended reading

Sydney D. Bailey, 1962, *The Secretariat of the United Nations*, New York, Carnagie Endownment for International Peace.

Seymour Maxwell Finger, 1974, *The Politics of Staffing the United Nations*, New York, City University of New York.

Gerard J. Mangone, 1966, *United Nations administration of economic and social programmes*, New York, Columbia University Press.

Theodor Meron, 1977, *The United Nations Secretariat; the rules and the practice*, Lexington, Mass., Lexington Books.

Robert W. Cox and Harold K. Jacobson *et al*, 1973, *The Anatomy of Influence: Decision-Making in International Organization*, Newhaven, Conn., Yale University Press.

Thomas J. Weiss, 1986, *International Bureaucracy: an Analysis of the Operation of Functional and Global International Secretariats*, Lexington, Mass., Lexington Books.

Part II

Institutions at work

4 The institutional basis of post-war economic cooperation

James Mayall

The present is a curious vantage point from which to survey the institutional landscape of the contemporary world economy. The institutions — the IMF, IBRD and GATT — that were established after the Second World War, as the framework for the reconstructed liberal economy, still exist; but they no longer perform the functions for which they were originally designed. Indeed, a sceptic, reviewing the record of exchange rate instability amongst the major currencies, the chronic debt problems of many countries and the problems of protectionism almost everywhere, could be forgiven for concluding that they no longer perform a useful function at all. The UNCTAD, which was created in 1964 to promote the interests of the developing countries, has created a sizeable and expert bureaucracy. During the 1980s, however, its substantive proposals were largely ignored by the industrial powers to whom they were addressed. Nor are the achievements of most regional organisations impressive.

The contemporary world seems to be dominated more by economic conflict than cooperation. Faced by a widespread retreat from multilateralism, it is easy to forget the fundamental problem to which the post-war economic institutions were addressed. This problem was how to reconcile competing national interests with the perceived need for common rules and procedures in an increasingly interdependent market order. Much in the world has changed in the past forty years, not least the structure of the world economy; but the fundamental problem itself has not changed. Perhaps for this reason governments continue to pay lip-service to the goals of international economic cooperation, even when their behaviour seems to suggest that they do not take it seriously.

It is beyond the scope both of this chapter, and the competence of its author, to prescribe what needs to be done to bring theory and practice into closer alignment, but if we are to understand the problem of doing so, it will be useful nonetheless to re-examine the basis of post-war economic cooperation. I shall proceed by discussing the historical and intellectual background to the system before turning to its achievements and the major contradictions that have developed within it.

The purpose of international economic institutions

The essential purpose of the institutional framework created after 1945 was to prevent a future breakdown of liberal capitalism. The economic peacemakers were determined to avoid what they perceived to be the mistakes of their predecessors after the First World War. In 1918, the intellectual hegemony of neo-classical economics was so powerful that the Covenant of the League of Nations contained only a single reference to economic affairs. This was an appeal to members of the League to return as quickly as possible to a world of free trade and to manage their monetary relations through the Gold Standard. Classical liberal orthodoxy held that long-run welfare would be optimised, if international markets were allowed to operate freely; there was no positive, or even regulatory, role for economic institutions.

This formula totally disregarded the political and social consequences of unregulated capitalism. During the late nineteenth century, a single market stretching to the four corners of the earth had finally emerged. Whatever welfare gains may have accompanied this development, it had the unfortunate consequence of making different parts of the world much more sensitive to international economics than ever before. So long as the capitalist world economy was underwritten by imperial Britain (whose navy also performed the important task of policing the major trade routes), the potentially dangerous political as well as economic consequences of such sensitivity were contained. However, the decline of British power after the First World War revealed the need either for a new hegemon, or for institutions to provide the basic framework of order, on which liberal capitalism depends. Neither was available during the great depression of the 1930s.

In their absence governments everywhere resorted to economic nationalism in order to try and protect domestic employment. They adopted a wide variety of 'beggar-your-neighbour' policies. In other words, in an effort to boost exports and curtail imports, they engaged in competitive tariff wars, or depreciated their currencies. But as one country's tariffs went up and its currency came down, so did those of its competitors. The result was a vicious downward spiral of deflation. Protection did not work. The central problem of mass unemployment was not solved anywhere during the 1930s except in Germany towards the end of the decade, under a programme of massive rearmament.

It matters less whether this is an accurate reading of economic inter-war history than that it was widely believed at the time. After the war, it became an article of faith that protection had not only exacerbated the economic problem of depression but that it had helped to poison the political atmosphere and so contributed to the drift to war. Economic liberalism was a fair-weather doctrine; regardless of the consequences, national authorities would have no alternative but to retreat behind their national defences when the weather turned foul. What was now required, the Americans passionately believed, was a set of institutions to manage the liberal market order, and so provide national governments with other alternatives during periods of economic distress. The Western Europeans generally shared the American view, albeit with varying degrees of enthusiasm.

Before turning to the institutions themselves, we need to note three compromises on which the new order was based, since in some respects it was their fragility that has created many of the subsequent problems that have faced international economic institutions in both the monetary and commercial fields.

The first, and in practice probably least troublesome, was a compromise with the ideological purity of liberal economic theory. The purpose of the two institutions created at the Bretton Woods Conference in 1944 — the IMF and the IBRD — and of the GATT, was to facilitate the freest possible movement of goods and services throughout the world. This objective, it was held, required the revival of private capital markets and the convertibility of major currencies. At the same time, since the system was intended to promote international harmony as well as economic growth, in principle, membership had to be open to all.

The requirements of universality raised an awkward question: how were states, whose economies were centrally planned (i.e. the Soviet Union and other socialist states), to be accommodated within a system essentially designed for countries with open or mixed economies? With hindsight, it is not clear how the bilateralism of the socialist and the multilateralism of the capitalist blocs could ever have been reconciled, although at the time the compromise reached was merely to ignore the problematic nature of integrating countries with different social and economic systems. In practice the compromise was not put to the test: Stalin denounced the Bretton Woods institutions (not without a certain justice) as the infrastructure of the Western Alliance, and prevented the socialist countries from participating in them. The question of their membership only arose in the 1970s, with the opening up of economic relations across the Iron Curtain, and then, as we shall see, the partial solutions that were found were essentially pragmatic.

The second compromise was between the principles of universalism and regionalism. In theory, economic liberalism addressed itself to the interests of individuals and private enterprises rather than states. All that the latter were required to do was to maintain domestic law and order which is necessary for business confidence, to underwrite the national currency for the same reason, and not to discriminate amongst suppliers from foreign countries. The post-war institutional order was designed to internationalise this limited conception of the state's role. To this end a system of agreed exchange rates was established, to allow the convertibility of the major currencies and to minimise the destabilising effects of speculation. At the same time, international trade was to be based on the principle of non-discrimination. The belief was that for a liberal system to be credible (establishing the trust without which it would inevitably break down) it would have to be universal and non-discriminatory.

However, from the start, the system had to coexist with regional aspirations which were dubiously consistent with it. Moreover, the political and economic interests of the new hegemony, the United States, were potentially in conflict. Politically, the Americans were strongly in favour of a united Western Europe, which could provide a second pillar to support the arch of the Atlantic Alliance. With this objective in mind, successive US governments backed the EEC. But they failed to foresee that a strong European Community would present a challenge both to American economic interests and to the theoretically universal principles on which the liberal system was to be based. As we shall see, many of the conflicts that have weakened international economic cooperation have their origin in this tension between European regionalism and American universalism.

The final and most important compromise underlying the post-war system was between nationalism (and the ultimate priority afforded to national policies) and the perceived need for some form of international order. The reasons for this compromise were twofold. First, national states would not voluntarily enter into binding agreements unless it was clearly understood that, in exceptional circumstances, they would reassert their own sovereignty. Of course they would have done so in any case, but for the new order to be credible the circumstances under which the new rules could be waived had to be spelled out. Secondly, by the end of the Second World War, all the major belligerents, with the possible exception of the United States, had accepted the revolutionary idea that the maintenance of full employment (or in the British formulation, high and stable employment) would henceforth be a major responsibility of democratic governments. The logic was simple: if national governments could require citizens to make the ultimate sacrifice in wartime, they could not subsequently, in peacetime, treat labour as a commodity like any other. It followed that the new institutions would justify themselves only to the extent that they were perceived as contributing to economic growth and stability. If and when international obligations were perceived as conflicting with the full employment goal, the latter would have priority.

The institutional framework

The core institutions established after the war shared a common strategic objective — the restoration of an open liberal economy in which private interests would be as free as possible from government interference — but were also designed to perform the functionally separate tasks of stabilising the international monetary system, establishing and policing a fair trading environment, and harmonising domestic economic policies so that the macro-economic policies of one country would not undermine similar efforts elsewhere. Very broadly, the first two tasks were the major responsibilities of the IMF and the GATT, while from 1960 onwards the OECD performed the third for the Western industrial countries. Let us consider each briefly in turn.

The international monetary system

Under classical economic liberalism one of the few positive functions that the state had to perform was to maintain the value of its currency. During the nineteenth century, it seemed for a time that this objective had been achieved internationally by the Gold Standard. The two great advantages of the Gold Standard, it was believed, were its impartiality and its predictability. Under it, the process by which the domestic economy adjusts to the international market, and vice versa, was automatic. All outstanding international transactions had to be settled in gold with the result that a country in balance of payments deficit automatically lost, and a country in surplus gained, gold. Under this system, all currency in circulation, was meant to be convertible into gold on demand. There was, therefore, neither an adjustment nor an exchange rate problem: an outflow of gold would lead automatically to a contraction of the money supply and hence of domestic demand; prices would fall, leading to improved competitiveness abroad and an increase in exports; this in turn would be followed by the development of a trade surplus, the inflow of gold and the expansion of domestic money supply and of domestic demand. The circle was now complete and the process would start over again. The system was not only automatic and predictable; it was also aesthetically pleasing: once a government had undertaken to back its currency with gold, everything else followed from this decision — there was no further need to involve itself in monetary policy; indeed it was positively required not to do so.

The great disadvantage of the Gold Standard was its notorious heartlessness. Deficit countries had to deflate regardless of the consequences for labour and capital, i.e. the inevitable rise of unemployment and bankruptcies that would accompany such action. In the event, the system broke down irretrievably during the great depression when governments were forced by the scale of the disaster to manipulate their exchange rates in an effort to boost exports and choke off imports in the interests of domestic employment.

The IMF was originally intended to preside over an international monetary order which would have the advantages of predictability and impartiality of the Gold Standard without its disadvantages. The former objective, it was hoped, would be secured by making the major currencies freely convertible into one another at fixed (and therefore known) rates of exchange; the latter by establishing in effect an international overdraft facility which would give countries in economic trouble time to adjust (e.g. by industrial restructuring and/or the retraining of labour), and so avoid the necessity of instant deflation.

There was much more controversy over credit than fixed exchange rates. It arose over both the criteria for establishing national lines of credit and their volume. Negotiations which led to the creation of the IMF were, in the first instance, largely an Anglo-American affair. The British economist, Maynard Keynes, proposed a scheme under which governments would have been left as free as possible to pursue their national economic policies without having constantly to worry about the state of their balance of payments. Deficit countries would have had access to generous overdraft facilities from an International Clearing Union (the size of the permitted overdraft essentially reflecting the country's historical dependence on foreign trade), and surplus countries similarly would have been required to bank their accumulated reserves with the Union.

The revolutionary aspect of the Keynes plan was that it made no moral distinction between deficit and surplus countries: one country's deficit was by definition another country's surplus; those who were in the black today could easily find themselves in the red tomorrow. The plan sought a technical solution to this problem by imposing a symmetrical code of discipline on all countries: those in deficit would find that the cost of credit rose the longer the situation persisted, thus providing them with an incentive to undertake the necessary structural adjustment; those in credit would similarly be penalised if their reserves continued to rise beyond an agreed point, thus providing them with an incentive to open their markets to foreign imports.

Had the negotiations taken place in 1960, by which time the United States itself was in chronic deficit, rather than in 1944, it is possible that some version of the Keynes plan might have obtained their support. But, like many of Keynes's ideas, it was ahead of its time. At the end of the war there was a chronic dollar shortage. In these circumstances the Americans were understandably afraid that unless they kept a tight reign on the new monetary system other countries would gain at their expense. What eventually emerged, therefore, was an organisation which established international drawing rights on a far more modest scale than Keynes had proposed, or even than had been suggested by his American counterpart, the Secretary of the Treasury, Harry Dexter White.

In the event, the resources available to the IMF could not meet the requirements of the deficit countries during the early post-war years of reconstruction. Since the demand for dollars was so high (and for other currencies virtually non-existent) it was not possible to move quickly to a system of convertible currencies at fixed exchange rates as envisaged by the negotiators at Bretton Woods. Instead, the Americans initiated a massive transfer of resources to their allies under the Marshall Plan and in effect managed the system unilaterally. It was only in 1958 that the IMF system began to function more or less as it had originally been intended. By this time the other industrial countries had recovered sufficiently to make their currencies convertible, although in the case of Japan it was not until 1964.

Between 1958 and 1971 the Fund played a major role in presiding over the monetary order and in providing a range of services to countries in economic distress. The system established a set of par values for currencies in relation to the dollar, which was itself pegged to gold at $35 an ounce. Theoretically, members of the Fund could only vary these values, without consultation, by 1 per cent in either direction, although in practice most of them, other than the United States, devalued or revalued unilaterally at different times. The drawing rights (overdraft facilities) available to Fund members ranged from the absolute to the conditional. Each country was allotted a quota within which a proportion (or in IMF terminology, 'tranche') was available on demand with subsequent drawings being accompanied by conditions relating to economic policy and performance. Although conditionality was 'built in' to the Articles of Agreement, governments always found it embarrassing to have their economic policies and administration publicly scrutinised by teams of international civil servants, if only because their political opponents invariably accused them of surrendering the country's sovereignty. This point is worth recalling because in much contemporary comment about the IMF's approach to the debt crisis, it is often wrongly assumed that it is only Third World countries that have had to engage in structural adjustment as a condition of obtaining IMF support. If there is a legitimate criticism of the IMF on this score, namely that its policies are insufficiently sensitive to the political difficulties and realities of individual countries, it applies across the board.

I shall return to some of the reasons which led to the collapse of the original Bretton Woods system in 1971 later in this chapter. The point to note here is that when the Americans finally suspended the convertibility of the dollar into gold and then terminated the fixed exchange rate system, the IMF did not cease to exist. Indeed, in some respects, its importance may have been enhanced. Apart from the notorious difficulty of disestablishing any international organisation once it exists, two other points may help to explain the apparent ease with which the Fund had shed its old functions and assumed new ones.

The first concerns the actual as opposed to the theoretical role that the IMF plays in the management of the international monetary system. In a sense this has not changed very much. As we have seen, the system was designed to be both universal and automatic. It turned out to be neither. Because the socialist countries excluded themselves it became essentially a Western institution; and because the resources available to the Fund were initially inadequate, it operated from the start in the shadow of the United States. A consequence of these developments was that the major decisions on monetary affairs, and such changes in the way the system was managed (e.g. the General Agreement to Borrow introduced in the early 1960s) were invariably agreed by the governments of the major powers outside the Fund and with little or no consultation with the other members. However, they were subsequently brought to the IMF for ratification and legitimation. Once the original system had broken down — for reasons unconnected with the activities of the Fund — the IMF's Articles of Agreement were changed to accommodate the new situation of floating exchange rates.

The second point with a bearing on the IMF's current role concerns its activities in the Third World. Although the Fund has always been a Western-dominated institution — a fact that has made it a natural target for Third World criticism — developing countries increasingly depend on its expertise and assistance. From the 1950s the IMF, in collaboration with the World Bank, became involved in coordinating Western aid programmes to countries whose development policies were accompanied by persistent and deepening balance of payments crises. Later the IMF established several special facilities, for example the compensatory finance and buffer stock facilities, to meet their special needs.

The major IMF involvement in the Third World, however, is a consequence of the debt crisis. Increasingly, Third World governments have found that to secure the continued support of the private banking sector, either for rescheduling old loans or establishing new credit, they need the IMF's seal of approval. Although the conditions imposed vary from country to country, they invariably involve a package of structural adjustment measures often requiring the devaluation of the local currency and the abolition of urban food subsidies. Some countries, for example Nigeria, have found it politically impossible to accept the IMF conditions openly but have been forced into similar policies on their own behalf and on the basis of private understandings with the Fund and the major banks. Others, for example Zambia, have accepted the IMF package, but then been forced by local political circumstances to abandon it and to attempt to go it alone.

For heavily dependent countries unilateralism remains a high-risk policy, and although some countries may be able to use the size of their outstanding debt as a weapon with which to bargain with their private and government creditors, it seems unlikely that the IMF will be excluded from influence in the Third World by an epidemic of massive and official default. Moreover, if at some future date the major powers agree to a general, as opposed to a piecemeal, approach to the problem of Third World debt, the IMF would almost certainly be heavily involved in an organising and servicing capacity.

The international trade system

The monetary system established at Bretton Woods was not an end in itself. It was intended to facilitate the freest possible movement of goods and services across international borders. The absence of stable and predictable exchange rates was only one impediment, albeit a very important one, to the achievement of this goal. In 1945 there were many physical and other obstacles to trade which had been built up during the 1930s, and during the war, when all the major trading countries operated command economies. The Americans had originally envisaged an International Trade Organisation (ITO) with parallel functions in the trade field to those of the IMF in the monetary field. By the time the Charter of the ITO emerged from the Havana Conference in 1947 it was hedged around with so many escape clauses and exceptions deferential to the interests of national sovereignty that President Truman concluded that it would be pointless to submit it to the Congress. However, the part of the Charter that dealt with trade negotiations was salvaged and subsequently formed the basis of the General Agreement of Tariffs and Trade (GATT).

The GATT is essentially a multilateral treaty which imposes on its signatories (the contracting parties) specific rights and obligations. (The fact that it is not an international organisation with a legal personality of its own has always been regarded by its supporters as a strength rather than a weakness.) Its purpose was to abolish all physical constraints on trade, i.e. quantitative restrictions, and to freeze and gradually to eliminate all trade preferences. In addition it sought to reduce the level of tariff protection through multilateral negotiations. To this end the contracting parties agreed to base their commercial relations with one another on the most-favoured-nation principle (m.f.n.) which implied non-discrimination, and to negotiate tariff reductions on the basis of reciprocity, i.e. all countries participating in the negotiations were expected to offer concessions.

Under the m.f.n. principle, any concessions exchanged by two countries in a trade negotiation are extended automatically to include more advantageous terms should either of their governments negotiate such terms with a third country. M.f.n. was established as a basic operational principle of liberal trade policy in the nineteenth century and was generally regarded as the minimum insurance that governments would require to persuade them to open their home markets to their competitors. The main innovation introduced by the GATT was multilateralism. Simultaneous multilateral negotiations under the m.f.n. rule meant that the effects of liberalisation were spread much more widely than when trade was conducted on a bilateral basis.

Only slightly less important than multilateralism was GATT's introduction of the idea of mutual surveillance into commercial diplomacy. The willingness of the contracting parties to open their markets to their competitors under the m.f.n. principle was conditional; in certain specified circumstances they would be permitted to close them again. Thus states could adopt protection for balance of payments purposes (Article XII), for economic development, i.e. infant industry protection (Article XVIII), as a defence against serious and unforeseen injury to domestic producers (Article XIX), and for reasons of national security (Article XXI). They were also permitted to discriminate in favour of certain contracting parties, if the purpose of discrimination was to create a Free Trade Area or Customs Union (Article XIV).

Except for Article XXI, which allowed states to take unilateral action, and Article XIV, where the waiving of the non-discriminatory m.f.n. rule had to be considered permanent, the other exceptions were regarded as temporary suspensions of the Agreement. Most of the signatories breached their obligations at some time, but during the heyday of the GATT they accepted the necessity of applying to their trading partners for a waiver of their obligations. If the time for which this was granted proved inadequate, they could reapply and reargue the case for an extension. This procedure represented a major departure from traditional interpretations of sovereign statehood.

Between the first round of tariff negotiations held at Torquay in 1947 and the implementation of the major cuts negotiated during the Kennedy Round in 1970, tariffs on manufactured goods were reduced from on average around 40 per cent to below 10 per cent, a point where they no longer constituted a major obstacle to international trade, at least amongst the industrial countries. Although the GATT has not fallen into disuse over the past fifteen years — indeed, there was a major round of negotiations (the Tokyo Round) in the 1970s and another (the Uruguay Round) got under way in 1987 — it has failed to check the general retreat from multilateralism and the rising tide of protectionism.

Two reasons for this relative failure should be noted. First, the world recession, the emergence of new industrial countries, which increasingly challenge the Western powers for market shares, and the failure of the international monetary system to provide either adequate credit or discipline, have combined to make governments more introspective and defensive and less mindful of their international obligations.

Secondly, further liberalisation depends on the elimination of non-tariff barriers to trade (NTBs). There is an enormous variety of these, ranging from subsidies and government procurement policies at one end of the spectrum to customs valuation procedures and health and safety regulations at the other. Their removal, or even rationalisation under agreed codes of conduct, represents a far more intractable problem than tariff reductions. One tariff is very much like another; it is a relatively straightforward matter therefore to measure the effect of a given reduction and then proceed to make concessions of equal value on the basis of reciprocity. By contrast, negotiation on NTBs raise problems of equivalence, similar to the classic problem that has always bedevilled arms control and disarmament negotiations, namely how many battalions equal a battleship. The difficulty in bringing agricultural protection within the purview of the GATT, and the similar difficulty that seems likely to accompany efforts to liberalise international trade in services will serve as illustrations of the general problem.

Like the IMF, however, the GATT seems destined to survive. Not only are

Western governments unwilling to reject publicly the idea of liberal trade, but the interests of giant multinational corporations (MNCs) also require national markets to be kept as open as possible. There is a paradox here. On the one hand, the governments which constantly urge a return to liberal orthodoxy are seldom prepared to practise what they preach. On the other, intra-firm trade within the multinational corporate sector accounts for a large and growing proportion of total world trade which is mostly beyond the reach of GATT. Yet the broad principles which the GATT upholds are those which best serve the interests of both governments and MNCs.

The harmonisation of industrial economies

The post-war order has been described somewhat glibly but not wholly accurately as being based on the doctrines of Adam Smith abroad and Maynard Keynes at home. The IMF and GATT provided an institutional framework for an open liberal economy whose objectives were essentially the same as those of classical economic liberalism. But the world of Adam Smith, in which private consumers were free to buy in the cheapest, and producers to sell in the dearest market, free from governmental interference, could only be made to work provided economic growth was sufficiently impressive to lay to rest the spectre of mass unemployment.

After the war, Keynes's belief that governments could and should manage the business cycle established itself as the new orthodoxy in all the major non-communist industrial countries. Implicitly, this raised the problem of harmonisation: in an economically interdependent world how were governments to avoid their anti-cyclical policies from undermining those of their trading partners? Since all the major governments insisted on the ultimate priority of national over international commitments, no institutional provision was originally made for handling this problem. But since the prosperity of each was perceived as involving the prosperity of all — the reverse image of what they had all experienced in the 1930s — a solution emerged nonetheless.

It was a condition of Marshall Aid that the recipients should take joint action to surmount the obstacles to the free movement of goods and services, and the restricted payments that they had established during the inter-war period. The Organisation for European Economic Cooperation (OEEC) was set up as a collective European response to meet this condition. When the task was completed, the OEEC was transformed into the Organisation for Economic Cooperation and Development (OECD). With its membership expanded to include all the major industrial countries, it developed as the agency where a substantial range of social and economic problems which are common to the industrial world could be identified and studied, and where, so far as possible, a common approach is worked out between governments.

With the general retreat from demand management policies at the end of the 1970s, and the rise of a more monetarist approach to national economic policy, the OECD's role in harmonising the domestic economic policies of its members is not so prominent as it once was. On the other hand, both the habit of intergovernmental cooperation that had been built up and the vast amount of data on the comparative economic policies which the OECD produces and on which the members have come to rely ensure that it will continue to play an important servicing role for the industrial countries in the future.

Errors and omissions

So much for the broad institutional design of the reconstructed liberal economy. Because all the major institutions involved have survived, we might conclude that they have proved not only the utility but their ability to adapt to rapidly changing economic and political circumstances. In a sense so they have. Closer inspection of the chaotic state of the world's monetary and commercial affairs may suggest that such a conclusion is unduly complacent. After all the original purpose of the post-war liberal order was to bring under law — and so to depoliticise — a major area of human activity and a potential source of conflict; whereas contemporary international economic relations are not only frequently highly conflictual, but are increasingly conducted on the basis of power relationships rather than agreed rules. Perhaps, as with national accounting, so with the liberal economic order as a whole, the books can only be balanced by allowing for error. In the final section of this chapter I will discuss the implications of three of these errors or omissions from the original design. They are respectively the false assumption that regionalism and universalism are in harmony; the dependence of the liberal trade order on an anachronistic conception of security; and the inadequacy of the institutional response to the economic problems of the Third World.

Regionalism and economic order

How can the potential conflict of interest between regional and universal organisations be overcome? The original answer to this question seemed straightforward. It was to ensure that the method of economic integration pursued by regional organisations should be consistent with the rules to govern economic relations at the global level. So, as we have seen, Article XXIV of the GATT permitted discrimination where its end result would be the creation of a Free Trade Area or Customs Union. The rationale for this major exception to the m.f.n. rule was that regional arrangements would reinforce rather than undermine the liberal order, providing they created new trade rather than diverted it.

There is nothing wrong with this reasoning in theory. Moreover, two post-war economic developments provided empirical support for it. The first was the structural change in the world economy during the 1950s and 1960s. Instead of the gains from trade flowing primarily to the producers of raw materials, as in the past, it became clear that the most beneficial forms of trade now consisted of exchanges of manufactured goods between industrial countries. The new pattern seemed to provide evidence of the potentially dynamic effects of regional integration within the EEC and EFTA — in both cases the enlargement of the home market allowing businesses to expand their operations and exploit economies of scale.

Secondly, the early success of the EEC in establishing a Common Commercial Policy (CCP), paradoxically strengthened the GATT as the umbrella under which wider international trade negotiations could take place. The EEC as a unit now had an interest in securing access to the North American and Japanese markets on the most advantageous terms; and for the first time the Americans had to take the Europeans seriously as economic competitors rather than merely as subordinate allies. The result was the Kennedy Round, which changed the basis of tariff negotiations from item-by-item bargaining to deep linear cuts across the board. Although in practice this proved almost as arduous as the previous method — the major argument shifting from those items to be included to those which would be excluded from the overall reduction — the result was nonetheless a more dramatic liberalisation of industrial markets than had hitherto been achieved.

In the Third World, there was also a strong theoretical case for regional cooperation. In many areas, both industrial development and the private investment that was needed to promote it were restricted by the small size of the national markets and/or the low level of per capita national income. In contrast to the industrial world, where integration was pursued as a means of rationalising and harmonising the economies of countries which were already heavily involved with one another, in Africa, Asia and Latin America, it was pursued as one of the preconditions of modernisation and development.

The tension between global and regional economic institutions arose from the historical situation not from their theoretical incompatibility. The process of regional integration, particularly but not only in Europe, has created at least three kinds of problems for international economic institutions.

The first concerned the role of preferences within the system. From the Second World War, it was a major American objective to abolish preferential trading, which they believed to have been a politically pernicious feature of the inter-war period. In the event the best they could secure within the GATT was the freezing of existing preferences, a necessary consequence of basing trade negotiations on the m.f.n. principle. The assumption was that as tariffs were negotiated down, the margin of preference granted to some countries (e.g. under the Commonwealth Preferential or Franc Zone schemes) would narrow and eventually disappear altogether. But as this goal was approached the EEC reintroduced preferences by the back door.

Initially this was the result of the French insistence on adding Part IV to the Rome Treaty which established the concept of association for the colonies of the member states. When the majority of these became independent in 1960 they retained their privileged position in EEC markets and then consolidated their right to Community preferences in the first Yaoundé Convention two years later. But the creation of the EEC put the m.f.n. principle under still more sustained pressure. Customs Union theory provides for the removal of all internal obstacles to trade and the simultaneous creation of a common external tariff. Once the Union has been established, therefore, all non-member countries should be treated on equal terms, i.e. under the m.f.n. rule. In practice, this is likely to disrupt traditional trading patterns as established suppliers find themselves ousted, through no fault of their own, by newcomers. Since these suppliers will have their outlets within the Union, there will be aggrieved interests inside as well as outside the newly created customs barrier. In such circumstances the governments of the member states are likely to come under both diplomatic and political pressure for some relaxation of the rules to accommodate the 'legitimate' interests of traditional suppliers.

The EEC responded to this unintended but predictable consequence of integration by negotiating a whole range of special trade agreements with third countries, particularly around the Mediterranean and in southern Europe. Britain's accession to the Community in 1973 led to a further proliferation of special trading arrangements. The African, Caribbean and Pacific members of the Commonwealth eventually joined with the associated states to sign the first Lomé Convention in 1975; special trade agreements were then negotiated between the enlarged Community and the South Asian Commonwealth countries and with the remaining members of EFTA who individually retained their tariff sovereignty with regard to the outside world. These arrangements were no doubt all practical *ad hoc* solutions to the consequential problems caused by the creation and subsequent enlargement of the Community; but they also inevitably reduced the coherence of the m.f.n. principle as the basis of the international trading order.

With few exceptions regional integration schemes in the Third World have not generated the development for which their supporters originally hoped. There are two major reasons for their failure. The first is the extreme difficulty which most developing countries have experienced in breaking with the colonial economy they inherited at independence: the national economies of most Third World regions (e.g. West Africa or the Caribbean) are competitive rather than complementary. Moreover, very little of their official trade is conducted within the region, with the result that the competition between them is for access to the markets of the industrial countries. Secondly, the fact that the benefits of integration are not distributed evenly amongst the members of a Free Trade Area or Customs Union has created even greater political difficulties in the Third World than in Europe.

Liberal economic theory holds that liberal trade policies will optimise welfare for all *in the long run*; it does not claim that all will benefit equally all the time. There is a problem in persuading governments to endorse such a programme: they are unlikely to enter into regional integration schemes unless they believe that it will be in their immediate interests to do so. In principle, of course, it is possible to build redistributive mechanisms into an agreement to counter the inequitable consequences of liberal integration, for example transfer taxes or progressive revenue allocations in favour of the poorer members. In practice, while many such mechanisms have been negotiated, where even the better-off members face formidable development problems (e.g. Kenya in the former East African Community) they have invariably proved unstable. Because they are generally unwilling to surrender sovereignty to supra-national institutions, Third World governments have either fallen back on economic nationalism —

negotiating the best deal for themselves that is available from the industrial countries on which they depend — or on limited cooperation amongst themselves on a preferential basis, in the hope of loosening their dependence on the industrial West — as in the Preferential Trade Area (PTA) in Eastern and southern Africa. Either way, the end result is to weaken rather than strengthen the international commitment to the liberal economic order.

The second problem created by regional integration concerns the process of negotiation itself. The point is simply that where multilateral negotiations can only take place after regional organisations have first reached a common position amongst their own members, the process is likely to be protracted and the end result limited in scope. The creation of the EEC, with its CCP, may have given the GATT system a new lease of life, but it also slowed down the pace of liberalisation. Reconciling the perceived national interests of twelve states takes time and effectively ensures that negotiations with the outside world are conducted on the basis of the lowest common denominator. In other words, the most reluctant rather than the most outward-looking members of the organisation dictate the pace and extent of liberalisation.

Thirdly, regional integration entrenches rather than weakens the pressures for protection in sensitive sectors of the economy. The most obvious example is agricultural protection. Originally, the GATT was intended to cover agriculture as well as industry. But because all industrial countries protected their agricultural sectors and, just as important, protected them by different kinds of support policy, it was put aside in favour of negotiations on the reduction of industrial tariffs where there was a greater prospect of success.

Ironically, it was the Americans, who were later to emerge as the major proponents of agricultural liberalisation, who in 1954 first applied for and obtained a general waiver from their obligations in respect of agriculture. But it is the EEC's Common Agriculture Policy (CAP) which continues to cause the most difficulty.

Ever since the dollar shortage of the early post-war period was transformed into a chronic American balance of payments problem in the early 1960s, successive US administrations have argued that their European allies should share the burden of financing the liberal economic order.

The Americans regarded agriculture as the most obvious candidate for European 'burden-sharing'. Under their own system they had developed the most efficient and productive agricultural sector in the world; the West Europeans, by contrast, pursued a policy of agricultural self-sufficiency on the basis of a very large, and relatively very inefficient, small-scale farming sector, particularly in France and Southern Germany. It followed, the Americans argued, that the Europeans should open their markets to US exports. Not surprisingly the Europeans viewed the matter differently: for them the CAP represented the central political deal — between German industry and French agriculture — on which the EEC had been constructed. They were not prepared to put at risk their own system of regional cooperation merely to please the Americans or to bring their economic policies more in line with neo-classical orthodoxy.

It is doubtful whether the CAP any longer performs the central political role within the EEC that it once did. It consumes a disproportionate share of the budget, not merely in American eyes, but in the view of several EEC member countries themselves, including Britain. However, the problem is now essentially institutional: other member countries, as well as France, have politically powerful farming constituencies which remain deeply attached to the CAP. Despite the strength of the arguments in favour of reforming European agricultural policy, to do away with the absurd over-production to which it has led, the problem has so far defied solution. Agricultural liberalisation together with services has been named as one of the major objectives of the Uruguay Round of GATT negotiations. There is little evidence to suggest, however, that substantial progress is likely to be made.

Security and the liberal trade order

If a choice had to be made, Adam Smith believed, defence was to be preferred over opulence: so did all the other classical and neo-classical economists. The reason was that while many of them believed that by replacing the world of passions by a world of interests, freely competing within an open market, war would gradually become irrelevant, they knew that in fact they lived within a war system. Since their own theory could not accommodate war, there was no alternative but to suspend it for the duration of hostilities.

As we have seen, Article XXI of the GATT reflects this tradition of economic thought. However, this Article, which allows contracting parties to disregard their international obligations and take whatever action is deemed appropriate to defend their vital security interests, has virtually never been used. The most plausible reason for its neglect is that the concept of international security on which it is based has very little relevance in the contemporary international system.

The original concept was designed for a world in which countries would be heavily engaged with one another economically and yet at any moment find themselves at war. In such a world it was only realistic to have a let-out clause to cover the eventuality of conflict. Moreover, the architects of the GATT looked back to the inter-war period when the major political, and ultimately military, conflict had been between capitalist countries. These countries were, indeed, heavily involved with one another economically. The major fracture in the post-war system, by contrast, has been between standing alliances, the membership of which is defined by different economic as well as ideological systems and allegiances. The major capitalist powers have many conflicts of economic interest, but in a nuclear world are unlikely to find themselves at war with one another. The recognition that this is so is probably amongst the reasons for the rise of protectionism in the industrial world since the mid-1970s: in effect the Cold War had made the world safe for economic nationalism.

Other explanations have been offered for the demise of the GATT system and the rise of the new protectionism, including the failure of the leading country, the United States, to ensure a properly regulated flow of credit in the free-for-all world that followed the collapse of the Bretton Woods monetary system. But without discounting the persuasive force of such arguments, it remains true that the reconstructed liberal order failed from the start to take account of the expanded concept of security that in practice underlay the post-war economic policies of all the capitalist countries.

The new responsibilities of the liberal state, for employment and welfare, implied that it also had acquired obligations to provide for the social as well as for the physical security of its citizens. Under the Bretton Woods and GATT systems these new responsibilities could only be catered for if high rates of growth were maintained. Moreover, the need to sustain a high level of economic performance increased with time, partly because demographic trends in the industrial countries meant that the state had to provide for a growing number of people who were either too young or too old to work, and partly because there were no obvious limits to a social security system.

The provision of public goods within a social security system which includes entitlements to health, education, environmental facilities and so on, is entirely open-ended. In these circumstances, once rates of growth slowed down, and major sectors of the economy came under attack from new and cheaper centres of industrial production, pressures for protection in the older industrial countries were often politically irresistible. The GATT Secretariat might bemoan the lack of political will shown by the contracting parties but there was nothing they could do about it.

Two issues are involved here. The first concerns the concept of strategic industries, the second the implications of welfare capitalism for commercial and industrial policy. On neither issue have the institutions of the liberal order worked out an adequate response. There are both similar and distinct reasons for their failure. Essentially the explanation lies in the radical separation of the private and public domain within classical liberal theory. For the classical liberals the state's functions were limited to the provision of defence from physical attack, the provision of internal law and order to protect civil society, and responsibility for the value of the currency. In all other respects the economy fell within the purview of civil society itself, that is the private domain, not that of the state.

The Bretton Woods institutions and GATT modified this classical view of the world to the extent that they were meant to perform the regulative and ordering function, at the international level, that the state itself performed nationally. As we have seen, there were certain concessions to the priority of national interests in the form of the exceptions to the GATT; but apart from Article XXI, these were not expressed in terms of the state's strategic or security interests. The underlying reason for this was that the system was designed to support private enterprise and to encourage the development of an international division of labour on the basis of the principles of comparative advantage and costs.

As regards the concept of strategic industries, two points should be made. The first is that the means of defence had always been excluded from liberal market philosophy. In practice all major arms producers have sought to develop an export trade — the extra production lowering unit costs. However, liberal economic theory is silent on this issue: once it is accepted that defence takes priority over welfare, states should presumably be prepared to subsidise the production of arms to the extent necessary. Not surprisingly, global economic institutions have steered clear of the issue also. It is noticeable, for example, that while the IMF has imposed stringent conditions on Third World debtors, as the price of its continued support, on no occasion has it attempted to curb their expenditure on armaments. Yet it is hardly deniable that in many cases where there is no self-evident external threat, the defence budget consumes a quite disproportionate share of the state's resources.

The second point concerns the theory of strategic goods. Once it is conceded that goods other than armaments play an important part in a country's overall war potential, it is impossible, even in principle, to solve the problem of definition. Any common good, even trouser buttons, as Khrushchev once quipped, may be regarded as strategic goods: it all depends on opportunity costs, on what a state must forgo in order to acquire what the authorities decide is essential to its security.

It is the impossible problem of defining inherently strategic goods which has bedevilled the work of COCOM, the committee of NATO which administers the strategic embargo against the Soviet Union and its allies. Broadly, the Americans have generally been in favour of a very wide definition covering many items of only marginal military significance, while the Europeans, with a much greater stake in East–West trade, have attempted to keep the list of embargoed items as short as possible. Their interest in restricting the list increased during the period of *détente* in the 1970s when several East European countries (although not the Soviet Union itself) were admitted to the GATT. This was achieved under a formula which gave them access to Western markets on m.f.n. terms, despite the fact that the nature of their own economies did not allow them to reciprocate in the normal way. The admission of Comecon states to GATT, in other words, was a political gesture, which depended on the Western powers taking a liberal view of the strategic goods issue.

The implications of welfare capitalism for national economic policies are paradoxical. The extension of the state's prerogatives to cover social security, 'from the cradle to the grave', grew out of the liberal tradition of social and political thought. (The chapter on 'The limits of *laissez-faire*' in John Stuart Mills's *Principles of Political Economy* lengthened with each successive edition as the author recognised that more and more 'vital' services were never likely to be provided by the private market.) Yet the result of the extension of the state's role in the management of the economy has undoubtedly been to reveal the latent mercantilism which liberal economic policy had sought to eradicate.

The attempt to define the concept of strategic industries from the point of view of economic history leads to opposing conclusions. The first is in line with the theory of strategic goods already discussed: there are no industries which are permanently or inherently strategic. The second is that, although the list may change over time, historically all the major industrial countries have regarded certain industries, e.g. steel, shipbuilding, automobile and textile production, as strategic in a sense that they have not allowed them to be exterminated as the result of foreign competition. From this perspective what appears to define a strategic industry is either its direct or indirect importance to the more narrowly defined defence industries and/or its importance to the national economy in terms of the numbers of people it employs directly and the secondary and tertiary industries that are dependent on it. At the time when the liberal trade order was constructed the major Western powers enjoyed the comparative advantage in all these industries. Consequently, liberalisation was seen as an opportunity not as a danger. The success, first of the Japanese and then other newly industrialised countries in capturing a growing share of world markets has forced the Western industrial countries on to the defensive.

In general terms, the problem was foreseen by the architects of the post-war order. They feared that a sudden surge of low-cost imports in a particular sector would have such disruptive social and political consequences that it might force governments to abandon their commitment to liberal trade policies. Article XIX of the GATT was included to safeguard against this possibility: in circumstances where they faced such a market challenge states were allowed to reintroduce protection of domestic industry. Article XIX (like the other exceptions to the m.f.n. rule) was subject to two qualifications designed to make it support liberal rather than mercantilist policies: first, waivers were to be temporary to allow countries time to adjust to the inevitable (and, under liberal theory, beneficial) shifts in the international division of labour; second, protection was to be applied on a non-discriminatory basis, i.e. to all suppliers of the products concerned.

Neither of these qualifications has worn well. To take the most notorious example, the international trade in textiles, successive attempts to regulate this trade, of which the Multi Fibre Agreement (MFA) is the most recent, have effectively been transformed from arrangements to provide temporary respite to declining industries in the industrial countries to an institutionalised and permanent form of protection. Moreover, protection is against low-cost Third World producers only, some of whom themselves acquire an interest in the protective regime against latecomers who find it difficult to establish a right to a quota. In the case of textiles, the MFA has been recognised by GATT, but in the 1970s and 1980s the trade in many other allegedly 'strategic' industries was regulated by voluntary export restraint agreements (VERs) or Orderly Marketing Arrangements (OMAs) which are not similarly recognised.

It is possible to exaggerate the significance of the reassertion of neo-mercantalism against the neo-classical orthodoxy of the Bretton Woods system and GATT. It can be argued that the market is a much more powerful mechanism than the institutional order set up to police it. World trade has in fact only declined in one year since the Second World War (1982) and, despite all the complaints, the Third World's share of the international textile market has continued to rise. Nonetheless the failure to devise rules, which command international respect, to cover the protection of industries which governments consider vital for reasons of social as well as physical security has undoubtedly weakened confidence in the ability of institutions to manage the international economy in the interests of all.

It is possible that the ground lost in recent years may not be recoverable. Ultimately what is at issue is a conflict between a view of internationalism in which institutions have a positive and hence a policy-making role in managing the world economy, and one in which they exist to perform essentially a regulatory function, to act as umpires in the application of a set of fair trading and other economic rules which have already been agreed by the states which make up the membership. The failure of the post-war institutional order to resolve this conflict is most vividly illustrated in relation to the role of developing countries in the world economy. By way of conclusion, therefore, I now turn to this final 'error' in the original design.

The Third World in international economic institutions

The literature on development is very extensive, and it is not my intention to trace in any detail the major issues involved. Rather my purpose is to suggest why international economic institutions have generally failed to meet the aspirations of Third World governments, even though their work has often been dominated by he North–South debate and a number of specific changes in the system have been introduced to meet Third World demands.

At base, the answer is both straightforward and fairly brutal. Third World countries have wanted an international economic system in which resources will be shifted on a large scale from North to South. To this end they have sought institutional changes which would take power from the market place, where they are weak, and transfer it to intergovernmental institutions where, assuming a reasonable level of Third World solidarity, they are strong. Such a reform of the existing system would obviously be at the expense of the industrial Western powers who have accordingly always resisted it.

This simple clash of interests, conceals a deeper conflict of institutional and political philosophies. We have seen that in the Western industrial countries, it was only after 1945 that the responsibility of the state for the overall performance of the national economy was unambiguously recognised. It is not surprising, therefore, that it took some further time before the idea of an international obligation to assist the economic development of politically independent but poor countries, gained widespread acceptance. Nor is it surprising that it remains a contentious subject even now.

It is not true, however, that the major Western powers were totally insensitive to the needs of the developing countries. Indeed, so long as the development problem could be viewed within a liberal perspective, they were reasonably responsive. During the 1960s both the IMF and the OECD played leading roles in coordinating Western aid policies, while in 1963 the GATT added a new chapter to the Agreement devoted to the special problems of the developing countries. Most importantly, this new chapter established the right of developing countries to full m.f.n. treatment and to participate, on equal terms, in international trade negotiations on the basis of non-reciprocity.

From the Western point of view these changes were seen as incremental reforms to a system which was fundamentally based on sound principles. From a Third World perspective the trouble with such tinkering was that it made very little impression on the development problem. In the Kennedy Round of GATT negotiations, which was the first to take place under the non-reciprocity provision, such were the difficulties in reaching agreement between the major actors in the drama that the interests of the developing countries were squeezed out.

Despite its good intentions, the GATT has also repeatedly failed to come to grips with the problem of escalating tariffs (i.e. rates of effective protection which rise with each successive stage of processing) which seriously restrict Third World development prospects. Schemes such as the EEC's STABEX, which provides automatic compensation for certain tropical products when their export receipts fall, have been limited by lack of funds. They have also helped, so their critics maintain, to freeze colonial trade patterns and to slow down the rate of industrialisation and diversification.

Such criticisms may not always be fair but they serve to dramatise the general crisis of confidence in the institutional order of the Western international economy. Except in a few countries the gap between the living standards of the majority of citizens in the industrial and developing worlds has steadily widened in the forty years since the end of the Second World War. At any other time in history a development of this kind would not have created a major diplomatic issue, but the existence of two sets of international institutions (those of the United Nations system and of the liberal economic order), has transformed it into one. Moreover, because the Bretton Woods institutions and GATT were widely, and on the whole correctly, viewed in the Third World as having been designed to serve the interests of the Western powers, the developing countries shifted the battle to the UN system where their numerical preponderance would ensure them a hearing.

In institutional terms their efforts were rewarded with considerable success, although, once again, the results in terms of major economic reform, let alone development, were unimpressive. The most notable achievement was the creation of the United Nations Conference on Trade and Development (UNCTAD) in 1964. Although a universal organisation, the UNCTAD has provided the nearest thing that exists to a Third World Secretariat, to some extent servicing the Group of 77 in the same kind of way that the OECD services the industrial countries. But neither the UNCTAD nor the UN Special Sessions in 1974 and 1975 which led to the formulation of the programme for a New International Economic Order (NIEO) has succeeded in shifting the economic balance of power. Nor did they introduce any major change in the organisation of the world economy. The most that can be claimed for them is that by generating a vast amount of detailed research into every aspect of the development problem, and by providing Third World governments with an international platform, they have both contributed to an understanding of the complexity of the development process and have succeeded in keeping the development issue on the international agenda, albeit hardly in a very prominent position.

In the midst of the general retreat from multilateralism in the 1980s, this itself is no mean achievement. Nevertheless it falls a long way short of the aspirations of most developing countries, let alone of the objectives of those who sought to establish the NIEO. A comparison between the two set-piece UNCTAD negotiations, those to establish a General Special Preference Scheme (GSP) in the 1960s, and for the Integrated Programme for Commodities (IPC) and Common Fund in the 1970s, illustrates the fundamental problem that developing countries collectively face in international economic institutions.

In the former case, there was initial opposition from the United States to the

Third World campaign for preferences for their manufactured and semi-manufactured exports to the industrial West. But in the end, even the US government was persuaded that such a general breach of the m.f.n. rule — under which *all* industrial countries would grant preferences to *all* developing countries — would lock the recipients into the system rather than exclude them. The GSP negotiations did not challenge the liberal order; the trouble was that the diplomatic investment was out of all proportion to the rather meagre results achieved. The reason, as immediately became clear once the GSP schemes were implemented at the end of the 1960s, was that very few developing countries had an industrial sector which would allow them to take advantage of the preferences. For the majority there was no alternative, for the foreseeable future, to remaining exporters of raw materials and tropical foodstuffs.

Negotiating internationally agreed programmes to help these countries shifted the focus of debate from the reform of liberal (i.e. arm's-length) trade rules to the creation of a system of managed markets and administered prices. For the major Western consumers of industrial raw materials, this shift raised the spectre of collectivism, and from the start therefore they were much less favourably disposed towards it. Nevertheless, the Western powers themselves were not united; and in the wake of the oil price rises of the mid-1970s, they agreed to negotiation within UNCTAD to create a fund whose purpose was to finance commodity price stabilisation schemes.

By the time the Common Fund Agreement was finally signed in 1978 the negotiations had revealed the deep divide which separated the two sides. The Group of 77, by its very nature, has to reconcile so many conflicting interests that it tends to proceed on the basis of the highest common denominator, putting together a package of demands which include something for everyone. Certainly in the IPC negotiations the more radical states not only wanted a transfer of real resources (either by raising prices or by generating money to assist research into new uses and new methods of exploitation), but also the creation of a new institution. They envisaged a Common Fund which would be largely under the political control of the Third Word, and would have sufficient resources to allow it to create new commodity agreements and intervene in the market. Faced with these demands the industrial countries engaged in damage limitation: to the extent that they were willing to contemplate the creation of new commodity agreements, they insisted that this had to be at the request of the consuming and producing interests of the commodity concerned. As the countries which would inevitably have to provide the majority of the finance, they also insisted in maintaining an important share in the management of any new institution. Although the Common Fund had not yet come into existence (initially because of a lack of the neccessary number of ratifications), not surprisingly the form of the final compromise was essentially designed to meet Western objections to the original proposal.

During the 1970s the UNCTAD provided the stage for an active North–South debate on international economic reform and the form that this should take. During the 1980s it has often seemed that the debate has been called off altogether because the governments of the major powers are in no mood to listen. These days, it is the UNCTAD, acting on behalf of an increasingly dispersed and demoralised Group of 77, which is most obviously engaged in damage limitation. The immediate explanation is clearly the political shift to the right in the major industrial countries. In the context of a major world recession, their governments have been markedly less internationalist in outlook than their predecessors.

But these developments, on the surface of political life, also illustrate a more fundamental problem of international cooperation. Intergovernmental institutions work best when the areas with which they deal fall unambiguously within the competence of governments. In the non-communist world, however, international economic cooperation must balance between private and public interests and competencies. For a time, after the Second World War, there was a broad international consensus that the purpose of international economic organisations was to establish a framework of agreed rules and then, on the basis of agreed procedures, to police them. No doubt the system never worked perfectly, but it nonetheless represented a major advance on the anarchy of the inter-war period. Now the contradictions which were present even at the creation have overwhelmed the system. While no government would willingly surrender access to international economic organisations which provide them with many useful services, their essential function has become increasingly obscure.

Recommended reading

Richard Gardner, 1969, *Sterling-Dollar Diplomacy*, 3rd edn., New York, McGraw Hill.
Robert Gilpin, 1987, *The Political Economy of International Relations*, Princeton, NJ, Princeton University Press.
A. MacBean and P. N. Snowden, 1981, *International Institutions in Trade and Finance*, London, Allen and Unwin.
Joan Edelman Spero, 1985, *The Politics of International Economic Relations*, 3rd edn., London, Allen and Unwin.
Susan Strange, 1986, *Casino Capitalism*, Oxford, Basil Blackwell.

5 The question of peace and security

A.J.R. Groom

Early history

During the nineteenth century war was becoming more salient both absolutely and relatively. The ability of man to do harm to man was increasing in absolute terms through the production of military equipment sufficient to supply armies of millions. War was becoming more important relatively because some of the other traditional curses of mankind, such as pestilence (at least until the spread of AIDS) and famine, were being conquered in so far as Western Europe and North America were concerned. Thus, during the nineteenth century radical thinkers turned their attention to international social problems. They thought in terms of developing a network of institutions for dealing with these problems in a way not dissimilar from that which had been created for dealing with social problems within society. Thus the stage was set for the development of a range of international institutions to deal with the problems of international peace and security.

However there was already in existence a *de facto* international organisation in the field of peace and security — the Concert system. The Concert system had its roots in the Congress of Vienna in 1815 but only properly came into existence in 1830. The system was predicated on the interests of the great powers of the day. It was a system which was primarily concerned with governing the relationships between those great powers and became in effect the institutional embodiment of the balance of power. Every state felt that each of the others wished to dominate the international system. Every state aspired to establishing the ground rules which would reflect its own interests and act as a constraint upon others. If that was the case then each would have to cooperate with the others to ensure that no one of them could dominate the system. It was, therefore, a system born in conflict, a conflict of the great powers struggling to establish their domination. But it engendered cooperation because, seemingly, the only way in which this conflict could be managed was through cooperation.

The institutional framework of this was first the Congress system and then the Concert system. In the period 1815–1914 a meeting was called on average once every three years. This may not seem to be a very rapid tempo of meetings but, bearing in mind the state of communications at that time, it was an impressive system. Typical of the Congress or Concert system is the meeting in Berlin in 1878. At that time Tzarist Russia was trying to establish a greater Bulgaria which would be a friend of its Tzarist patron and which would also enable the Russian government to establish a dominance in the Balkans and over the

Ottoman Empire (and in particular a favourable regime in the Straits). This was viewed as being unacceptable to all the major powers in the system. In particular, Turkey, the traditional sick man of Europe, and the temporarily weakened Austria–Hungary felt their interest to be threatened. Moreover, Britain and France did not wish to see the Russian government have easy access into the Mediterranean and establish a position of dominance over the Ottoman Empire. Bismarck acted as 'honest broker' in calling a Congress in Berlin. The Russian government found itself isolated and therefore did not press with its plans for the establishment of a greater Bulgaria. Later, in the mid-1880s, a Great Bulgaria was established, but at that time it posed no threat since Austria–Hungary had re-established its position and the Ottoman Empire was in a healthier condition.

This incident illustrates the working of the Concert system, particularly after the Congress of Paris which ended the Crimean War. It was the great powers seeking to put a check on their mutually conflicting ambitions. It required a good deal of diplomatic fleeting of foot to ensure its proper working, but it did operate successfully to a remarkable degree for a century. However, it was a system which was primarily concerned with the interests of the great powers of the day and not with the small powers. Frequently, in order to preserve the balance of power, the interests of the small powers were ridden over roughshod. At the beginning of the period, for example in 1815, Poland had been divided between Russia, Austria–Hungary and Prussia. It was thus a system that was no respecter of national pride and ambitions on the part of the smaller powers. Moreover, it was a system that ultimately failed.

The League system

The occasion of the failure was the cataclysmic events of the First World War, properly known at the time as the Great War. This gave the social reformers their chance. For they were able to say that the traditional means of handling peace and security questions not only trampled on the interest of smaller powers and flew in the face of the rising nationalism, but were also unacceptable in terms of the costs that were involved. The Great War, in which millions used the products of the Industrial Revolution to tear European civilisation to pieces in the name of nationalism was surely, in the eyes of the progressive social reformers, a sufficient condemnation of old-style politics.

The progressive reformers had already begun to develop their ideas. As early as 1843 the first Universal Peace Congress had been held in London with representatives from the Continent and the United States. In Britain and the United States, safe behind the seas dominated by the Royal Navy, reformers put the accent on pragmatic and piecemeal peace proposals. On the Continent, where states with land frontiers were more immediately vulnerable, the emphasis was more on European unity as a panacea for peace. In the second half of the century the debate waxed and waned (as did the movements), ringing the changes on a repertoire of ideas that was little different in conception from that of previous centuries. However, matters were to change, first as governments became more involved and then, in the aftermath of the Great War, as institutional building for peace and security on a hitherto unknown scale was achieved. In 1899 there was the first Hague Peace Conference followed by a successor in 1907 in which the codification of the laws of war were agreed, the first timid steps in the direction of arms control emerged, and an attempt was made to begin, by institutional means, to modify the crude workings and machinations of the balance of power. The reaction due to the First World War indicated that this was the trend to develop. The end result of the great debate of the first two decades of the twentieth century was the establishment of the League of Nations.

The League of Nations was based upon the idea not of a traditional balance of power, but of collective security. Collective security assumes that there is a basic set of agreed and shared values between the state members of a collective security system. On the basis of these values a set of rules of behaviour agreed to by all can be enunciated which all states will then follow. In addition to this there should be some institutions which will allow peaceful change to take place and, in the event of there being any dispute these institutions will also be able to handle any difficulties which arise, including the imposition of sanctions on any deviant actor within the system. It is thus different from an alliance which seeks to preserve security against an outside threat; rather it is a system which seeks to preserve security among a group of states.

Typical of the progressive radical thinkers was President Woodrow Wilson of the United States who was a founding father of the League. Wilson was critical of and sought to reform the system of balance of power allied to Great Power Congresses as a means of maintaining peace and security. His view was far more radical. He believed that people were fundamentally peace-loving and therefore one of the conditions for international peace and security was that nationally the people would be able to make their voice heard. Thus a prime prerequisite of peace was democracy. Moreover, he argued that each state had not only to be democratic but also national: states as institutions should be made to fit nations as socio-political-economic entities. In short he wanted to see a world of democratic nation-states. If such a world was created then the foundations for peace were laid and this was one of his objectives in the negotiations at Versailles at the end of the First World War.

The particular international framework which was to regulate the relations of democratic nation-states was the League of Nations. The League of Nations framework embodied three ways of preserving peace and security at least in philosophy if not always in practice. First of all, it sought to promote a working peace system by creating acceptable conditions for international exchanges whether in the economic, social, cultural or humanitarian sphere. Secondly, it provided a mechanism to promote peaceful change, not in this general way, but in a more specific manner. It was to be an institution whereby government could identify future problems or present trends and together arrive at a solution for resolving those problems or creating a framework in which those trends, if favourable, could flourish. Then, thirdly, the League was a mechanism for the handling of disputes. War was not outlawed in the final sense, but it was unlikely that countries which followed the procedures laid down by the League would ever arrive at a state of war. Thus, if any government did not follow the procedures it made itself automatically a deviation and an outlaw and could justly be brought back into the fold, if necessary by coercion wielded through the institution itself.

These assumptions of collective security, which underlay the philosophical and institutional practices of the League, were based on the notion that all the major actors in the system had a set of shared values. However, it was particularly unfortunate that the Covenant of the League of Nations was the final part of the Treaty of Versailles because the Treaty of Versailles was viewed by the Germans as a *Diktat*. In other words, whether or not the theory was fine the practice most certainly was not, and the League of Nations was a set of values imposed by the victors on the vanquished and those who had put themselves beyond the pale — Germany and the new Soviet Union.

Germany was disarmed, it was not allowed to join the League until 1926, it had massive reparations inflicted upon it and later, when it could not meet its payments, sanctions were applied, particularly in the occupation of the Ruhr by France and Belgium. The Soviet Union for its part was not allowed to join the League until 1934 and the major League powers all intervened in the Soviet Union during the time of the Civil War attempting to crush the Bolshevik government. Indeed, not only did Britain and France intervene but so too did the United States, Japan, Czechoslovakia, Poland and a host of other countries. There can be little surprise, therefore that both Soviet Russia and Germany rejected the consensus which underlay the League and although they both later joined it, one left and the other was subsequently expelled.

The League could not therefore act as a collective security system because it did not reflect a value consensus. It was not a matter of merely policing one occasional deviant actor but a question of a fundamental disagreement on the part of the two major powers, Germany and the Soviet Union, and a lesser disagreement, which was later to come out into the open, among two of the victors who had had a much smaller say in the creation of the League, namely Italy and Japan. Moreover, the principal architect of the League, the United States, did not join although this mattered less since it shared the philosophy if not always the practice of the League. Nevertheless, the absence of global consensus involving the major powers meant that it was hardly surprising that the League collapsed as a peace and security organisation. However, it flourished as a body for promoting functional ties and during the 1920s, when it was still a working body in the peace and security area, it did manage, in some instances, to introduce elements of arms control, and to handle successfully one or two disputes. But in the face of general disagreement, an organisation which was predicated upon continual agreement was bound to collapse. There were undoubtedly lessons to be learned when consideration was being given to a new general post-war organisation as negotiations started between Britain, the United States and the Soviet Union during the course of the Second World War.

The UN Charter

When the three principal members of the United Nations separately and collectively began to consider the future of international organisation, it was evident that the war that was still raging was uppermost in their minds. Their problem was a difficult one since Britain, the Soviet Union and the United States were not only heavily involved in the war but they had different conceptions of the desirable nature of the post-war world and, within it, the role of international organisation for peace and security purposes. The negotiations, therefore, did not proceed easily, but in the end the Charter was ready for signature in San Francisco in 1945.

The fundamental desire of the drafters of the Charter of the United Nations was to avoid another world war. Their strategy was not so different from that which underlay the Covenant of the League of Nations. It was a three-part strategy: first of all, to base peace and security upon the notions of collective security; secondly, to promote peaceful change; and thirdly, to promote the necessary background conditions for the peaceful development of international relations generally.

The doctrine of collective security was applied in a rather different way from the Covenant of the League. The three major powers insisted that security questions should be the province of a restricted-member Security Council of which they would be permanent members, along with France and China, and have a veto. It was thus more like the Concert system. Their view was that realistically the provisions of collective security could not be applied against any great power and that this should be recognised in the institutional framework. The Charter of the UN set out in its Chapter Six the notion that disputes must be settled peacefully. It enumerated many ways in which that could be done, whether through the processes of international law or through arbitration, mediation, conciliation and the like. Moreover, these processes could be applied at the bilateral level, at the regional level or at the universal level. Should a member state not follow the processes designated in Chapter Six, then it would leave itself open to the possibilities envisaged in Chapter Seven. Chapter Seven concerned itself with threats to the peace, breaches of the peace and acts of aggression, and the Security Council was empowered, in certain circumstances, to apply economic sanctions. It could even go further and apply military sanctions against those found to be in breach of their obligations to handle their disputes in a non-violent manner. In fact military sanctions have never been applied and the only mandatory sanctions that the Security Council has passed were economic sanctions against Rhodesia and a ban on the sale of arms to the Republic of South Africa. Chapter Six has, therefore, dealt with the non-violent management of disputes and Chapter Seven remains available to deal with the failure or breakdown of such processes.

The Charter also urged the development of peaceful relations in trade and the facilitation of contacts in all areas of national life. Specialised Agencies, each with their own separate constitution, membership, secretariat and budget, were created. Their purpose was and remains to promote normal conditions for good inter-state relations and to provide a framework through which groups and individuals can develop their contacts on a global basis. This range of Specialised Agencies often made specific reference to peace and security questions in their Charters. UNESCO, for example, refers to its view that wars begin in the minds of men at the beginning of its founding document. The promotion of human rights, too, are a major concern expressed in the Charter and they quickly gave rise to the Universal Declaration of Human Rights. The Charter of the UN itself is clearly an imperfect instrument. For although it goes far in giving mandatory powers to the Security Council, the UN Charter also contains two statements which obviously limit such powers — acknowledgement of the inherent right of individual and collective self-defence, which has been interpreted to include regional alliance systems provided that they are based on UN principles, and also a protection of the sovereignty of member states by the statement that the domestic jurisdiction of states would be treated as sacrosanct. Thus when it is a question of a dispute states could easily claim that a matter was one of domestic jurisdiction or, should they get involved in hostilities, that this was part of their inherent right of individual or collective self-defence.

Not too much should be made of these imperfections in the Charter. Any international lawyer worth his salt could have tightened them up in half a day's work. This was not a problem. The problem was that of securing a degree of political agreement that was acceptable to the three major sponsoring powers of the Charter — Britain, the Soviet Union and the United States — as well as to its potential members. The conceptions of these three powers, and indeed of potential members, about the ways in which to deal with peace and security varied greatly and so the Charter is inevitably a compromise document. It also reflected some of the unhappy aspects of the experience of the League. But the Charter is not thereby an insignificant document, because it provides a potential for growth and a framework in which useful work can be undertaken. The Charter of the UN has been a success not only because it has provided a framework for the routine conduct of international relations and, indeed, for the handling of disputes, but because it also has an element of growth. That element is exemplified by the expansion of the activities of the United Nations Secretariat under the leadership of Dag Hammarskjöld into the area of preventive diplomacy and the development of the conception of peacekeeping.

Peacekeeping is one of the major activities of the United Nations in the field of peace and security. As the ideas of collective security fell to the ground, and with it many provisions of the Charter, when the lack of consensus between the great powers revealed itself soon after the founding of the organisation, so the Secretariat was able to pick up the pieces and develop a useful role for the organisation in the handling of disputes and particularly those arising from the process of decolonisation. Thus, although collective security between the alliance systems of the Cold War was an impossibility, both conceptually and practically, the development of preventive diplomacy and of peacekeeping enabled the process of decolonisation to move forward and the disputes arising therefrom to be handled in a way which did much credit to the United Nations even if it was fraught with difficulty and with a potentiality for disaster. The Charter therefore worked in that it provided a framework in which this imaginative development of the new role was possible. It is to this new role of UN peacekeeping that we now turn.

Preventive diplomacy

Preventive diplomacy is a phrase used to describe a range of diplomatic techniques and activities pursued by Dag Hammarskjöld when he was UN Secretary-General. It has since been adopted and adapted by his successors in various ways. In a sense the whole gamut of United Nations activity is geared towards preventive diplomacy since the institution contains continuously functioning processes for the establishment, improvement and expansion of international relations in a vast range of human endeavours: it seeks to create a working peace system. Yet short-term crises can prejudice this long-term endeavour and it is the purpose of preventive diplomacy to avoid just such an eventuality. Hammarskjöld concentrated on those 'conflicts which are initially only on the margin or outside the bloc conflicts, but which, unless solved or localised, might widen the bloc conflicts and seriously aggravate them'.[1]

Sometimes this process gave rise to the establishment of a UN 'presence' in a troubled area which Ralph Bunche, one of Hammarskjöld's principal advisors, described as

the establishment of some sort of UN arrangement on the spot with a purpose of watching local developments, holding a finger on the pulse and keeping UN Headquarters fully informed about developments in the area. For the most part those who constitute and lead the 'presence' operation, whatever its form, are expected to play their role pretty much by ear, to give well considered advice where needed and requested, to intervene as necessary but always delicately and diplomatically, and to keep constantly in consultation with the Secretary-General for advice and guidance.[2]

Such a 'presence' obviously requires the consent of the host government and its effectiveness is likely to be enhanced if it has at least the tacit approval of other local parties and is looked upon benignly by the superpowers. It is, however, a part of the diplomatic repertoire of the Secretary-General which he can use on his own initiative stemming from his personal involvement in peace and security questions which is clearly implied in Article 99 of the Charter. Nevertheless, no Secretary-General needlessly antagonises any of the parties to a dispute or the permanent members of the Security Council. He may decide that he should 'live dangerously' politically in the interests of peace and security even if, in the long run, it loses him the support of a permanent member and ultimately his job, but he is not likely to do so in a heedless manner.

The UN experience of using a 'presence' in a troubled situation has been a mixed one, but expectations should not be set too high since the technique is only resorted to when a significant crisis appears to be in the offing. Preventive diplomacy is an attempt to relieve an already difficult situation and its success rate reflects the difficulties of such situations. The present Secretary-General, Mr Perez de Cuellar, has been giving thought to ways in which conflicts, including those within states, may be monitored before they deteriorate into an intractable and protracted conflict. A division in the Secretariat is also examining means of facilitating acceptable and supportive intervention by the UN and other bodies in such conflicts. The establishment of a UN 'presence' is a relatively small scale intervention in such a situation, usually involving no more than a few individuals from the Secretariat with perhaps an international personality as the Secretary-General's special representative. Peacekeeping, on the other hand, may be a palliative on a grand scale involving thousands of soldiers and civilians with a budget of millions.

Peacekeeping

Peacekeeping emerged in its fully-fledged form in the Suez crisis and its genesis owed a great deal not only to Dag Hammarskjöld but also to Lester Pearson, the Canadian Minister of External Affairs, among others. It was formulated as a device that enabled Britain, France and Israel to withdraw from dangerous and untenable positions. In the context of the UN the definition of peacekeeping is a substantive issue, since the relationship between what is defined as peacekeeping and what is considered to be enforcement is symbolic of differing attitudes towards the control of UN peacekeeping operations. For present purposes peacekeeping is taken to mean operations undertaken by an international body, usually of an actual or potential military character, in an actual or potential conflict or crisis situation, which are based on the consent of all of the significant parties to such a conflict.

The definition is deliberately broad and its essential elements are the consent of the parties, the actual or potential military character of the operation and an element of impartiality by the peacekeeping force as between the parties and also in the fulfilment of its mandate. Since the consent of all parties is the vital factor, the military character of an operation does not assume a momentous importance because the consent of the hosts will presumably not be available for enforcement activities against themselves and enforcement without consent is not peacekeeping. Indeed, peacekeeping forces are usually deployed between parties or in situations to act as a buffer. At the other end of the scale observation groups and 'fact-finding' missions are included since they are often concerned with military matters and are frequently conducted by military personnel. In the case of operations by the UN the conflict or crisis will have an international character and the parties will normally be states. Thus the UN is very restricted in the forms of conflict in which it can intervene and the history of the UN has already demonstrated the difficulties it encounters when a conflict is essentially internal in origin between parties not all of whom are state actors. Yet it is in this very sort of conflict that the demand for a UN peacekeeping force may in future be greatest.

The definition begs the question of the purpose for which actions are being taken. While actions are supposedly taken for purposes of conflict resolution, at least in declaratory terms, in fact they are usually taken for purposes of the restriction of overt violence. Peacekeeping would have a greater relevance if it could be fashioned in a more meaningful way to fulfil the needs of peacemaking and conflict resolution. It is for this reason that a nominal distinction is made between conflict settlement and conflict resolution. Conflict settlement occurs when organised manifest violence is eliminated, but when the parties remain at odds. This may be due to the 'victory' of one of the parties or to intervention by more powerful outside forces. Thus, if the coercion that eliminates overt violence is removed violent conflict is likely to be resumed. Conflict resolution occurs when the parties no longer feel the pursuance of their conflict to be functional, even when no constraints are put upon them. Relationships are legitimised. Conflict resolution also demands that structural violence be absent. 'Peace' is thus real and self-sustaining. The situation is not merely one of 'non-war', as is the case with conflict settlement. Clearly 'peacekeeping' frequently goes no further than the stage of conflict settlement.

As peacekeeping is often resorted to at a time of crisis, when humanitarian concerns with death and destruction and fear of escalation predominate, it is not surprising that the overriding sentiment should be to stop the fighting. However, the techniques used may be such as to perpetuate the conflict so that it is relevant to consider the extent to which, and if so how, peacekeeping operations merely settle or actually resolve conflicts. Are they condemned to be a palliative in conflict or can they become a prelude to peace?

The three touchstones of a peacekeeping operation — consent, no enforcement and impartiality — are all fraught with difficulty. The consent of the host country (as well as that of the donors of contingents and the sponsoring countries — usually the superpowers) removes peacekeeping from the ambit of Chapter Seven of the UN Charter. Yet its obvious military characteristics, and its occasional forays into military activity, suggest that it goes beyond the traditional pacific settlement of disputes outlined in Chapter 6. Peacekeeping is thus in a limbo between Chapters 6 and 7 in that it involves military activity of a non-enforcement character, the essence of which is the consent of the hosts to such activity as well as that of the donors and sponsors. It is a political concept and so is the consent that underlines it.

From the UN point of view it must be able to secure adequate conditions for the fulfilment of its mandate, while the host country wishes to ensure the plenitude of its legal sovereignty, and political independence. For a host country a peacekeeping force is, at best, almost by definition, a lesser evil. The consent of the host country is thus given but grudgingly. The parties to a peacekeeping operation — host, sponsor, donors and managers (the Secretariat) — need to establish a consensus and to maintain it in the face of an evolving situation. The 'good faith', which is the cement of such a consensus, thus needs to produce concrete which can withstand a significant degree of political pressure.

Consent is a many-faceted concept for it may be given in principle for the establishment of a peacekeeping operation on a country's territory but not for particular aspects of that operation such as specific military contingents. Hammarskjöld quickly asserted his right to choose donors: the host country could not specify which countries should be included, and no state had a right to participate, but the host country did have a tacit right of veto over contingents.

The element of consent by the host country has a further aspect in that Hammarskjöld claimed

that United Nations activity should have freedom of movement within its area of operations and all such facilities regarding access to that area and communications as are

necessary for successful completion of the task. This also obviously involves certain
rights of overflight over the territory of the host country . . . Their application requires
an agreement on what is to be considered as the area of operations and as to what facilities
of access and communications are to be considered necessary.[3]

Such an agreement is more likely to be difficult to obtain, and especially to
secure its full implementation, where the host is in effect a non-state actor in
an internal conflict situation.

While the initial consent of the host country is a *sine qua non* for the establishment of a peacekeeping operation the consent of the sponsors can act as a
countervailing and even a prevailing power. Consent is now usually given
formal expression in a Security Council resolution. Even if the peacekeeping
operation takes place at the request of a government the relationship is not a
contractual one with the government. The government gives its consent to an
operation based on a resolution and it is to that resolution, the body that passed
it and the UN Charter that the Secretary-General is responsible, not to the host
government. Neither the Secretary-General, the donors nor the sponsors are
likely to accept a contractual relationship with a host government. On the other
hand once consent has been given by a host government that consent is not given
for all time. If it were then few host governments would give their accord
because the risk of a peacekeeping operation becoming *de facto* enforcement
would be great. A host country can easily make the conduct of a peacekeeping
operation impossible by withdrawing its co-operation in a myriad of possible
ways. Peacekeeping forces, after all, are usually militarily insignificant in
comparison with those of the parties, nor are they equipped or deployed to fight:
in short, they cannot function independently of the co-operation of the host
country.

Formally, a host country can request the termination of an operation. From
the legal point of view it might be possible to argue that once a government has
given its consent to an operation in the form of a Security Council resolution
then the operation will continue until completion of the mandate. The host
country cannot therefore withdraw its consent. Such a view is, however,
unrealistic since the willing co-operation of the host country is a necessity for
a viable peacekeeping operation. Termination of an operation is thus a
touchstone of a host's rights and, thereby, of its attitude towards the operation.
This will be most obviously so if a peacekeeping operation has strong support
from the superpowers who are putting some pressure on a host country to accept
it. The matter is also of evident concern to sponsors and donors, as the rancour
felt after the withdrawal of UNEF in 1967 attested.

The end of a conflict is not always self-evident. Indeed, it may well be a
fundamental political question for sponsor, donor or host. Host governments are
unlikely to accept 'fulfilment of the mandate' as the only criterion for
withdrawal and they usually have the means to enforce withdrawal by the simple
process of non-cooperation with an operation. On the other hand, instant
withdrawal on demand almost puts the peacekeeping operation on a contractual
basis to the host government and this is likely to be unacceptable to the
Secretary-General, the donors or the sponsors. One way in which the interests

of both sides can be safeguarded is to authorise the operation for a limited, but renewable period, thus giving the host country consent by instalments. Adjustments can thus be made from time to time to maintain the initial consensus in the light of an evolving situation. An alternative might be to write into an agreement the notion of a 'cooling-off' period between a request for termination, by either the hosts or sponsors, and its implementation. Donors can withdraw from time to time for a variety of reasons to be replaced by another country. In all events it is necessary to ensure that there is not enforcement if the peacekeeping character of the operation is to be preserved.

The relationship between consent and the absence of enforcement is an obvious one, but it is, nevertheless, a complex matter and nowhere more so than in peacekeeping operations in internal disputes such as the Congo, Cyprus and the Lebanon. In such situations the consent may have been obtained from the host government but not from other parties to the dispute operating in the country. The informal requirement is thus that the consent of all the significant parties be obtained to ensure that they do not oppose forcibly the UN's fulfilment of its mandate. If there is such forcible opposition then the UN may back down or it may move into an enforcement posture *vis-à-vis* the opposing party and seek to impose the mandate, as it did in Katanga. In such cases, whether it acts in concert with the host government or not, it has lost its impartiality and become a party to the dispute.

Consent, no enforcement and impartiality are the distinguishing features of peacekeeping. However, complete impartiality is impossible since action must be decided on some criteria the incidence of which on the interests of the parties will vary over time. This is as true of the selection of criteria and the application of criteria as it is of their consequences for the parties. Nor does equal treatment ensure impartiality, since the parties are not equal. In any case impartiality is not an objective phenomenon; it is a subjective perception and it only exists when it is perceived to exist by all parties. Thomas Franck has summed the matter up well:

The impartiality of the international decision-maker is not the absence of partiality, but rather a partiality to the values and mores of the international [community] . . . Where he differs from the parties, and the only unique quality he brings to a dispute, is that *his* subjectivity is *not that of a* disputant. His detachment gives him an opportunity to make a subjective determination on the basis of the greatest possible openness, sensitivity and receptivity.[4]

This is, again, more difficult when non-state actors are effective, if unofficial and only tacitly recognised, parties to the dispute as the situation in the Lebanon exemplifies. Such difficulties require that the UN strive even more rigorously to 'avoid actions which could prejudice the rights, claims and positions of the parties concerned' as the Secretary-General put it in the context of the Lebanon.[5] There exists, as Georges Abi-Saab has pointed out, 'an obligation of *due diligence* whose fulfilment can be verified in each case, in the light of the general background of the measure or the decision in question'.[6] The degree of due diligence in pursuit of impartiality, as well as the principles of consent and no enforcement, is crucial to the establishment and maintenance of a consensus between host, donor and sponsor upon which a peacekeeping operation is based. Without such a consensus an operation will fail or will turn into an enforcement measure.

Disarmament

Preventive diplomacy and peacekeeping are innovations in terms of the UN Charter, but the UN has not ignored the traditions of institutional concern over disarmament stretching back to 1899. Disarmament has a prominent place in the Charter of the United Nations. Both the General Assembly (Article 11) and the Security Council (Article 26) are competent to act in the area which must necessarily thereby involve the Secretariat. In addition, the Secretary-General's independent political role, as set out in Article 99, also gives him the opportunity to be a major actor in the field. The Security Council, with the assistance of the Military Staff Committee, is charged with the responsibility of formulating plans to be submitted to members with a view to establishing a system for the regulation of armaments and the Assembly is empowered to study the principles governing disarmament and thereupon make recommendations to members of the Security Council. Over the years the Security Council has done so, and continues to do so.

Early efforts in the UN context gave prominence to the atomic question and, in particular, to discussion of the Baruch and Gromyko plans. Over a decade later the question of general and complete disarmament came to the fore, but to no greater avail than in the case of the Baruch and Gromyko plans. Thereafter arms controls rather than disarmament became the order of the day with the main political impetus being outside the UN framework as, for example, in the cases of the Partial Nuclear Test Ban Treaty, the Demilitarisation of Antarctica and SALT. The United Nations thus has no exclusive proprietorial rights in the area either functionally, where the superpowers discuss their peculiar relationship in a separate bilateral framework, or geographically, as in such discussions as MBFR, a Latin American nuclear-free zone or the CSCE. But if security is the goal then it has to be recognised that it is indivisible: in the long run no one is fully secure if anyone feels significantly insecure. The United Nations therefore has a necessary and important role to play as a universal organisation and one that is adept at formulating norms on a basis of which limited functional or geographical agreements can be made. Through the years the General Assembly has espoused several principles which it judges to be appropriate as a basis for disarmament questions. These include the notion of general and complete disarmament under international control; a priority to be given to nuclear disarmament, the illegitimacy of nuclear weapons, and a model of a nuclear-weapon-free zone; the special responsibility of the superpowers in the disarmament effort; and the role and responsibility of the United Nations. To this the Special Sessions of the General Assembly have added two complementary principles — that of a global approach to disarmament and a positive role for public opinion.

Special Sessions of the General Assembly on any subject are a relatively infrequent phenomenon.[7] Thus, to devote only the tenth such session, in 1978, to disarmament (UNSSOD I) was not only to bring the subject back into the mainstream of the UN's preoccupations, but also to give it a special salience. The calling of a Special Session is a signal to governments, NGOs and the world at large, as well as to the participants themselves, that something unusual is about to happen. UNSSOD I and II (in 1982) were only the tenth and twelfth such sessions respectively. But since Special Sessions are on different topics there is no direct spillover as such except in the unusual case of UNSSOD II (and now of UNSSOD III). Moreover, for most delegates and the Secretariat, a Special Session is an out-of-the-ordinary occurrence. Even the expert delegates have been bloodied in other fora. Thus the absence of routine, especially a confrontational routine, helped UNSSOD I to get off the ground. An air of expectation was created which, if judiciously managed as it was in UNSSOD I, could lead to the emergence of a salient idea or formula, a structure, and then to an outcome. Moreover, UNSSOD I was important for the Secretariat as it was an occasion for it to get back into the mainstream of a central aspect of one of the UN's prime concerns, namely peace and security. It was a challenge accepted by the Secretariat in the mid-1970s, but the low morale of the Secretariat in the early 1980s in general, the new Cold War and the lack of progress over substance in disarmament, were contributory factors in the setback in UNSSOD II. The financial crisis of the organisation in the mid-1980s bodes ill for UNSSOD III, but an arms control agreement between the superpowers could create a more propitious climate.

UNSSOD I needs to be seen in the context of the four main functions of the UN in the field of disarmament as spelled out by the Secretary-General in 1978. The first is to provide a forum in which disarmament would be given its proper pre-eminence; then it is to give a sense of direction and a hierarchy of priorities on a global basis reflecting the interests, needs, concerns and problems of all states and not just the nuclear powers; it should act as a resource centre of some significance; and, finally, it can develop a capacity to supervise arms control and disarmament agreements. The Special Session was the occasion in which progress was made on the first three counts.

The Final Document agreed at UNSSOD I consisted of an introduction, a declaration, a programme of action and a consideration of machinery. UNSSOD I initiated some important and necessary reforms. It was recognised that

for maximum effectiveness, two kinds of bodies are required in the field of disarmament — deliberative and negotiating. All Member States should be represented on the former, whereas the latter, for the sake of convenience, should have a relatively small membership.

In general, the UN should play a more active role in disarmament affairs and the

General Assembly has been and should remain the main deliberative organ of the United Nations in the field of disarmament measures . . . The First Committee of the General Assembly should deal in the future only with questions of disarmament and related international security issues.

It was thus designated what it had in fact already almost become — a specialised body. The Disarmament Commission was reactivated as a deliberative body and a further Special Session was envisaged. Moreover, the

General Assembly is deeply aware of the continuing requirement for a single multilateral negotiating forum of limited size taking decisions on the basis of consensus. It attaches great importance to the participation of all the nuclear-weapon States in an appropriately constituted negotiating body.

And, indeed, France and China duly took their place in the Committee (later Conference) on Disarmament as the outworn Soviet–US dual chairmanship along with the previous body was abolished. Besides the Special Session, 'At the earliest appropriate time, a world disarmament conference should be convened with universal participation and with adequate preparation'. As for the Secretariat, the Centre for Disarmament was to be strengthened, the Secretary-General urged the constitution of an Advisory Board of eminent persons, and 'there should be increased participation by non-governmental organisations concerned with the matter, through closer liaison between them and the United Nations'.[8]

Besides enriching the body of principles for approaching the question of disarmament, the Final Document, which was reaffirmed in UNSSOD II, stressed the global approach to disarmament and the General Assembly was enjoined to establish an international strategy of coordinated efforts to be pursued with perseverance in order to achieve general and complete disarmament under effective and strict international control. The aim was to achieve genuine security through the ending of the arms race and to promote real disarmament by means of a gradual process. Furthermore, the Declaration set out a programme of action, with priorities, to achieve this goal and although the nuclear powers were put in the hot seat, they were not alone. Besides nuclear questions, chemical and biological weapons and conventional weapons were to be considered concurrently. The General Assembly had taken itself, in its entirety, to task.

The Final Document had become the loadstone of the global disarmament process and constitutes a minimum programme and a basis for operation. Moreover, it was the starting point for UNSSOD II (and now for UNSSOD III) and a rationale for the second disarmament decade. In addition, it linked disarmament with the other great questions exercising the global community such as development, self-determination, human rights, the peaceful settlement of disputes and collective security. Unusually for it is governments and not 'we the peoples. . .' that rule the roost in the UN, it brought in public opinion. The Declaration, in short, constitutes an integrated whole providing principles, goals, priorities, structure and mechanisms. The United Nations had put its house in order and was back in the mainstream of the disarmament business. The UN was not in exclusive control, but it was to have an important say in disarmament questions globally, a say enhanced by its representivity, and a say based on a Declaration to which all had subscribed and were thereby, politically if not legally, to be held accountable. However, even if you lead a horse to water you cannot make it drink. The UN framework is an appropriate one for disarmament negotiations but it cannot, of itself, bring about disarmament: that is for governments and peoples to achieve. And failing that, governments will resort to self-help in a desperate striving for security.

Self-help

Given the failure of collective security, the slow progress towards disarmament and the lack of a guarantee that the processes of peaceful change, preventive diplomacy and peacekeeping would be sufficient to handle problems, it is hardly surprising that members of the United Nations and, indeed, all states look to self-help as a means of dealing with their security problems. Security, after all, is a basic preoccupation of foreign policy. Indeed, the ability of state authorities to provide their citizens with an element of security is one of the *raisons d'être* for the existence of government. However, security is not the only preoccupation of governments, particularly since the notion of absolute security is impossible to achieve. There is always likely to be some way in which a hostile individual or group could threaten or damage the interests of any actor. The question, therefore, is not whether absolute security can be obtained but how much insecurity is tolerable. The unthinking pursuit of absolute security would be costly in the extreme and would entail the sacrifice of many other perceived valuable goals. It is thus a question of balancing a degree of insecurity with the pursuit of other goals such as development. This trade-off is exemplified by the slogan of 'guns or butter'. How many guns, how much butter?

In the pursuit of self-help it is important for us to understand what is meant by security. There are two basic types of definitions. The first seeks to get as near to absolute security as is possible. It puts emphasis on the *capabilities* of others to harm the interests of the state concerned and frequently assumes that what others can do, they are likely to do. This is what is meant by 'worst-case' analysis. The security that they are seeking to provide is based on the worst case rather than the most likely case. Any policy based on such a worst-case analysis usually leads to the creation of an armed camp as the chimera of absolute security mesmerises decision-makers. However, the creation of an armed camp is self-defeating since others acting on similar premisses view it as a threat to their own security. Thus one armed camp begets another opposing armed camp and an arms race and a climate of hostility ensues. Even where there are attempts to negotiate it is, in this conception, usually viewed as a case of negotiating from strength. However, the difficulty arises that if one side negotiates from strength, the other must negotiate from weakness. It is unlikely to be prepared to do so and therefore the net result as it, too, tries to negotiate from strength, is much strength and little negotiation. Thus the creation of an armed camp has a tendency to be self-defeating in that it generates not security, but insecurity as hostility grows, arms races intensify and power politics reigns.

The second definition of security is one which concentrates not so much on capabilities but on *intentions*. It asks not what others *can do* to harm the state which is seeking security, but what they are *likely to do*. The goal of policy is thus to influence the likelihood that others may follow policies which are detrimental or hostile towards the interests of the state which is trying to enhance its security. This gives rise to a positive notion of security — security by association.

The essence of security by association is that a state's security is best safeguarded in a situation in which it plays a valued role in the eyes of others in international society. If a state is providing services which are acceptable to others, and to itself, then the pursuit of hostilities or threats against it would prejudice a continued provision of such services. It is thus unlikely that other states will deprive themselves of such services by attacking or threatening the state which provides them. International security thereby grows out of a network of cross-cutting ties between states so that each becomes dependent upon the other for valuable and valued services. Such dependencies are, of course, not based upon coercion but freely undertaken. Thus, to pursue a coercive policy against any other state would be to risk losing the benefits provided by that state: it would be a clear case of cutting off the nose to spite the face. While history provides many examples of where such has been the case, nevertheless, the obvious price of pursuing conflict in such an instance has stayed the hand of many states in the contemporary world. A classical example of this is a comparison of the relationship between France and Germany between 1860 and 1950, when they each sought security against the other by the first definition, that is by the armed camp, with the relationship between France and Germany since 1950 in which security has been pursued by the second method, that is by association.

With these definitions of security in mind it is perhaps useful to look at the range of possible means of self-help. These vary from alliances to neutrality, isolation and to non-alignment. Such foreign policy options reflect these two very different conceptions of security.[9] The quest for interdependence and security is common; but the means to these ends are very different. Moreover, two of these options give rise to international organisations — alliances and non-alignment.

Alliances

Few sovereign and independent units have ever had full confidence in their ability to establish their own 'armed camp' from entirely within their own resources. They have, therefore, sought safety in numbers by aligning themselves with like-minded states. An alignment is a general disposition in political and security affairs to cooperate with another power or powers in order to deter or prevail in the face of a possible threat. If the consequential relationship has a substantial military component then it takes the form of an alliance. NATO is a case in point. In general terms an alliance describes an understanding between two or more actors (they need not be governments) to act in concert to promote specified interests, which are usually held in common, and which are opposed by third parties. It is the element of potential or actual opposition by third parties, together with the willingness to coerce third parties, that is at the heart of an alliance. In short, alliances are a technique in manipulating the balance of power.

A striking feature of some alliances since the Second World War is that they have given rise to international organisations. NATO and the Warsaw Treaty Organisation are dramatic examples of this. Moreover, general-purpose regional organisations have developed a security function that has both elements of an alliance and of collective security. The OAU, OAS and Arab League are, in effect, alliances against South Africa, Cuba and Israel respectively but they also act as collective security bodies seeking to manage disputes between their members. In this latter function they use techniques similar to those of the UN, including peacekeeping. On the other hand, NATO, a formal alliance, also seeks to reconcile its disputing members such as Greece and Turkey. In all of these activities secretariats can be found performing functions familiar from a UN setting. However, membership of an alliance, while the dominant experience in the developed world, is not the norm among the newly independent countries.

Non-alignment

More than 100 states have concluded that to join alliances in the contemporary world is more detrimental to their own and the community interest than to adopt a non-aligned stance. Non-aligned states are not passive or neutral; they have an active interest and concern in world politics at all levels. They wish, in a non-discriminatory manner, to make an independent judgement on the issues of the day and to participate in their management. Since they are in a loose consultative association of a non-binding character, they do not, and do not wish, to form a bloc. Indeed, they wish to overcome the dangerous consequences of bloc politics. Moreover, they pursue an independent approach to the parties based on the issues in dispute, even if on a specific question they come down on a particular side. In this they contrive to arrive at a consensus. Thus the non-aligned movement as a whole is able to exert an influence in UN affairs and not least in questions of peace, security and disarmament.[10]

In order to be non-aligned a state must not be dependent on either of the Cold War alliance systems in an exclusive or coerced manner in any major dimension of its activities. However, non-aligned states are neither isolationist nor autarkic; they are interdependent. Their interdependence has certain important characteristics: it is not exclusive in the sense of a dependence on one other state or group of states, and its asymmetries are balanced between partners and between dimensions so that a dominant flow in one direction in, say, cultural ties, will be compensated for in, say, the economic domain, both in terms of partner and direction of flow. But it is difficult to be a non-aligned state if there are serious internal disharmonies since disaffected groups turn to external sources for succour. This leads to an association of internal forces with external actors, thus creating alliance linkages across the state's boundaries. If a state is not at peace with itself it will find it difficult to be at peace with the world.

A non-aligned stance can be in relation to all external ties in all dimensions or limited to a specific set of transactions. A state can avoid permanent ties with any actor in relation to any situation. Alternatively, it can act in a non-aligned manner towards a particular set of relationships, but not necessarily universally. Thus India has acted largely in a non-aligned manner in the Cold War, but in an aligned manner in the Sino-Soviet dispute.

Non-alignment leads to some states playing a supportive third-party role in regard to the parties in systems of power politics. They endeavour to move such systems towards the resolution of conflicts and the establishment of more legitimised relationships. This was the case in the first Cold War. However, in the second Cold War of the late 1970s until the Reykjavik summit they failed to achieve this goal. With over 100 members the non-aligned movement is too heterogeneous and bureaucratised to be effective in global peace and security questions. Its consensual procedures lead it to a minimal lowest common denominator. Two of its important members have fought a terrible war since 1980. By attacking the West on economic issues it lost its standing as a helpful neutral on East–West issues. Perhaps, too, it is also because most of these states are plagued with internal economic and political instability.

There is a need to distinguish between a non-aligned policy and the non-aligned movement. The policy in the guise of a concerned independence holds its theoretical validity, and, on occasion, its practical utility. Indeed, there is a crying need for more states to follow a genuine supportive policy of non-alignment and concerned independence. However, non-alignment as a movement has lost its way. It maintains an effective existence as a caucus in the UN, especially in New York. But as a security policy and a factor for peace it has not fulfilled the aspirations of its founders when in 1961, after the first non-aligned 'Summit', delegations were sent to the two superpowers in an attempt to ease the tensions of the Cold War.[11]

Some forms of self-help may be useful in the promotion of international peace and security of which non-alignment or concerned independence are examples. But the promotion of international peace and security is not a question for governments and international governmental institutions alone. It is also a question of vital concern to peoples and groups and this is reflected in the non-governmental international organisational framework.

The role of non-governmental organisations

It would be surprising if a problem which touches potentially every individual in the world in an important manner should be left entirely to governments and international governmental organisations. Thus, a large number of non-governmental and international non-governmental organisations have an active role in questions of peace and security. It is often forgotten that while there are some 300–400 international government organisations (IGOs), there are more than 4,000 international non-governmental organisations (INGOs) and a roughly equivalent number of business international non-governmental organisations (BINGOs!).

In a very real sense it is the INGOs that make the world go round, particularly in questions of peace and security, for they provide the background of cross-cutting ties and the transmission of goods, services, ideas and people from one part of the globe to the other which is an integral part of the creation of a working peace system. They also create shared goals. Of course it is possible for such organisations to act in a coercive manner towards each other but, nevertheless, the dominant characteristic of these relationships is that of ties on a basis acceptable to all those participating, at least to a substantial degree. They, in short, help to create some sense of world community. But not always so. Besides creating this sense of world community they can also be an important and sometimes deleterious factor in the structural relationship between North and South. Not only can they be a medium for exploitation but also they tend to be heavily skewed in their participation towards countries in Europe and North America. Moreover, membership is of elites from those countries as well as from the Third World. Notwithstanding this, however, their general contribution to the promotion of international peace and security should not be underestimated. While individually they may not be of any great moment, cumulatively, both in terms of quantity of transactions and also in terms of substance, their influence is immense.

There are a large number of organisations dealing specifically with questions of peace and security. The International Committee of the Red Cross, which is a committee of Swiss businessmen, concerns itself with the amelioration of the conditions of war, whereas the League of the Red Cross Societies is an organisation of national Red Cross societies dealing with Red Cross matters in times of peace, for example, aid to countries which have earthquakes or other natural or man-made disasters. In a more overtly political vein are the Quakers, the Palme Commission and the Pugwash movement, all of which seek actively to alleviate tensions, particularly East–West tensions. Indeed, the Quakers have their own quasi-diplomatic service with permanent representatives at the United Nations in New York and Geneva and field representatives in various parts of the world which are conflict-prone, such as the Middle East. The Quakers have been known to intervene in many tense situations with their own special brand of quiet diplomacy which has alleviated tensions to a significant degree in some instances. Some, such as the Palme Commission, have a very specific concern with peace and security, and especially with disarmament questions.[12] The Pugwash movement is also an example of this type of organisation.

As the full potential horrors of the nuclear age became more and more evident in the 1950s, a group of eminent scientists, including Albert Einstein and Bertrand Russell, made an appeal to the leaders of the major nuclear powers. As a result of this appeal, scientists, who very often were working in government research establishments in the United States, the Soviet Union, Britain, France and other leading actual or potential nuclear powers, met together in the town of Pugwash at the invitation of a Canadian millionaire and philanthropist Cyrus Eaton. Pugwash in Nova Scotia was his birthplace and the movement has taken the name of that town. The purpose of this movement and these meetings was for scientists to discuss questions of international peace and security in their private capacity. However since they were often governmental scientists they were able to take the results of their discussions into the governmental framework. This was a very useful process at a time when the major nuclear powers were not on speaking terms. It is quite likely that the subsequent arms control agreements such as the Partial Nuclear Test Ban of 1963 were greatly influenced by initiatives that grew out of these series of meetings which continue to this day and have considerably broadened their scope. Finally various academic organisations, such as the International Institute for Peace in Vienna, brings together social scientists from Eastern and Western countries and the UNESCO-sponsored IPSA and IPRA (International Political Science Association and International Peace Research Association) have a universal vocation. Once again it is important to get a proper sense of perspective. Individually these organisations, and many more like them, are not of any great significance, but cumulatively they create a climate of opinion and a conventional wisdom which moves in the direction of an amelioration of international problems. Occasionally, of course, they can be the conduit for the conduct of coercive activities, but more usually the opposite is the case. They therefore help to build an important, if often neglected, aspect of the international institutional framework for the handling of questions of peace and security.

A further example of this is the 'organic' participation of NGOs in most aspects of UNSSOD I and II. Not only did they have their own preparatory conference but also they addressed the delegates in the official Special Session. In addition, their parallel meetings and events, as well as their newspaper, during the Special Sessions had an impact. They forced themselves on to the disarmament stage but they did not always have the maximum substantive effect. In part this was because.they had, or at least put forward, few new ideas for the consideration of the delegates or the attentive public — there was an intellectual failure in that they appeared in too many cases to be doing little more than back-stopping foreign offices. In part their impact was mitigated by the fact that NGOs do not cooperate together easily and their structures cannot command such cooperation. The enthusiasm of individuals can evaporate quickly if their cause or organisation has to compromise to create an effective network. Given the world public concern over disarmament, and the vested interests of governments and the military–industrial complex, it is not surprising that the NGO world has responded to public opinion nor that they have made relatively little impact. But the structure has responded, they have an assured place and if they put their own house in order they will be able to have a more significant impact. The preamble of the UN Charter referring to 'We the peoples. . .' will then have a more authentic ring about it.

This survey is a sobering exercise. It started with an optimistic search for a brave new world in which peace and security would be built through an institutional framework. With the collapse of such hopes during the onset of the Second World War, a new 'realism' resulted. The UN was less ambitious, but it, too, failed, and failed before it even started. Yet out of this failure new efforts emerged: peacekeeping was an inspired palliative, even if it remained a palliative. A new movement of concerned independent states, such as the five-continent independent initiative, the EC in the Near East or the neutrals and non-aligned in the Helsinki (CSCE) process, acting in concert might develop to play a role in ameliorating superpower conflicts as the non-aligned movement has tried to do. But in essence the problem is political. In the last resort, however, it is the people who pay the price and it is from the people that peace must come. Must we pay the price of the destruction of world civilisation or are we now for the first time ready to pay the price of peace? It means for those likely to read this essay a high price in forgoing our privileges, but it is better than the alternatives and, perhaps, in the long run, better for us, too, if it makes for a peaceful world.

Notes

1. From UN Document A/4390/Add. 1 as quoted in Georges Abi-Saab, 1978, *The United Nations Operation in the Congo 1960–1964*, Oxford, Oxford University Press, p. 2.
2. As quoted in Brian Urquhart, 1972, *Hammarskjöld*, London, The Bodley Head, pp. 294–5.
3. As quoted in Lincoln P. Bloomfield, 1964, *International Military Forces*, Boston, Little, Brown, p. 273.
4. Thomas M. Franck, 1968, *The Structure of Impartiality*, London, Macmillan, p. 261.
5. See Maureen Boerma, 1979, 'The United Nations Interim Force in the Lebanon: peacekeeping in a domestic conflict', *Millenium*, Spring, p. 60.
6. Abi Saab, op. cit., p. 65.
7. See Paul Taylor and A.J.R. Groom (eds), 1988, *Global Conferences: the UN Experience*, London, Macmillan.
8. Quotations from the Final Document which has been published complete in brochure form by the UN Department of Public Information.
9. These opinions are discussed further in J.W. Burton, A.J.R. Groom, Margot Light, C.R. Mitchell and D.W.D. Sandole, 1984, *Britain between East and West: A Concerned Independence*, Aldershot, Gower.
10. See A.J.R. Groom, 1984, 'The Commonwealth and the non-aligned movement: back to the source', *Non-Aligned World*, April.
11. For a contemporary relevance of non-alignment as a security policy, see A.J.R. Groom, 1983, 'The new Cold War: a need for a concerned but independent Western Europe?', *Non-Aligned World*, April.
12. The proposals of the Palme commission can be found in *Common Security*, 1982, London, Pan.

Recommended reading

Evan Luard, 1982, *A History of the United Nations*, Vol I, London, Macmillan.
F.S. Northedge, 1986, *The League of Nations*, Leicester, University of Leicester Press.
I.J. Rikhye, 1984, *Theory and Practice of Peacekeeping*, London, Hurst.
Brian Urquhart, 1972, *Hammarskjöld*, London, The Bodley Head.

6 The origin and development of the ILO and international labour organisations

George Foggon

From the early nineteenth century, the industrialisation of Europe, particularly in Britain, Germany and France was reflected in long hours of work, poor working conditions and inadequate wages. Women and children in the work-force were often the worst sufferers. Employers could impose whatever wages and conditions they liked with virtually no governmental interference until well into the century. Collective action by workers was slow to gather strength, inhibited everywhere by the hostility of factory owners to workers' associations and the restrictions of the law. The situation was defended by the need to be competitive. It was no good improving wages and conditions in Britain unless others followed suit; unemployment would result and destitution would take over from poverty. Here and there a few enlightened employers like Robert Owen sought to demonstrate that improved working conditions meant better productivity, and that health, family life and respect for human dignity were more important than profits. But the threat of external competition was continually raised against those who sought reform. It was inevitable, therefore, that men's minds should turn towards the possibility of action on an international scale which would permit improved living and working standards to develop which would not harm the competitiveness of any particular country.

Robert Owen tried hard for a wider acceptance of his ideas which he embodied as early as 1813 in his book *The New View of Society*. At the international level he approached the Congress of the Holy Alliance in Aix-la-Chapelle five years later, proposing that they appoint a Commission to visit New Lanark and see his ideas in action; but the Congress ignored his pleas.[1]

A more direct effort at international action came much later — in 1840 — when Daniel Legrand, a prominent industrialist in Alsace, sought to stir the French, British, German and Swiss governments into concerted action to remove abuses in the factory system. He believed that only by negotiation and agreement between governments could progress be made to improve the lot of working people.

His ideas found many sympathetic hearers; nothing positive emerged from his efforts, but a ferment of thought had begun in Europe. The iniquities of the existing system, with its hardships and degradation, began to be questioned by more acute minds than that of Daniel Legrand. If society could not be reformed by persuasion then perhaps fundamental changes were called for. In 1864 the First International was formed in London by Marx and Engels.[2] It had a profound and continuing influence on political thought, but its practical achievements in the period before its collapse in 1872 in improving the lot of the working population were negligible.

The collapse demonstrated that an international organisation of workers could not succeed unless it was based on established workers' and political organisations in their own countries. Within the First International, however, there was developed a central council which brought together information about social conditions, facilitated the exchange of information between countries, and within which reasoned and informed debate about labour conditions could be undertaken. It was the seed from which an international labour organisation was eventually to grow — long after the First International had disappeared. The path was a long one, through the disappointments of the Second International,[3] until the Swiss government, in March 1889, proposed the setting up of an international centre for the translation and circulation of labour legislation, and periodic conferences to discuss minimum labour standards. But the initiative might have been stillborn had it not been for help from an unexpected source. In 1890 Kaiser Wilhem II, Emperor of Germany, called a meeting in Berlin of the fourteen West European countries to consider international agreement on improved working conditions. And what an agenda! It included proposals for an eight-hour working day for mineworkers, with reduced hours of work if conditions were particularly bad, restrictions on Sunday labour, a minimum age for the introduction of children into employment, and the abolition of night work for women. This was 1890. (It was 1908 before the then President of the Board of Trade stood up in the House of Commons and presented an Eight Hour Bill for mineworkers. That man was Winston Churchill, then a member of the Liberal government, under Mr Lloyd George, which laid the foundations of the British welfare state).

The British delegation at the Berlin Conference took the lead in opposing any binding agreements: 'They are forbidden to put their industrial laws at the discretion of a foreign power'.[4] There was little support, moreover, from the governments represented there for proposals that there be regular interchanges of information between the participants and periodic meetings of delegates. The Swiss government did not give up and, through a series of diplomatic initiatives, gained agreement in 1900 for an International Association for Labour Legislation.[5] It was hoped that the research on labour hours and social conditions undertaken by the International Association would influence governmental policies in Europe: this was, indeed, the case, notably in the Franco-Italian labour treaty of 1904, which governed the conditions of employment of nationals of each country working in the other.[6] The great leap forward took place in the following year (1905)[7] when the Association, through the good offices of the Swiss government, initiated a Technical Labour Conference in Berne attended by France, Great Britain, Germany, Spain, Portugal, Denmark, Greece, Romania and Italy. For the first time, the essential elements of international standard setting emerged. There was agreement that the night work of women should be arranged to ensure a rest period of not less than eleven hours, and that the manufacture, sale and importation of matches containing white phosphorus should be prohibited. These agreements were subject to ratification by all the governments represented at the Conference and, in addition, by Japan. The formal agreements, in the form of two conventions, were drawn up at a Diplomatic Conference held in 1906. The 'Convention' — the key to supranational standard setting — had been born.

Nevertheless doubts about the structure and membership of the International Association had begun to develop — it was unrepresentative, not subject to official supervision, and did not command the resources for wide-scale research and investigation. Should some more formal intergovernmental institution be established? The Great War (1914–18) brought these bureaucratic gropings towards an international policy into the hands of trade-union leaders, determined to see that the voice of working people should be heard at the making of the Peace Treaty.

During the war, labour leaders in the United States, France and Britain (Britain was represented by William Appleton of the British General Federation of Trade Unions) began to exchange ideas.[8] William Appleton had taught himself French and he was able therefore to correspond with his trade-union opposite number in France, Léon Jouhaux (later awarded the Nobel Peace Prize). The theme of what they were talking about between themselves was brilliantly expressed by William Appleton in a letter to Prime Minister Asquith in August 1916. What William Appleton said was this:

Nearly all other wars have ended with treaties which conserved the rights of kings, the boundaries of nations and the privileges of property. The poor people have had no part in the making of war or peace; they have suffered, they have endured contumely, and they have died, but never yet has monarch or statesman made their situation a determining factor in a treaty of peace. The time has arrived for better methods; for the consideration of the common rather than the particular interest; for the wide conception of human rights rather than the narrow one, and a beginning may be made on the lines indicated.[9]

This letter was sent following a special Trades Union Congress held in Leeds, attended by Léon Jouhaux, Secretary of the French Confédération Générale du Travail, who lived long enough to assist in the regeneration of the German trade unions after the Second World War. The Conference expressly called for the creation of an international labour organisation and for detailed workers' rights to be incorporated into the Peace Treaty.[10]

The British Ministry of Labour had carefully monitored these developments and was ready at the end of the war in 1918 with proposals that might be put to any Labour Commission established when the Peace Treaty was being negotiated. They favoured the setting up of a permanent organisation for dealing with international labour problems with a permanent Secretariat and an Annual Conference, which would be tripartite, representing governments, employers and workers. The ultimate shape of the ILO derived from these far-sighted ideas, which in their final form as presented on 2 February 1919 to the Labour Commission established at Versailles as part of the peace negotiations also included the definition of the status of a Labour Convention, procedures for notification, reporting procedures and action against member states failing to meet their obligations.[11] Finally, the British proposed that the new labour organisation should be part of the new League of Nations! After strenuous negotiation, and many amendments to the British proposals, the main structure and concepts survived and the International Labour Organisation was established by Article XIII of the Treaty of Versailles. Its outstanding characteristic of tripartism has been a fundamental element in the stability and success of the Organisation and remains unique to this day among the Specialised Agencies of the United Nations.

The methods of the ILO

How does the ILO work? The tripartite principle was new, but they still had to face up to the problem which was raised in 1890 by the British delegation in Berlin: how do you get over the sovereignty question? There were more governments than Britain who were not prepared to have laws made externally which would automatically be applied within a country. Out of this thinking, they picked up the earlier idea of international labour conventions. This is briefly how a labour convention operates.

A standard is elaborated at the annual International Conference — say, a minimum age for entry into industrial employment, protection of workers against ionising radiation, protection of workers against the use of carcinogenic chemicals, the rights of public servants to bargain collectively (something which many governments exclude), and so on. Once that standard has been elaborated and worked out in detail in tripartite committees, with representatives of governments, employers and workers present, all with the right to speak and vote, and has been adopted by at least two-thirds of the delegates attending the International Labour Conference, it becomes formally a Convention. It has no binding force at that stage. But under the Constitution every member state of the ILO must refer that Convention within one year to its appropriate national authority, in the case of Britain, Parliament, with an indication of what the government intends to do.

The process in Britain is as follows. The Department of Employment consults the other interested departments in Whitehall. A White Paper is prepared, and cleared in Whitehall, setting out the government's policy on the Convention and that is laid on the table of the House of Commons by the Secretary of State for Employment. There is thus an opportunity in Parliament for it to be debated. Usually, if the government says it is going to ratify, there is no problem. But if the government says it is not going to ratify, for such and such reasons, there usually ensues debate, and perhaps, pressure on the government, often instigated, of course, by Labour MPs or trade-union-sponsored MPs. Assuming that the British government has decided to ratify the Convention, the Foreign and Commonwealth Office then prepares a formal instrument of ratification in the form of a Treaty which is deposited with the ILO in Geneva.

At that stage a binding obligation is created between the British government and the International Labour Organisation; it is an obligation that in law and practice the requirements of the Convention are being applied in the United Kingdom. There is also an obligation to report biennially; these reports are examined by independent experts of international standing whose report is thereafter published. There is another safeguard; when the British government reports to the ILO on a Convention, a copy of the report must be sent to the CBI and to the British TUC. Both the TUC and the CBI can check on what is being said. That is a requirement of the Constitution of the ILO, something that has to happen in every member state, i.e. that the trade unions and the employers receive copies of reports made by governments on the application of Conventions.

It should be mentioned that one reason why Britain has ratified fewer Conventions than, shall we say, France is that historically in Britain many matters have been left to collective bargaining which in other countries are dealt with by labour laws. It follows that if a matter is left to collective bargaining it is not possible for the British government to enter into a treaty obligation to apply particular standards, even though the British standards reached by collective bargaining may be, for the majority of workers, higher than those required by the Convention. The record of Britain, from the moment it took part in the foundation of the ILO, has been one of strong support. One of the staunchest supporters was Ernest Bevin. He made his first visit to the ILO in 1928 and was profoundly seized with the concept that instead of working to improve the lot of the dockers and transport workers of Britain alone, he could, through his work in Geneva, help workers on an international scale. Thereafter, as a trade unionist and later as Minister of Labour, the ILO enjoyed his constant and unstinting support. Later, in 1945–6, when the United Nations was being created, it was he who intervened — he was then Foreign Secretary — to ensure that the ILO was not absorbed into the United Nations, but remained as a separate Specialised Agency of the UN.

The structure of the ILO

A vital part of the structure and procedures of the ILO is the Annual Conference. On the first Wednesday in June each year the International Labour Conference assembles in Geneva. Each member state's delegation must consist of four people — two government representatives, one worker, one employer. There are now 151 member states. Each delegation may bring along advisers, as one delegate could not be expert enough to be able to make a useful contribution on the wide range of issues under consideration in the various committees.

The worker and employer delegates are not to be appointed by their governments; they are appointed in agreement with, and after consultation with, the most representative workers' organisation, or the most representative employers' organisation respectively. In Britain that is the TUC and the CBI. All the expenses of delegations are met by the respective governments. It has to be admitted, though, that the methods of choosing delegates have sometimes been a subject of disagreement. In the 1970s, United States authorities were particularly concerned with Soviet workers whom, they argued, were chosen by the Soviet government. There is, of course, a Credentials Committee at the Annual Conference, and if the credentials of any delegate attending are challenged, it goes before that Committee, which is, of course, tripartite.

Every three years the Conference elects the Governing Body which might be called the cabinet or executive council of the ILO and which comprises fifty-six members, twenty-eight governments, fourteen workers and fourteen employers. When the elections take place, the whole conference — delegates only (advisers are not involved), that is, four from each country — split up to create a government electoral college, a workers' electoral college and an employers' electoral college. All the workers' delegates elect fourteen people to represent them on the Governing Body: they must have regard to geographical spread, to the performance of individuals within the ILO, to the contribution they have made to the work of the organisation, their degree of dedication and so on. Eventually, after a tremendous amount of hard work in the corridors, fourteen workers are elected to the governing body, plus fourteen substitutes. A similar procedure is followed by the employers.

There are aspects of the election which are necessarily somewhat political in character. For example, there are two main trade-union international groupings in the world, the International Confederation of Free Trade Unions (ICFTU), which is Western orientated, and the World Federation of Trade Unions (WFTU), based in Prague, which broadly represents Eastern Europe, the Soviet Union and some communist affiliates around the world. These two trade-union power blocs inevitably contend for control of the workers' group of the Governing Body of the International Labour Organisation.

With governments there is a difference. Those who drew up the Constitution of the ILO in 1919 wrote into it that the ten countries of principal industrial importance should have guaranteed seats. That means that only eighteen seats are voted for. The Group of 77, that is, the newly developing countries, believe profoundly that all government seats on the Governing Body should be voted for. A Structure Committee has been established to seek ways and means of compromise, which will ensure an equitable geographical spread, and which will also ensure that at least some of the countries that meet most of the budget of the organisation will always be represented. The fear of those who wrote the original Constitution was that there might be 'taxation without representation', that those who were in fact meeting most of the budget, because they were wealthier, could fail to be elected to the Governing Body, which controls the Organisation's budget and programme. After many years of discussion, proposed changes in the ILO's Constitution have now been put to member states: the abolition of the special position of the ten countries of principal industrial importance; the doubling in size of the Governing Body; and a system of voting proposed on a regional basis for a specific number of places which will ensure an equitable geographical representation. These changes are subject to ratification by 75 per cent of member states. In the background, servicing it all, is the International Labour Office, the secretariat and research heart of the organisation, with about 1,800 staff of some 100 nationalities.

Creating a Convention

How is a Convention created? One example is as follows. A few years ago, anxiety was expressed about the hours of work and rest periods for transport drivers. There had been many serious accidents in Europe and elsewhere and there was a feeling that it was about time that international standards were set in this area. The Governing Body decided to place the subject on the agenda of the Conference. That was in 1976, two years in advance of the date stipulated for decision. The Office then had to gather information from all round the world about actual working conditions, the laws involved, and the views of the trade unions, employers and governments. These were incorporated into reports which were circulated to all concerned. These are called 'law and practice reports': they simply describe how countries manage these affairs.

The Conference met in 1978 with the subject of hours of work and rest periods of transport drivers on the agenda, and immediately a tripartite committee was set up to consider the question with the 'law and practice report' as the basic document. Any worker delegate, any employer delegate, any government delegate can put his name down to work in a committee. But what happens if there are say, fifty-nine workers in a committee, about 102 governments and only sixteen employers? The votes are then weighted so that each group vote is equal in value whether it is government, worker or employer.

It should be noted, however, that in a technical committee discussing a technical subject, the voting is 1:1:1, not 2:1:1. It is worth describing how this came about. It was the view of Samuel Gompers, the American trade-union leader who chaired the Labour Commission at Versailles, that the ILO should be strictly tripartite, 1:1:1, all the way through. The attitude of governments was that any combination of workers and employers, if the vote were 1:1:1, would defeat the governments. This sort of vote would not always convince governments; they, after all, had to pass the laws, they had to meet the costs, and if they were not party to the decision, then their adherence to it could be very limited indeed.[12] A compromise was reached which provided that, when the report of a committee went to the whole conference, which was necessary for its endorsement, voting would be two government, one worker, and one employer in each delegation. The governments have half the votes, but as every convention requires at least two-thirds of the votes of all those entitled to vote, it has to be a convincing document. After the first discussion in the first year — in this case 1978 — the subject was put on the agenda for a second discussion in 1979. In the meantime the report of the first discussion had been circulated around the world, to trade-union centres, employers and governments. The second discussion, therefore, closely focused on the actual terms of an Instrument. In this case it resulted in the adoption of International Labour Convention No.153. That is how a Convention is created.

The ILO was originally unique in international institutions in having a system of checks on the performance of countries. There was established in the early 1920s an International Committee of Experts — there are eighteen of them — to examine reports coming from governments. Sir John Wood, Professor of Law at Sheffield University and Chairman of the Central Arbitration Commission, the CAC, is a member of that Committee of Experts. He is not a 'British' member. He does not represent Britain at all. He is appointed personally by the Director General of the ILO, at present Francis Blanchard, in his personal capacity and he has taken the same oath as a judge of the International Court of Justice of absolute independence from governments. The Chairman of the Committee of Experts at the moment is Sir Adetokunbo Ademola, former Chief Justice of Nigeria. Other members are the famous Professor Ago, a judge of the International Court of Justice, from Italy; a judge of the Supreme Court of India; the Chief Justice of Barbados; Grigory Tunkin, Head of the Department of International Law at the University of Moscow and a Corresponding Member of the Academy of Sciences of the USSR, and so on. They are drawn from all around the world and represent probably as eminent a cross-section of individuals as could be found, skilled in the examination of evidence and particularly skilled and experienced in matters of labour law and labour standards.

They are backed up by an experienced secretariat which specialises in the examination of the reports of governments on the application of conventions. Reports on Conventions must be accompanied by copies of any new laws and regulations, of any important arbitration or courts of inquiry decisions, and so on. But in addition, the ILO monitors newspapers and other publications, and has its own sources of information. The other safeguard was mentioned earlier: when a government reports it must send a copy to the local TUC and CBI, or the appropriate bodies in each particular country. In March each year the Committee of Experts convenes. They meet in private so that they can talk quite frankly and freely among themselves. When they have reached their conclusions their report is printed and sets out country by country, Convention by Convention, their views and observations.

Naturally, if a country is in complete conformity with its obligations, then nothing is said. The United Kingdom normally is a very good conformer and if it has obligations it actually carries them out. But to show how carefully the Committee of Experts works, one might refer to Convention 122 which is concerned with full employment as being a central element of government policy and which was ratified by the United Kingdom. The Report of the Experts included the following:

The Committee notes the information supplied by the UK Government in its report. Much of its information relates to the measures taken to deal with special problems of unemployment and underemployment, for example in respect of the disabled and the young. It also describes at length the policies adopted to assist those who have lost their employment to find work.

It is not clear to the Committee from the report what positive steps are being taken to develop a policy to deal with increasing unemployment. According to statistics published by the Government, in mid-February 1981 there were over 2,400,000 registered unemployed persons, representing a seasonally-adjusted unemployment rate of 9.6 per cent of the labour force, and the Government recognises in its report that this rate, which has risen from 6.2 per cent in February 1980, will continue to rise during the year and is likely to remain high for some time.

In these circumstances, the Committee would have wished to find detailed information on the current situation and trends in employment and on the measures being implemented in the Government's report, which covers only certain limited aspects of an active employment policy as called for by the Convention. The Government states moreover that the conquest of inflation is seen as a necessary precondition of the conquest of unemployment, and that future employment opportunities are seen as depending on the ability of industry to respond to the opportunity offered to enterprise and efficiency.

The Committee emphasises that under the Convention a policy aimed at ensuring that there is work for all who are available for and seeking work should be a major goal, and requests the Government to provide particulars of the measures taken or contemplated to this end.

The Committee requests the Government to provide particulars of the consultations which have taken place with representatives of employers and workers concerning employment policies during the period covered by the report.

This is an example of the care with which reports are examined. The Report of the Committee of Experts on the Application of Conventions represents, one might say, the conscience of the world in relation to labour standards. Where there are injustices, it is in this Report that they are exposed, and not only with regard to labour standards but also to human rights.

The Report of the Committee of Experts is laid before the annual conference and immediately, as with a technical item, a committee is set up — in this case a Committee to consider the Report of the Committee of Experts. Again, the Committee includes workers, employers and governments with votes of equal strength. About 200 delegates attend that committee to debate the report. The debate is sharper and closer to the bone than is usual in international gatherings. In the main, governments do not bite each other publicly (or they avoid it as far as possible). But the workers' group — if the matter under discussion is, for example, a complaint about Chile or Bolivia, or the efforts of some people to form a free trade union in Soviet Russia — will want to know the facts, and they have the government representatives there to question.

Having gone through the Experts' Report, the Committee selects what it regards as salient points. It ignores minor infractions for the main part. The Committee concentrates a good deal on countries which year after year have been in default of their obligations; and they draw up a 'Special List' of such countries. Governments fight very hard not to be on the list since the Committee's Report is debated publicly in full plenary session.

There are currently 160 Conventions. The people who founded the ILO were concerned at first with basic labour standards — protection of women and children, extension of workmen's compensation to agricultural workers, and so on — but gradually considerations of human rights and broader questions have come into focus. It was, for example, not until 1947 that two key Conventions of the ILO, Conventions 87 and 98, the first concerning the right to freedom of association and the second the right to bargain collectively, were concluded. Those two key Conventions have probably had more ratifications and exerted more influence on the welfare and status of workers than virtually any other pair of Conventions. A special Standing Committee on Freedom of Association has been established to which complaints can be addressed even though a country may not have ratified Convention 87.

The experience and work of the ILO

The ILO, apart from being a setter of standards, is a gatherer of information. On the health and safety side, if a union, for example, has any anxieties about a particular process or a particular chemical, the ILO in Geneva can say what the experience has been, if any, around the world. The information about industrial diseases, dangerous chemicals, incidences of accidents of a particular kind repeating themselves, are recorded and are available. For a modest annual fee, any firm or trade union can have access to these records and the world's literature on health and safety at work. The translations cover every country; there are articles from the USSR as well as from the USA; subscribers can ask for a computer search in any particular area required.

There is a large technical assistance programme. At any one time there are about 800–1,000 experts and specialists around the world helping countries in a practical way. In the whole field of labour affairs, manpower planning, manpower statistics, vocational training and education, the improvement of job centres and employment exchanges, workers' education, workmen's compensation, increasing knowledge about industrial diseases, there are specialists working world-wide doing a practical job on the ground. There is a flow the other way under the same programme of technical assistance: medical doctors from Kenya studying occupational health in Britain under a United Nations scholarship, a Commissioner of Mines and Labour from a developing country who will be making a specialist study of certain industrial diseases in which he has particular interest in relation to his job back home. These examples could be multiplied. In Britain alone there are about 300 scholarship-holders, taking up one kind of training or another in a year. So quite apart from the standard setting there is this additional, practical work.

Some of the gravest problems faced by the ILO are in the field of human rights. It is disheartening to find that attacks on trade-union freedom are more widespread than they have ever been before. The number of complaints which are coming into the ILO has been rising steadily over the past four or five years. Partly this may be that people have learned the ropes a bit more and know how to handle complaints. But, as mentioned earlier, it was long ago decided in the ILO that the freedom of workers (and employers) to associate was a basic freedom. Without the ability to bring collective pressure, things would not happen. Therefore, even though a government may not have ratified Convention No. 87 on Freedom of Association, that country can nevertheless be called to account for any infraction of standards of freedom of association. It is an exception to the general rule that governments must ratify conventions before they incur any obligations. The tripartite Committee on Freedom of Association consists of three government, three worker, and three employer representatives. Any trade-union centre, including international trade unions recognised by the ILO, any government member, or any employers' organisation can put in a complaint duly documented to the Committee on Freedom of Association. The reports of the Committee are published and widely distributed.

A striking example of the ILO's defence of human rights in the field of freedom of association occurred in 1983. The Committee of Experts produced a report strongly critical of Soviet violations of Convention No. 87 which was later adopted by the Conference by a substantial majority in spite of strong Soviet bloc opposition. The Soviets reacted by proposing changes in the ILO supervisory machinery which would have had the effect of seriously weakening the procedures by which the Soviet violations had been exposed. This was heavily defeated by delegates in a secret ballot. The decision later to appoint a Commission of Enquiry into the Solidarity problem and the critical report which followed led to the Polish government giving notice (in 1985) of its intention to withdraw from the ILO.[13] The threat has so far not been carried out.

Like many other institutions in society it is moral pressure which alone in the end can prevail. We live in an imperfect world, but if every time there was some kind of infraction or another one began to think in terms of boycotts, sanctions and so on, there would be a confrontation, which in the end might make situations considerably worse. So long as there are sufficient people in the world who believe in what is right and continue repeating their views, and there is continual publicity for the things that they regard as wrong, in the end mankind will move in the right direction.

Trade-union standards in developing and developed countries

One must be careful, however, about looking at trade unions in developing countries from the standpoint of the experience of an industrialised country. In most developing countries, the wage-earner is in a privileged minority. It is important to note that people in developing countries who work for wages or a salary are a small minority of the total working population. This is not generally recognised. Nigeria, for example with a population of 70–80 million, probably has no more than 2,500,000 people working for wages and salaries. That includes government, transportation, docks, power, public service, manufacturing industry, commerce, and wage-earning plantation workers. The rest of the people must live off the land or their relatives. A high proportion one would regard as unemployed.

But 'unemployment' is a smoke-screen word that conceals basic poverty: no social security, no old-age pensions, no family allowances, no state sickness benefit, no unemployment benefit. Ministers and politicians take a much harder line about the right to strike, for example, because they are looking at it in an entirely different context, in a country beset by poverty and with great economic needs which can never be fulfilled in the short term. Thus they tend to act less sympathetically and sometimes more repressively than their Western counterparts. We need to understand the underlying causes which make ministers in developing countries rather more sensitive about the losses occasioned by strike action than those in richer economies.

The history of the trade-union law of Britain is one of pushing back the frontiers of the law, the common law as it affects unincorporated associations, the common law as it affects restraint of trade, the law as it affects breach of contract, and so on. The total effect has been until recently to allow employers and trade unions to negotiate and bargain collectively untrammelled by legal restrictions. Now in most other countries the law works in the opposite direction by imposing procedures and obligations on the relations between employers and workers. During the colonial period Britain exported her trade-union laws to territories for which she was responsible: the 1871 Act based upon the report of a Royal Commission after the steel strikes in Sheffield in 1869; legislation enacted in 1906 after the Taff Vale case, the 1927 Act which resulted from the 1926 General Strike. The trade-union laws which had been hammered out in Britain as a result of these events became part of her industrial and social history, but were too often exported uncritically overseas. Many colonial countries, as they became independent — this was also true of French overseas territories — inherited trade-union laws which did not derive from their own history or from their own background and problems.

It is perhaps a criticism of some governments and indigenous trade unions that they have not thought more deeply about what they need in their industrial relations, in their particular context, deriving from their own history and their own difficult economic circumstances, and have not challenged this colonial inheritance. But there have been exceptions. For instance, the Australian Federal Labour party leader, speaking to the Australian Parliament in 1903, said:

Although the Labour party as a whole throughout Australia has adopted the principle of compulsory arbitration, we find that even today there is a considerable section of extremists who scoff at any idea of handing over their liberties to a tribunal, such as is contemplated in this Bill. This feeling on the part of the extremist reformers is perhaps similar to that which moves the British and American trade unionists in their opposition to compulsory arbitration.

Then he went on:

In most countries they are practically without representation in Parliament and they have not even had an opportunity of making their voices heard, much less their votes felt, as far as the action of the judiciary is concerned.[14]

In other words, unlike the situation in Britain, there was in Australia a Labour party in power. There was a confidence that institutions of this kind involving compulsory arbitration, in their own national circumstances, had an effective part to play. Similarly, President Nyerere of Tanzania said in December 1960:

I have spoken before of the need for the African to think out for himself what is the essential meaning of democracy. Too often we have been led to accept an Anglo-Saxon or an American definition without realising that we are allowing ourselves to be sold not simply the democratic ideal but the particular form it has taken in these countries. I think the time has come also to re-examine our ideas about the union movement in Africa . . . particular patterns or traditions grow up in different countries because of the historical circumstances peculiar to those countries during the period of growth and those habits of thought tend to become accepted as essential to trade unionism when in fact they are not.

Though there may be a single International Labour Convention on Freedom of Association — Convention 87 — there cannot be a single perfect legal model for trade-union and industrial-relations law which will work in the same way in all parts of the world, under all sorts of conditions.

In looking at questions of trade-union freedom it is well to reserve judgement until one has looked closely at the local circumstances. It would be a great mistake automatically to criticise some aspect of trade-union freedom or trade-union law overseas because it differed from that in Britain.

International trade unionism

The idea of trade unionists getting together on an international basis has deep roots running right through the whole of nineteenth-century thought. It has in it a strong political element before the voice of the trade unions began to predominate.

In 1864 in London the First International was created. The opening words of the famous address to working men said what it was all about: 'It is a great fact that the misery of the working masses has not diminished from 1848 to 1864 and yet this period is unrivalled for the development of its industry and the growth of its commerce.' The founders of the First International felt that one reason for this was that working people in Britain and on the Continent had not taken common action to improve their conditions. But it was individuals not organisations spread right across Europe who founded the First International. There was no strong trade-union base. Even the British TUC had not yet been established. The First International broke up in 1872.

The Second International was constituted in 1889 in Paris. It was made up of socialist parties and trade unionists, but soon the trade unionists were saying that this kind of organisation, a mixture of trade-union leaders, a few workers' organisations, politicians and political organisations, had no real foundation. What they wanted was active trade-union memberships working together. In 1898 the first International Federation of Trade Unions was created. That survived and was given a great impetus after the trauma of the First World War by the foundation of the ILO in 1919. This gave the International Federation of Trade Unions an international platform where it could begin to work with trade-union people from unaffiliated countries.

Setting up the WFTU

It was a profound belief of the late Walter (later Lord) Citrine, then General-Secretary of the TUC, and those around him that in the post-war reconstruction period it was vital that the workers of eastern Europe and the Soviet Union, and also of Germany, the United States and the Western European countries, should get together and create for the first time a true workers' international with its roots deep in the trade-union movement of each country. That, they thought, would give it the kind of base which would survive and in time iron out some of the ideological and varying philosophical ideas on trade unionism. In 1946 the World Federation of Trade Unions (WFTU) was founded.

History suggests that a mistake was made in the appointment of the General-Secretary. He was a dedicated communist from France, Louis Saillant, and he surrounded himself with people of similar views. The WFTU rapidly became a platform for the views of the Soviet Communist party and the Cominform. The strains escalated quickly with the political differences between East and West reflected sharply in the Executive Bureau of the WFTU. As early as 1946 Walter Citrine had to warn the Executive Bureau and Executive Council of the WFTU in Moscow that persistence in the policies then being pursued would result in the British TUC's reconsidering its position. The WFTU, he said, was an international trade-union organisation, not an extension of the political views of the countries from which the membership was drawn. It would only ensure its existence by concentrating on trade-union, social and economic demands.

An early cause of conflict was the desire of the Communist membership of the WFTU that the International Trade Secretariats should be absorbed within the organisation. These Trade Secretariats — the Mineworkers' International, the International Transport Workers' Federation, etc., had long histories of independent existence and were understandably reluctant to submerge their identity in a new untried organisation. More important, however, was the reaction of Louis Saillant and his sympathisers to the proposed European Recovery Programme (ERP) — the Marshall Plan. Moscow had refused to participate, as had the puppet governments of Eastern Europe. The Western European unions called for a discussion of the ERP within the WFTU which was met with a refusal by Saillant even to put the matter on the agenda. The ERP, the Executive Bureau declared in November 1947, was 'a devilish scheme of Wall Street to enslave the free countries of Europe'. Since it proved impossible to arrange any discussion of the Marshall Plan within the WFTU, the trade-union centres in Western Europe and the United States organised their own ERP Trade Union Conference and set up an ERP Trade Union Advisory Committee. The Cold War, meantime, took on a new and dangerous aspect with the blockade of Berlin which began in May 1948 and lasted until June 1949. The spectacle of two and a quarter million Berliners having to be fed and maintained by a massive and expensive airlift was a sombre backcloth against which the Western trade unions sought to return the WFTU to its proper purposes.

All efforts were unavailing and in January 1949, in Paris, the three non-communist representatives (British TUC, American CIO and the Dutch NVV) announced the withdrawal of their respective organisations from the WFTU. Things moved swiftly thereafter and in July 1949, at the initiative of the British TUC, a conference was called in Geneva attended by fifty delegates from thirty-eight national centres. A preparatory committee was formed and a few months later, in November 1949, a conference held in London decided to establish a new trade-union international — the International Confederation of Free Trade Unions (ICFTU), now firmly based in Brussels. The International Trade Secretariats agreed to cooperate with the new organisation, but retained their autonomy and independence. (The full history of these momentous events is recorded in the TUC *Congress Reports* for 1948 (Margate) and 1949

(Bridlington).) Today these two trade-union blocs dominate the trade-union world. They do not cooperate; they do not meet.

In the wings is a third small confederation. It used to be called the IFCTU (the International Federation of Christian Trade Unions), but is now the World Confederation of Labour (WCL). The WCL is a product of that feeling in nineteenth-century Europe that Roman Catholicism and socialism did not always mix. In the strongly Roman Catholic areas of Western Europe, the Christian trade unions took root; they transferred their ideas to other parts of the world and, as might be expected, the WCL is strongest in areas where Roman Catholicism is dominant.

The unfortunate divisions in the world trade-union movement have been reflected in Third World countries. For example, in the 1950s and 1960s there were two main trade-union groupings in Nigeria, one affiliated to the WFTU and another affiliated to the ICFTU. Both groupings were being supplied with money, typewriters, transport and so on. This led to the artificial generation within Nigeria of Western European differences, which had no relevance to Nigeria or to the basic union problems of Nigeria: probably the workers would have been better off without either of the two groupings. The problem has only recently been resolved. It would have been pleasant had the dispute been resolved by the two trade-union groupings deciding to amalgamate, but in fact it was done by a government edict. In France's colonial possessions the position was made worse by the extension to them of the deep political divisions within the trade-union movement in metropolitan France. Some African governments, in Kenya, Malawi and Zambia, for instance, prohibit the central trade-union federation from having external affiliations, but the work of the international trade secretariats is seldom interfered with.

Thus potential worker unity throughout the world has been converted by historical pressures into two strong blocs contending with one another and fighting for influence. Later came the creation of the European TUC. Obviously such a grouping creates the problem of whether WFTU affiliates, such as the CGT in France and the CGIL of Italy, can become members. The European TUC is represented on the Economic and Social Committee of the European Community and, as a result, has considerable influence and pull. As trade unions have emerged in Portugal and Spain they have, therefore, applied to join the European TUC. The problem of political affiliation has broadly been dealt with as follows. The rule which in general is applied by the ETUC is that, irrespective of the political complexion of a trade-union grouping, if it maintains affiliation with the WFTU or if its policies seem to be identical with those of the WFTU, they will not be admitted. (See General Council's *Report to Congress*, Blackpool, September 1981.)

There are regional organisations of the ICFTU in Asia and in Latin America. These regional organisations are valuable because they bring together trade-union leaders within a region who have common problems for the main part, who can discuss them freely in their own area of the world and devote proper time to them, without having to listen to the more esoteric problems of the Western Europeans or the North Americans. Africa, after many false starts, has created its own independent trade-union federation —

the Organisation of African Trade Union Unity (OATUU).

Policies of the ICFTU

The ICFTU represents about 70 million unionists in over ninety countries and it represents, of course, a confederation of trade-union centres, not individual trade unions.

The TUC is affiliated to the ICFTU: it is not open to any individual British union to affiliate. In some countries there may be rival trade-union centres and on occasion both have been admitted. Where that has happened it stems from the belief that if the ICFTU were to affiliate only one grouping it would widen the divisions within the country itself and, therefore, unless there are overriding political objections, it is better to have both in the ICFTU.

The ICFTU has followed a strictly anti-colonial policy. Its attitude on apartheid and conditions in South Africa has been exemplary. Through the generosity of affiliated unions, including the TUC, they have been able to pursue a quite active policy of support for the black unions in South Africa in difficult circumstances. The ICFTU is active in intervening where trade unionists have been arrested, imprisoned, or where trade-union freedom is at risk. In this they line up very often with Amnesty International and, of course, they take up cases in Eastern Europe whenever they can get hold of facts which can support a complaint. On the ground there are the international trade secretariats. The oldest, the International Transport Workers Federation, was founded in 1896 even before the International Federation of Trade Unions. These are international organisations of trade unions from the same trade, industry or occupation.

The affiliates of the trade secretariats are individual unions and the organisations have a particular strength because they talk from common ground, from a common work experience, from shared work problems, from common relationships. Again, it is easier through the trade secretariats to help the weaker unions of the developing world than it is through other forms of organisation. Apart from shared experience, they are less susceptible to charges of political bias. Trade secretariats are in a position to do something positive and active. Perhaps the most dramatic example of this is the International Transport Workers' Federation (ITF). They have long had a policy of opposing flags of convenience. If a ship flying a flag of convenience goes into an ITF-controlled port it may be held there until the owners agree to pay ITF minimum wages and conditions and the master can then be given a blue ticket, preventing the ship from further interference by ITF affiliates.

The trade secretariats have in recent times faced problems when supporting local trade unions. There occurred some years ago in Malaysia, for example, a series of incidents which upset the Malaysian government. There was a dispute involving pilots and ground crew of Malaysian Airways. Some people were sacked, others allegedly arrested. The International Transport Workers' Federation moved in to help them, they got Malaysian Airways grounded in Sydney Airport and another plane grounded in Frankfurt Airport: essentially the overseas activities of Malaysian Airways came to a standstill. In the end a compromise was patched up, but ministers in Malaysia have protested that this is an undue extension of trade-union action, that is to say, that a national problem, a national trade-union difficulty should not become the subject of interference from people outside who have no stake in the country. The Public Services International has also had a few problems in that direction. So whatever the solidarity trade unionists may feel for each other around the world — with the increasingly complex world in which we live and the interrelationships between one country and another in shipping, air lines and communications — international action is for the first time being applied and is arousing resentment and doubts.

Trade unions and multinational companies

Multinational companies have been increasingly a subject of concern within the International Labour Organisation and indeed the international community. The ILO has produced a Declaration of Principles governing the social policy of multinational enterprises. This was hammered out by government, workers and employers in Geneva and represents the only tripartite agreement on the social policy of multinationals that exists. Periodic reports are called for from governments and these are examined and discussed within the ILO by the same procedures described earlier in relation to conventions. The OECD in Paris has also issued guidelines for multinational companies and established machinery for a limited degree of supervision with a reporting point for complaints in each member country. The Trade Union Advisory Committee (TUAC) has played a valuable part in the formulation of these guidelines (TUAC is the successor of the ERP Trade Union Advisory Committee referred to earlier).

In New York there is the UN Commission on Transnationals (the UN term for multinationals) which has been discussing the problem since 1974, but nothing much of value has yet emerged. There has not so far been a successful set of collective bargaining negotiations with a multinational company which bridges international boundaries. Attempts have been made, for example, with Philips and certain chemical companies. The motor manufacturers have remained rigidly opposed. But it is a foremost aim of the international trade-union movement, whether at the international trade secretariat level, or at the international confederation or world federation level, to get some kind of grip on the activities of the multinationals, and thereby reduce the power they have to move their resources from country to country according to wage differentials or political amenities or for other reasons.

The international trade-union movement is not an area of unity. It is most unlikely, given the deep political differences that exist in the world, that the gulf which divides the great trade-union groupings can be narrowed down. The British TUC has been active in trying to improve relations. One result has been occasional meetings between trade-union representatives from Eastern Europe and the USSR and trade-union representatives from Western Europe. They do not represent the ICFTU at these meetings, nor do the other side represent the

WFTU. The trade-union leaders participating confine discussions to a chosen technical subject; there are no resolutions and the press release is mutually agreed, i.e. it is a very cautious coming together on technical labour matters between East and West. The Soviet AUCCTU would like to see a secretariat set up, but so far there has been no agreement on this. In addition, there are numerous individual trade-union delegations and TUC delegations visiting Eastern Europe and the Soviet Union as fraternal delegates, and there is also traffic the other way.

The ILO has been a powerful force since its foundation in 1919 for improving living and working standards in all parts of the world. It was largely the influence of the ILO which steered the United Nations into linking social objectives with economic objectives in the strategy for the UN Second Development Decade (1970–80): 'The ultimate objective of development must be to bring about sustained improvement in the well-being of the individual.' It has lived up to its Constitution 'by international action to improve living conditions, raise living standards and promote productive employment'.

Notes

1. J.W. Follows, 1951, *Antecedents of the International Labour Organisation*, Oxford, Clarendon Press; G.A. Johnston, 1924 *International Social Progress*, London, Allen and Unwin.
2. John Price, 1945, *The International Labour Movement*, Oxford, Oxford University Press, pp. 2–10.
3. ibid., pp. 11–13.
4. James T. Shotwell (ed.), 1934, *Origins of the International Labour Organization*, Vol. 1, New York, Carnegie Endowment for International Peace, p. 25.
5. ibid., pp. 29, G.A. Johnston, op. cit., pp. 25–8.
6. Leon Eli Troclet, 1952–62, *Législation Sociale Internationale*, 8 vols., Brussels, Université Libre, Cahiers No. 4, pp. 136–49.
7. J.W. Follows, op.cit., 1951; James T. Shotwell, op. cit., Vol. 1, pp. 36–47; G.A. Johnston, op.cit., pp. 29–30.
8. James T. Shotwell, op.cit., Vol. 1, Chapter III by Carol Riegelman, pp. 55–79.
9. James T. Shotwell, op.cit., Vol. 1, p. 65 (the full text of the letter is in Vol. II, Doc. No. 5). (Note: the TUC did not have an International Department, hence the GFTU initiative.)
10. G.A. Johnston, op.cit., pp. 34–5.
11. James T. Shotwell, op.cit., Chapter IV, Vol. 1, pp. 108–10, 'The Phelan Memorandum'.
12. G.A. Johnston, op.cit., pp. 51–2.
13. ILO Document, GB 230/19/4, June 1985.
14. J.H. Portus, 1958, *The Development of Australian Trade Union Law*, Cambridge, Cambridge University Press, p. 248.

7 The United Nations and human rights

Andrew Williams

Introduction

No individual and certainly no state representative will ever oppose the idea of the furtherance of human rights. Since the defeat of Nazi Germany it has been to say the least unfashionable to advocate policies which discriminate against any section of a national or regional population so as to infringe upon their 'fundamental' rights or 'liberties' on whatever grounds, be they religious, racial, sexual or political. All states that have constitutions and many that do not have implemented legal instruments specifically banning any such infringement by government organ or individual. Given this quasi-unanimity, it must therefore be asked why the world needs a body, or bodies, to remind us continually that human rights, variously defined, need to be protected. The sad truth is that the United Nations (UN) is made up of human rights violating states, just as it is made up of states that break other self-imposed limits on their actions. This translates into often nauseating and hypocritical pontification by state representatives defending their indefensible record, and the United Nations paper machine faithfully reporting their justifications and excuses in reams of legal hyperbole. This is one of the areas where it is easiest to find a divergence between stated intention and sorry practice. A dispassionate and objective account of the UN's activities in this field is, therefore, not easy to draft. But while the application of a double standard must occasionally be admitted we should ourselves not let 'political broadsides masquerade as evaluation'.[1]

The first section will try to define what is meant by the expression 'human rights'. The second will put the human rights debate into historical perspective by showing what the UN has achieved in terms of legal instruments. A third section will look at how the UN deals with human rights violations, with some examples from recent years. Lastly it will be asked whether the UN is the best place to organise the improvement of a sorry record and whether other organisations, notably such bodies as Amnesty International, might not do better.

What are human rights?

Social scientists have often noted the difficulties inherent in classification and definition. Confucius wrote that the definition of terms was at the basis of good government: 'If names are not correct, language will not be in accordance with the truth of things.'[2] Language has perhaps suffered incommensurate abuse this century and many believe that it has become devalued in the process to the detriment of civilisation in general. Orwell's famous 'Newspeak' and the French expression '*langue de bois*' are generally directed against the excesses of the totalitarian regimes that have flourished since 1918, but the tendency towards a lack of linguistic accuracy can be found in many places. Deplorable as this may be, language has a social function; it is a mirror of clarity or confusion.

Analysis of the term 'human rights' demonstrates the problems inherent in the twentieth-century dilemma. In the United Nations many different cultural heritages confront each other in what is often uneasy debate. Consequently one of the major areas of disagreement is in the formulation of international 'codes', which emerge as official documents. In his recent report, Maurice Bertrand identifies 'long-windedness' and its corollary 'lack of realism' as two of the key problems in giving credibility to the UN as a whole. He admits that imprecision often facilitates discussion but that this has dangerous limits and that in the field of human rights we are perilously close to these limits.[3]

The general malaise gives ample support for Bertrand's view and an examination of problems in human rights gives an insight into why some of the wider problems exist. The first realisation has to be that the whole idea of 'rights' has a long history that goes to the basis of what various cultures mean by 'government'.

In Western political thought it has often been observed that there are two major traditions of democratic thought that have coexisted uneasily down the centuries. The secularising revolution of 1642–88 in England produced thinkers like Hobbes and Locke who recognised the selfish individualism of human beings and urged, respectively, a form of benevolent despotism or pluralist democratic structures to channel these energies. C.B. MacPherson summed up this pattern of thought as 'possessive individualism'.[4] This idea was restated forcibly in the American Declaration of Independence as a 'self-evident truth', while coming down on the pluralist or Lockean side of the suggested solutions. Successive American governments have of course defended the individual rights enshrined in their constitution in many foreign policy initiatives. Naturally their self-perception has not gone unchallenged.

Collectivist ideas also derive some of their legitimacy from the great modernising revolutions of the Western world. Rousseau is perhaps the most famous writer in this tradition, when he pointed out that Lockean democracy was often only for the few and for the rich. His counter-attack was the idea of a 'general will' where all citizens' rights would derive from the greater good of society.[5] Such thinking can be found writ large in the constitutions of the French Republic as well as in those of the great revolutionary states of the twentieth century, as it can in the writings of Karl Marx and other thinkers on the left.

Elements of these two main currents can be found wherever ideological debate is engaged. The currently popular free-market ideas of people like F.A. Hayek are a reiteration of Lockean principles. Those who talk of positive state action to eradicate inequality are echoing Rousseau's emphasis on the necessary role of the state to protect the underprivileged. To demonstrate that this dichotomy is even present in discussion of human rights at the international level a small example can be used. In discussions about the idea of genocide as a crime against individual lives or against a broader ideal of group aspiration, the UN working group defining 'apartheid' favoured the former when it interpreted the term 'genocide' as meaning 'any act calculated to destroy the individual or to prevent him from participating fully in national life'. This is a somewhat wide definition that many would find unacceptable. Likewise, in discussing how to eradicate the crime of genocide a delegate admitted that 'sincere differences of opinion exist as to whether this problem is best dealt with by education and constant vigilance or by the influence of legislation.'[6]

Can rights therefore be equated with 'values' and, if so, who is to say which ethical appeals shall be made law and enforced, or can such legislation be wise or effective?[7] Do we not also have the problem of successive governments in a country changing those whom they deem 'eligible' for proper treatment? In both Nazi Germany and the early American Republic 'enemies of the people' were persecuted. These are not just philosophical niceties, they are reflected in harsh realities. In the human rights debate the struggle has essentially been over whether individuals' rights should be put before or after those of the collectivity, over whether political rights should have primacy over social and economic rights.

The horrors of Nazi Germany gave a first impetus to a truly international attempt to define and improve the definitions of human rights. But the make-up of the 'basket' of individual and collective rights has proved elusive. The history of UN organs in the field has largely been one of trying to find the common ground necessary for this definition. Shue has argued famously that four rights are 'basic': the right to no detention without trial, to freedom from torture and from extra-judicial execution, and the right to subsistence. Without these all other rights have no meaning since they are the minimum necessary to survive and function. But they leave a lot of areas very hazy, both in the context of individual and collective rights.[8] The United Nations has slowly come to terms with this debate, even if it has by no means resolved it.

The UN and forty years of human rights

From the outset the main agencies created as part of the United Nations system attempted to address practical problems in a practical fashion. As the GATT, IMF and World Bank grew out of the economic disasters of the 1930s, so human rights activity grew out of the experiences of the concentration camps. But the transition from vague principle to definite acts was more difficult. The British and United States governments had given some impetus to the idea in the Atlantic Charter, signed as quid pro quo for the Lend Lease Agreement in 1941 by Churchill and Roosevelt. Roosevelt's 'Four Freedoms' were those of freedom of speech and worship, freedom from want and for 'all persons everywhere'. Vague indeed, but even British and American views differed on key areas of what 'freedom' meant, in the colonial context for example. In the early discussions for a United Nations Organisation at Dumbarton Oaks in 1944 and San Francisco in 1945 this vagueness persisted. At the first conference there developed a rather bizarre alliance of the British and the USSR, concerned that any reference to human rights would open the way to gross violations of the internal affairs of states. The United States insisted that such reference be made, which the Soviet Union in the end conceded, followed by the British. The compromise was that the Charter reference stayed vague even if it was, in the words of Evan Luard, 'a substantial advance on anything that existed in the League'.[9]

The problem was essentially one of a possible infringement of sovereignty, and this has remained as perhaps the major impediment to progress on human rights as in other areas. Very real fears exist of one state seriously infringing the sovereignty of another in the human rights field. Sovereignty is a basic guaranteeing principle of the international system, and one state will usually be a rather poor judge of another's record. Equally there is an unavoidable uncertainty about the outcome of an intervention by one state in another's affairs and very little guarantee that an external action will meet with any genuine response if not given mass internal support. There are unhappily many examples in twentieth-century world history where at least the last two problems have been very evident.

On the other hand, the claim of immunity from non-intervention in domestic affairs can cover up a multitude of ills within a state upon which the international community may decide it has a *right* to comment. Here lies the hoary old discussion of 'political will' to let international organisation play a real role in improving the conditions of the world's population. It could well be argued that intervention can and must be justified when it does not mean interference but rather an encouragement of discussion.

When the infant UN was discussing its possible activity in the human rights field it therefore had initially to make compromises. The Charter determined that the United Nations should 'reaffirm faith in human rights, in the dignity and worth of the human person, in the equal rights of men and women and of nations large and small' (UN Charter, *Preamble*). To this end the General Assembly was given responsibility for 'assisting in the realization of human rights and fundamental freedoms for all without distinction as to race, sex, language or religion' (Article 13). Article 55 gave the UN the task of promoting 'respect for and observance of' the said rights and freedoms, thus implying a research, publicity and at least moral enforcement role. The umbrella for this activity was to be the Economic and Social Council (ECOSOC), made up of eighteen member states in 1945 (now numbering fifty-four). In turn ECOSOC set up a Commission for Human Rights to implement the Charter provisions.

It must be added that the same problems encountered at Dumbarton Oaks, over sovereignty, re-emerged during the Charter discussions, with the US delegation, under strong pressure from human rights pressure groups, being the prime supporter among the 'Big Five' states for human rights clauses. The small states were the greatest supporters outside the United States, ironically with hindsight, since they included Chile, Cuba and Panama who especially urged protection of particular rights from the start.[10] It should also be said that some of the major input to the Charter provisions came from General Jan Smuts of South Africa, also a citizen of a country without a faultless human rights record since 1945.

The Commission and its secretariat immediately embarked on the drawing up of a Universal Declaration of Human Rights which embodied a series of aspirations that included both individual and collective rights, with the emphasis on the former, perhaps reflecting the major role played by Eleanor Roosevelt in its drafting. Its very rapid acceptance was contingent on a clear understanding that the Declaration had declaratory, but not legislative, power. That it was passed at all is perhaps a miracle given the atmosphere of 1948 when it was voted in the General Assembly. In the event the USSR and the whole of Eastern Europe voted against it, as well as South Africa and Saudi Arabia. The Eastern bloc objected to the individualistic emphasis of the Declaration and its relative lack of emphasis on social and economic rights. It also objected to the low profile given to the role of the state as arbiter of, and responsible party for, social justice, and to the implication in Article 28 that the 'social and international order' was already a good one. This was certainly not the implication intended but it enabled the USSR to shun any responsibility for injustices deriving from colonial regimes, a line of reasoning used elsewhere in the UN to evade its responsibilities.

To put flesh on the bones of the Declaration, and to implement it, has been and will continue to be the prime aim of the UN Commission for Human Rights. Supplementary work has been done in other agencies, such as the International Labour Organisation, whose Conventions are generally respected. But certain areas of the Declaration have given rise to problems of interpretation, even where good will exists. The Anglo-Saxon and Latin systems of law differ significantly on the rights of the individual. There are differences of social and economic emphasis within the capitalist and socialist systems and, perhaps most importantly, there are great differences of economic and social development in what are now called 'North' and 'South'. The first twenty years of the Commission's life were, therefore, spent trying better to define the area of agreement between these differing conceptions of what human rights are all about. A key writer on human rights has put it thus: 'human rights are more than a collection of formal norms; they are dynamic political, social, economic, juridical as well as moral, cultural and philosophical conditions, which define the intrinsic value of man and his inherent dignity.'[11]

The period until the signing of the more binding Covenants on Civil and Political Rights and Economic, Social and Cultural Rights in 1966 might be seen as a complete waste of time and energy. David Forsythe says that 'pessimists see this period as one of inaction' whereas 'optimists say human rights diplomacy turned to indirect protection or promotion efforts through seminars and publications'.[12] We can nonetheless accept that the period until 1954 was one of the elaboration of basic Charter provisions. In a book written in 1967, Luard commented that the Human Rights Commission remained 'almost totally unknown to more than 99 per cent of the world's population'.[13] Given Luard's 'optimistic' views it may be said that the pessimists carry the vote on the pre-1967 period. There were UN actions before 1967 to try and implement the Charter in Southern Africa and a half-hearted attempt to condemn The People's Republic of China (then not a member of the UN) for its repression in Tibet during 1959. Successes over decolonisation could be attributed to an already existing Western desire to decolonise which the UN could at best accelerate.

Here consensus already existed and, where it did not, the UN's actions had little effect, as with apartheid.

The signing of the Covenants should have immediately ushered in a new era of action, but it took until 1976 for enough countries to ratify the Covenants to make them operational. The ratifying states numbered eighty-eight for the Economic, Social and Cultural Covenant by mid-1986 and eighty-four for the Covenant on Civil and Political Rights. An 'optional protocol' to the latter Covenant which had thirty-eight signatories by mid-1986 makes the signatory state recognise the competence of the Human Rights Committee, set up in 1977, to receive individual depositions.

We can summarize briefly the make-up of the various main organs dealing with human rights in the UN orbit as at the end of 1985 as follows;

(a) The ECOSOC has fifty-four member states and established the:
(b) Commission on Human Rights, which has forty-three states represented. Each year one-third of the mandates are renewed by vote in the General Assembly. The states are geographically divided into eleven African, nine Asian, eight Latin American, five East European and ten Western. The Commission appoints a:
(c) Sub-Commission on the Prevention of Discrimination and the Protection of Minorities. This is made up of twenty-six independent experts who theoretically do not represent their national governments, again geographically distributed into seven Africans, five Asians, five Latin Americans, three East Europeans and six Westerners.
(d) The Covenants mentioned above also led to the appointment of the Human Rights Committee. The signatories to the Civil and Political Covenant elect an eighteen-member committee made up of independent experts. It reports straight to the General Assembly.
(e) The Centre (formerly the Division) for Human Rights, within the Geneva Secretariat of the UN, services all the above bodies in spite of its small size (only a few professional and general service staff). As will be shown below, the views of its members can play a key role in agenda formation and development.
(f) The General Assembly, and its 'Third Committee' in particular, has *overall* titular responsibility for the actors of the other bodies.

United Nations action in human rights

It must be said from the outset that none of the UN's bodies responsible for human rights carries out actual physical protection work, any more than does the International Committee of the Red Cross or Amnesty International. UN bodies must respect the principle of national sovereignty, even if there are greater or lesser lengths to which this respect can be taken. As with the Commonwealth's condemnation of Amin's Uganda in the 1970s, there have been occasions on which the Commission, the Committee, and even the Secretariat have gone much further than simply noting human rights problems in a country. This has especially been the case since 1977 and the entry into force of the two Covenants mentioned above. It might even be said that in the field of human rights there has been a notable departure on many occasions from the usually acquiescent attitude of secretariats in other UN bodies. But before discussing particular cases, we should examine the process of dealing with human rights violations at the international UN level.

Procedures

Marc Bossyut has summed up the activities of the Commission, Sub-Commission and Committee on human rights as well as the ECOSOC deliberations that derive from these bodies as the examinations of violations of human rights and the examination of communications. The first category, that of violations, can be divided into a 'country oriented' and a 'thematic' examination. The second category is a part of the procedure that is confidential, the first is generally in public. Both must be seen in tandem.[14]

As has been inferred, the General Assembly does have some responsibility for human rights questions, but it generally contents itself in a crowded schedule with broad political resolutions. The main broad areas of interest to it in this context are of course Israel, South Africa, Chile and Central America at the moment. In so far as there is detailed discussion, this takes place within the so-called 'Third Committee'. Discussion in the General Assembly tends to mobilise along fairly predictable lines, often with a strong North–South divide, leading to often voiced Western condemnations of 'politicisation'. Some degree of consensus has been reached recently on the Namibia question.[15]

Each year the ECOSOC requests that the Sub-Commission on Prevention of Discrimination and Protection of Minorities prepare a series of reports on thematic issues, such as (currently) torture, apartheid, slavery, and other racial and political discrimination. This is done by special rapporteurs who are experts in the field in question. The Sub-Commission, with the help of the Centre for Human Rights, also summarises the communications it has received from governments, organisations and individuals. This has been possible since 1947 under ECOSOC Resolution 75(V) of that year. Since 1970 and ECOSOC Resolution 1503 (XLVIII), individuals and organisations can submit their reports confidentially. The reports are scrutinised by a five-member working group of the Sub-Commission before being sent to the Commission or, as sometimes happens, dropped.[16]

The Commission considers the reports forwarded to it and transmits them to the governments concerned. It can then recommend dropping the subject, keeping it under review, or forwarding it to the ECOSOC for further, public, consideration. Only on four occasions has the latter happened, at the request of the government in question after a change of regime in 1979 with Equatorial Guinea, in 1985 with Argentina and Uruguay, and in 1986 with the Philippines. Bossyut prints the following collation of countries that have been discussed in the Commission, all under the confidential procedure, by the end of 1985.

— 1978: Bolivia, Equatorial Guinea, Ethiopia, Indonesia, Malawi, Paraguay, Republic of Korea, Uganda, Uruguay;
— 1979: Bolivia, Burma, Ethiopia, Indonesia, Malawi, Paraguay, Republic of

Korea, Uganda, Uruguay;
— 1980: Argentina, Bolivia, Central African Republic, Ethiopia, Indonesia, Republic of Korea, Uganda, Paraguay, Uruguay;
— 1981: Afghanistan, Argentina, Bolivia, Central African Republic, Chile, German Democratic Republic, El Salvador, Ethiopia, Guatemala, Haiti, Indonesia, Japan, Mozambique, Uganda, Paraguay, Uruguay, Republic of Korea;
— 1982: Afghanistan, Argentina, German Democratic Republic, Haiti, Paraguay, Uruguay, Venezuela, Republic of Korea;
— 1983: Afghanistan, Argentina, German Democratic Republic, Haiti, Paraguay, Uruguay, Indonesia (concerning East Timor), Iran, Turkey;
— 1984: Albania, Benin, Haiti, Indonesia (East Timor), Paraguay, Philippines, Turkey, Uruguay; for the first time the Chairman announced that the situations relating to certain countries (Afghanistan, Argentina, Malaysia and Pakistan) were no longer under consideration;
— 1985: Albania, Haiti, Paraguay, Philippines, Turkey, Zaïre; the situations relating to Benin, Indonesia (East Timor), Pakistan and Uruguay are no longer under consideration.[17]

Separately, and since 1977, the Committee for Human Rights also considers state reports submitted by signatories of the two Covenants. It can also consider submissions from individuals or organisations from within states that have signed the 'Optional Protocol' to the Covenants on Civil and Political Rights. After consideration of the reports the Committee can ask for further information, offer its good offices to help improve the situation, refer the situation to a working group for further consideration, and finally submit its reports directly to the General Assembly for further action.

The Centre for Human Rights (until 1982 called the Division for Human Rights) can have a varying impact on this procedure which is basically one of putting pressure on countries felt to be demonstrating a 'consistent pattern of gross and reliably attested violations of human rights'. The kind of pressure varies from 'quiet diplomacy' to overt publicity in all the UN's human rights bodies. The Centre is in a better position than anyone to oversee the whole process since it services all the meetings considered above. It actually prepares the papers, agendas and reports and keeps everyone informed. The Director of the Centre advises the Secretary-General of the UN on human rights matters and plays a vital role in providing information. The personality and actions of the Director of the Centre can therefore have a major influence on the other procedural attacks on human rights violations.

The Directors of the Centre/Division have always been Westerners. In the recent past the most important of these was Theo Van Boven who headed the Division from the beginning of what has been termed the 'active' period in 1977 until his dismissal in 1982. His actions and the manner of his departure were, to say the least, controversial. His period of office coincided suspiciously with the Carter presidency in the United States when, of course, the President made human rights observance a prerequisite of United States aid and foreign policy support. The lesser emphasis given to such issues by President Reagan meant that Van Boven had less protectors in high places for his policy of a high-profile exposure of abuses. The generally accepted account of his departure is that the Americans gave way, particularly to Argentinian pressure, as well as there being an amount of personal friction between Van Boven and the new Secretary-General Perez de Cuellar, who had crossed swords with Van Boven earlier. It would perhaps be too much to say that Van Boven was 'silenced', but his departure does prove that the Centre's Secretariat can make the great tremble on occasion.[18]

The dispute may be put into the wider context of the status of the Centre and of human rights in general within the United Nations. There is not a 'High-Commissioner' for human rights in the way that there *is* one for refugees. The reason for this goes back to the initial discussions about how binding the UN's strictures about human rights should be. A High Commissioner would have far more authority to exercise power. Khruschev's phrase 'there are no neutral men', applied by him to the Secretary-General of the UN, is seen as even more pertinent when applied to the human rights field. The USSR has also often made the (dubious) point that to have a High Commissioner would be to create a 'World Conscience' as, for example, Prince Sadruddin Aga Khan became over refugees, when only states and international organisations are subjects of international law. Lengthy discussions continue along these lines without much prospect of resolution.[19] The Van Boven episode perhaps proves that all the states of the globe (or most of them) prefer the UN secretariats to keep their own counsel and let countries pursue their own 'collegial' activities.

Evaluation

To return to Bossyut's division into country and thematic reports on the one hand and the examination of communications on the other, it is clear that there is a great amount of overlap between the different interested bodies. The sheer number of subjects under discussion, and countries involved, makes a comprehensive discussion of even a few cases rather difficult. What will now be attempted is to highlight the problems faced in one area and in the discussion of one country in the context of the foregoing discussion.

We should ask ourselves whether an evaluation of UN activities in this field is possible, and if so on what criteria. Remarkably little serious academic work of this kind has been attempted. It is generally accepted that critiques of the UN are usually in the form of negative broadsides. Studies of the international bureaucracy in the last fifteen years are rare and evaluation of its actions, except in the security field, even rarer.[20] In the human rights field they are virtually non-existent. One member of the UN's Centre for Human Rights, B. Ramcharan, has nonetheless attempted the definition of some parameters.[21] These he defines as the implementation of international instruments and procedures, research and studies and their impact on the ending of discrimination and the effect of advisory services and publications.

On the principal area of UN human rights action since the Second World War, the elaboration of international instruments and procedures, it should be quite easy to evaluate progress. But as the Covenants prove, it can take a long time to secure enough ratifications to bring them into force. Again, only a relatively small number of states signed the 'optional' protocol allowing submissions by individuals under the Covenant. Other possible areas to evaluate include the extent to which there exists dialogue within any one country about human rights, especially between the government and citizens groups under the influence of the instrument in question. Of course, to this must be added the extent of the international legislation's incorporation *in good faith* into national legislation. On procedures the most important points are: does fact-finding result in the finding of facts? Is there a clear identification of the problems? Promptness here is a key test since an abuse of human rights usually means direct suffering by an individual.

To set standards, topics need to be presented in a sensible way that will encourage change. Here Ramcharan admits that it is difficult to generalise about what indicators to use in reports — measurement of progress has to be 'mainly in relation to particular societies'.[22] This development has yet seriously to take place. Lastly, to evaluate national performance in terms of the provision of information the non-governmental organisations (NGOs) have to be considered. Their 'state of the world reports' (Freedom House in the United States or Amnesty International are two organisations who produce such reports) can have an immense corroborative or denying effect to government statements of progress.

If we try and apply this to only one field where some evaluation has been seriously attempted, slavery, we can see the problems of such efforts.

Slavery as a 'thematic' area

Slavery is one of the oldest forms of human rights abuse. It is still present today in many states of the world, although it was universally condemned in this century by the League of Nations in the 1926 Slavery Convention. Its treatment by the UN has demonstrated many of the problems facing such 'themes' eradication. It encompasses both individual and collective rights in that slavery is both an economic institution, whether it be the selling of people into service or to the 'sweat shops', and an individual constraint or denial of civil and political rights. It was broadly defined by the 1926 Convention as 'the status or condition of a person over whom any or all of the powers attaching to the right of ownership are exercised'. A 1975 Sub-Commission working group stressed the complexity of the phenomenon and included a rider to this definition including any form of 'dealing with human beings leading to the forced exploitation of their labour'. One member of the group, Mr Singh, is said to have remarked, 'The real problem was that old and evil practices frequently assumed new guises'.[23]

The problem of cultural specificity is here a major problem both in definition and information-gathering. Do arranged marriages or the Indian caste system count as slavery? Of course, there is no doubt that prostitution, debt bondage and child labour are condemned by all, but how then does a poor family survive in, say, Calcutta without certain members of it being involved as victim in such practices? The state would have to provide alternative arrangements and often cannot.

So what does the UN do? Since 1966 and earlier it claims that it has done much: 'There is no doubt that the action on newly independent governments to eliminate slavery has been encouraged both by publicity and by discussion at the United Nations'.[24] However, it might be said that, like disarmament, the more it is tried the less it happens. Zoglin points out that the membership of working groups, such as the one mentioned, makes a great difference: 'Some members such as Whitaker [Special Rapporteur] . . . have made significant contributions to the progress and development of issues studies . . . Others, by contrast, have not . . .'. Nonetheless, Zoglin notes that although some state representatives have criticised some of the working practices of the group, certain reports, such as Whitaker's, have been generally accepted as 'appropriate and beneficial'. Also, on the question of information-gathering, it is clear that working groups have to rely heavily on HGO input, which is often criticised for relying on press reports.[25]

Implementation of such groups' work at the international level, that is to say ECOSOC or the General Assembly, or at national level, is naturally crucial. Given that the 1975 and later working groups reported first to the Sub-Commission, which then referred it to the Commission, the latter's role became crucial. It is clear that certain members of the Commission felt that the Sub-Commission often exceeded its mandate, as did the NGOs reporting to both it and the Sub-Commission. Here we have a clear case of independent experts (or the Sub-Commission) being prepared to go far further than state representation on the Commission. In addition Zoglin makes a strong case for demonstrating the inaction of the political bodies (General Assembly, ECOSOC) and the concrete action undertaken by some functional bodies of the UN, especially the International Labour Organisation. ILO representatives attended the working groups regularly and provided information of a high quality as well as taking action, as against the Dominican Republic and Haiti in 1983, under the relevant ILO conventions. On the other hand, UNESCO, Zoglin stresses, did nothing ('passing the buck') and the UN Development programme refused to take action.[26]

On the theme of slavery, it is clear therefore that the UN record is patchy. The functional organisations gave a mixed response. The Commission may be criticised for noting the Sub-Commission's working group reports but feeling it can do little. But we can praise the Sub-Commission report for its energy and for not fearing to embarrass.

Poland as a country case

Very few people in the West would disagree that the 1981 crushing of *Solidarnosc* was a flagrant breach of the Covenant on Civil and Political Rights by one of its signatories, Poland. The ILO conference in 1980 was marked by the appearance of Lech Walesa as head of the Polish Workers' delegation to the annual conference of the ILO. The Polish government report under Article 40 in 1986 of the Covenant to the Committee for Human Rights makes interesting reading. The report states that the period 1979–87 'witnessed extensive reconstruction of the legal system resulting from socialist revival of social, economic and political life'. Especially

legislative changes which were undertaken remained closely correlated with the postulates of various groups of Polish society, particularly the workers, put forward, *inter alia*, in the 1980 social agreements and within the spontaneously-born structures of the Patriotic Movement for National Rebirth.[27]

The Committee for Human Rights largely dismissed this report as a whitewash and some comments were much stronger.

This case, and many more could be cited, illustrates the problems inherent in respect for sovereignty. However, it might be argued that the Polish state's response to *Solidarnosc* showed a considerable improvement on Eastern bloc reactions to 1956 and 1968. The fact of the report being sent (and it was due in 1984) demonstrates the defensive attitude of the government in question and its felt need to embellish its tarnished image. In a truly power politics world, why should it have bothered?

The Human Rights Committee with its special powers under the Covenant therefore plays much the same spoiling role for authoritarian governments as the Sub-Commission plays on 'thematic' issues. Neither believes in 'quiet diplomacy'.

The future relationship between various UN bodies concerned with human rights

The departure of Van Boven and the impact of the Committee and Sub-Commission has led to an increasing debate about these bodies which has by no means been completed as yet. A brief examination of this debate does shed some light on positions taken.

A first point, made by Forsythe among others, is that we should guard against seeing this debate purely in terms of a North–South divide. Certainly the Eastern bloc has played a very dubious role in improving the UN's efficacy in human rights violations, but the same cannot be said of Third World countries, many of which have made a substantial contribution in the 'right' direction. This applies both in the Sub-Commission and in higher bodies, right up to the General Assembly. On civil and political rights Forsythe cites a vote where forty-six non-aligned states voted with the West.[28] However, he also points out that on the primacy of economic and social rights there is no such agreement.

The so-called 'right to develop' illustrates where the traditional splits still exist. Whenever debate takes place, and it has done almost annually since 1977 (cf. General Assembly Resolutions 32/130, 34/46, 35/174, 36/133), the vote is made up of all the developing nations voting for and all the Western nations abstaining or voting against. The idea is essentially an extension of the concept of economic and social rights. The problem is that all Western states see this as putting individual rights lower than those of the 'community', and, what is more, applying only to developing countries. The Italian delegate who pointed to this last problem saw great possibilities for the abuse of political rights in this formulation. The idea is also linked strongly to the New international Economic Order ideas, or what a Ugandan delegate at the same meeting called the 'democratisation of international economic relations'. Add to that the Eastern bloc emphasis on the need of the *state* to ensure that these rights were upheld and we have the Locke/Rousseau debate writ large.[29] It is doubtful that the inclusion of this item has done anything to further the effective work of the UN in human rights, given that it resurrects old ghosts and makes the task of implementation more difficult. Some of its sponsors undoubtedly intend this to be the case.

Since 1981 there have been lengthy discussions under Item XI of the Commission's agenda to improve the work of that body. Apart from the upgrading of the Division to what is now a 'Centre', not much can be said to have been achieved. Many of the suggestions involve 'time-saving' to 'rationalise' the agenda of both Commission and Sub-Commission. (Lest it be thought that using these terms implies cynicism, these are the terms employed.) A ten-member working group has operated since 1982, hampered by a need to work only on consensus when such a consensus did not exist, as on the 'High Commissioner' proposal. However, here we find Costa Rica and Senegal being for the idea and Brazil and India being against, a confirmation of Forsythe's contention about cross-bloc voting.[30]

Given the bickering in this working group, Perez de Cuellar, whether on his own or on the Centre's advice, has tried to get movement to improve UN performance. Mr Herndl, the present head of the Centre, introduced this at the 1985 meeting of the working group under agenda Item XI. For de Cuellar, the work of bodies such as the Committee on Human Rights was important, but his emphasis seemed to be more on action 'geared to provide practical forms of assistance to states to enable them to comply with their international obligations'. Technical assistance was, therefore, to be the new watchword with the Centre leading the way. The Commission has already been increased in number in 1979, and a consensus developed at this meeting that the Commission's role should continue to be enhanced. This, of course, pleased the socialist countries since it confirmed the importance of the state over that of 'unofficial' experts. The USSR went even further and stressed the 'realism' of putting more emphasis on ECOSOC, the Third Committee and the General Assembly as fora for human rights questions. In short, as the Irish delegate pointed out, the ten-member group had achieved very little in really defining the relationship between the different bodies in question.[31]

The Committee for Human Rights, and especially its concern over individual cases under the optional protocol, is clearly of key importance. The independence of the experts that make it up means that their actual and potential nuisance value to states with blemished records is immense. The future of this body will therefore be a weather vane of the credibility of the UN in this field. One ominous sign is that the deliberations of the Committee were severely constricted in 1986 as an 'economy' measure.

Can the UN (or anyone else) do better?

The above remarks will make it clear that the gathering and dissemination of information to put pressure on human rights violators is the main aim of the UN and other bodies in the field. The UN itself is made up of member states, thus ensuring that the secretariat plays a secondary servicing role and that no action is taken that could be construed as interfering in the sovereign rights of states. Given this inevitable constraint, might not NGOs do better? After all, more people have heard of Amnesty International than of the Commission on Human Rights. The Van Boven example probably shows that quiet diplomacy is now to be the rule. Yet as Jacobo Timmerman, the Argentinian activist, has put it, 'quiet diplomacy is surrender': the public espousal of his case by President Carter is perhaps proof of the need for very overt publicity.

NGOs have played a vital role at every stage of the UN's development as a force in human rights. Many of them now have consultative status with ECOSOC, which gives them access to the Commission. They also have an important role to play in the confidential activities of the Committee and the Sub-Commission. They can even point to concrete results, in private at least. Undoubtedly Amnesty's revelations about Emperor Bokassa's predilection to child murder embarrassed his 'ally' the French into arranging his downfall.[32] Naturally Amnesty denies such influence and acknowledges that its actions can backfire to the detriment of its reputation (as in local support for the *Rote Armee Fraktion* in Germany). The efficacy of such organisations, and even bigger ones such as the International Committee of the Red Cross, is undeniable.[33] However, the NGOs *themselves* cannot implement major change — they need a governmental forum to do so. Hence their relationship with the UN has to be symbiotic, if usually uneasy.

It must be said that this uneasiness sometimes is provoked more by NGO crassness than by UN intransigence. Some rather amusing if bizarre episodes figure in every meeting of the Commission to show this.[34] But often one can hear the authentic voice of an oppressed minority speaking through an NGO. A Ugandan delegate replying in 1983 to NGO criticism, stating that 'all people living in Uganda enjoyed full freedom of conscience, religion and worship' hardly rings true, even if it is understandable that he should assert it.[35] Those NGOs who have learned how to play the system can have a major impact on it. And naturally quite often the human rights experts that make up the Committee and Sub-Commission are often affiliated to NGOs in their home countries. Any discussion of a human rights 'regime' should include discussion of such bodies.[36]

As has been said before, human rights cannot be removed from their social, political and cultural context. NGOs act as the conscience for, particularly but not exclusively, the Western tradition of civil and political rights and are also accepted by large numbers of developing countries. The NGO can, therefore, act as a double mediator within the UN — between peoples and governments and between governments themselves, but only in an international framework. They play a vital role in information-gathering and dissemination. They can act as 'unofficial diplomats' to great effect by using the oldest arts of persuasion and threat of exposure within the United Nations system. Undoubtedly this is why their number has grown so vertiginously in recent years.[37]

So even the most vocal critics of UN bureaucracy cannot do without it. Could it be argued that states' bilateral actions might have more effect? It is often said that only those states that have good records feel any guilt about being accused of violations. This is probably not true. The assault on human rights violations in South Africa has led to massive heart-searching in that country. United Nations discussion of Argentina did much to bring about change there, although the Falklands/Malvinas war obviously helped. Perhaps the best summary of the impact of the UN in this field comes from a former United States representative

---

to the Commission, Dr Abrams:

Despite the harsh realities of power politics world opinion *is* a force to be reckoned with. Governments *do* devote much time and energy, both in and out of the UN defending and embellishing their own human rights image and demeaning that of others.[38]

Notes

1. Kathryn Zoglin, 1986, 'United Nations action against slavery: a critical evaluation, *Human Rights Quarterly*, vol. 8, no. 2, pp. 306–39 (Hereafter *HRQ*).
2. Quoted by Leonard Shapiro, 1972, in *Totalitarianism*, London, Pall Mall, p. 7.
3. Maurice Bertrand, 1985, 'Some reflections on reform of the United Nations', Geneva, United Nations, JIU/REP/85/9, p. 16.
4. C.D. Macpherson, 1962, *The Political Theory of Possessive Individualism*, Oxford, Oxford University Press.
5. See Jules Steinberg, 1978, *Locke, Rousseau and the Idea of Consent*, London, Greenwood Press, for further discussion of these ideas.
6. United Nations, ECOSOC, Commission on Human Rights, E/CN.4/Sub.2/1985/6, pp. 22–3.
7. Useful collections on this vast field are: E. Kamenka and A.E.S. Tay, 1978, *Human Rights*, London, Edward Arnold; and J.R. Pennock and J.W. Chapman, 1981, 'Human rights', *Nomos XXIII*, New York, New York University Press. See also Jeremy Waldron (ed.), 1984 *Theories of Rights*, Oxford, Oxford University Press.
8. For a discussion of Shue's ideas, see Robert Matthews and Cranford Pratt, 1985, 'Human rights and foreign policy: principles and Canadian practice', *HRQ*, vol. 7, no. 2, May, pp. 159–88.
9. Evan Luard, 1982, *A History of the United Nations*, vol. I, London, Macmillan, p. 32.
10. John P. Humphrey, 1967, 'The U.N. Charter and the Universal Declaration of Human Rights', in Evan Luard (ed.), *The International Protection of Human Rights*, London, Thames and Hudson, p. 41.
11. Moses Moskowitz, 1974, *International Concern with Human Rights*, Dobbs Ferry, NY, Oceana, p. 3.
12. David Forsythe, 1985, 'The United Nations and human rights, 1945–1985', *Political Science Quarterly*, vol. 100, no. 2, Summer, pp. 249–69, 250.
13. Evan Luard, *The International Protection of Human Rights*, op. cit., p. 323.
14. Marc Bossyut, 1985, 'The development of Special Procedures of the UN Commission for Human Rights', *Human Rights Law Journal*, vol. 6, pp. 179–210, 179–81.
15. United Nations, 1983, *United Nations Action in the Field of Human Rights*, New York, United Nations, pp. 272–4.
16. Marc Bossyut, op. cit., p. 182.
17. Marc Bossyut, ibid.
18. 'Human Rights Internet Reporter', edited by Laurie Wiseberg and Harry M. Scobie (hereafter HRI) is an NGO publication that followed this affair with great interest; cf. the first two editions of HRI in 1982 (January–February and March–May).
19. This idea was first mooted in ECOSOC in 1967 (E/4393/1967). For a detailed discussion of arguments for and against, see Roger Stenson Clark, 1972, *A United Nations High Commissioner for Human Rights*, The Hague, Martinus Nijhoff.
20. David Pitt and Thomas G. Weiss, (eds), 1986, *The Nature of United Nations*

Bureaucracies, London, Croom Helm, point out that recent studies of this type are almost non-existent. One of the best is still Jean Siotis, 1963, *Essai sur le secrétariat international*, Geneva, Droz.

21. B.G. Ramcharan, 1981, 'Evaluating human rights performance: some relevant criteria', *HRI Reporter*, September–October, pp. 12–15.
22. B.G. Ramcharan, ibid., p. 13.
23. Benjamin Whitaker (Rapporteur), 1984, *Slavery*, presented to the Sub-Commission on Prevention of Discrimination and Protection of Minorities, United Nations, E/CN.4/Sub.2/1982/20/Rev.1.
24. ibid., p. 18.
25. Kathryn Zoglin, 'United Nations action against slavery . . .', op. cit., pp. 315–23.
26. ibid., pp. 331–4.
27. Human Rights Committee, 1986, *Second Periodic Report of States Parties Due in 1984: Polish People's Republic*, CCPR/C/32/Add.9, 17 January, p. 3, para. 7.
28. David Forsythe, 'Human rights', op. cit., pp. 254, 258–9.
29. UN Commission on Human Rights E/CN.4/1982/S.R.30, pp. 7–18.
30. E/CN.4/1983/S.R.54/Add.1, pp. 5–14.
31. E/CN.4/1985/S.R.53/Add.1, pp. 20–1.
32. See Jonathan Power, 1981, *Amnesty International: The Human Rights Story*, Oxford, Pergamon.
33. A recent study is that of Georges Willemin, Roger Heacock and Jacques Freymond, 1984, *The International Committee of the Red Cross*, The Hague, Martinus Nijhoff.
34. For example, see E/CN.4/1983/S.R.55, pp. 14–16.
35. E/CN.4/1983/S.R.56, p. 10.
36. Jack Donnelly in his recent 'International human rights regimes' in *International Organisation*, Summer 1986, vol. 40, no. 3, pp. 599–642, shows up the main weakness of some regime analysis, its state-centricity, by making very little reference to NGOs except to say that 'NGO efforts . . . can be of considerable significance in the day-to-day operations of all the regimes [UN and regional] that we have considered' (p. 631).
37. See Harold K. Jacobson, 1984, *Networks of Interdependence*, 2nd edn., New York, Alfred A. Knopf, Introduction; and Peter Willets (ed.), 1982, *Pressure Groups in the Global System*, London, Frances Pinter.
38. Roger Stenson Clark, *A United Nations High Commissioner for Human Rights*, op. cit., p. 92.

Recommended reading

Ian Brownlie, 1981, *Basic Documents on Human Rights*, 2nd edn., New York, Oxford University Press.

Jack Donnelly, 1986, 'International human rights: a regime analysis', *International Organization*, vol. 40, no. 3, Summer.

David P. Forsythe, 1985, 'The United Nations and human rights', *Political Science Quarterly*, vol. 100, Summer, pp. 249–70.

John P. Humphrey, 1984, *Human Rights and the United Nations*, Dobbs Ferry, Transaction Press.

Walter Laquer and Barry N. Rubin (eds), 1979, *The Human Rights Reader*, New York, New America Library.

Theodor Meron, 1986, *Human Rights Law-Making in the United Nations: A Critique of Instruments and Process*, Oxford, Clarendon Press.

R.J. Vincent (ed.), 1986, *Foreign Policy and Human Rights: Issues and Responses*, Royal Institute of International Affairs and Cambridge University Press.

8   The United Nations:
a suitable place for disasters?

Randolph Kent

'It was pluralism run riot,' mused the former US Assistant Secretary of State for Refugee Affairs. 'These sorts of situations have a considerable degree of efficiency losses. You've got to measure this in terms of marginal systems. Not as many died as might have; perhaps that is the key.'[1]

In the wake of the civil war which raged in Kampuchea between 1979 and 1982, two types of disaster began to command the attention of the international community.[2] The first was conventionally defined as a man-made disaster, the direct product of a civil war. Starting in 1979, hundreds of thousands of Kampucheans began to flee from Kampuchea for the relative security of neighbouring Thailand. They came to Thai sanctuaries malnourished, diseased and in constant fear of retribution. The second disaster was that normally regarded as a 'natural disaster'. Within Kampuchea, the horrors of the Pol Pot regime from 1975 until the end of 1978 had led to massive destruction of the country's agricultural infrastructure. Many agriculturalists had been killed, the urban population had been dislocated, farming communities had been disrupted. Now the country, under the leadership of the Vietnamese-backed Heng Samrin regime, faced the prospect of severe food shortages. Mass starvation seemed to many to be the inevitable prospect.

The plight of millions of Kampucheans finally was brought to the attention of the international community through the mass media and through the lobbying of special interest groups throughout the world, particularly in Western Europe and North America. Confronted with two disasters, both of mega proportions, the international community felt compelled increasingly to respond.

Yet an effective international response would have to wend its way carefully through the highly emotive and explosive political situation which bedevilled South East Asia. Despite the apparent genocidal policies of the Pol Pot regime, it was that regime alone which the majority of governments continued to recognise. Only the Eastern bloc formally recognised the authority of the new Heng Samrin government installed in the Kampuchean capital of Phnom Penh. Since Vietnam had been the major supporter of the new government, the United States and most of its allies were reluctant to work overtly with the new Phnom Penh authorities, and hence famine relief inside Kampuchea became encumbered with all sorts of 'difficulties'. The plight of the refugees fleeing from Kampuchea, however, was not; for those refugees were deemed to be symbols of the repressive nature of the regime in Phnom Penh.

The initial stances of the major Western governmental donors placed the government of Thailand in an excruciating dilemma. To curry favour with the

West, Bangkok allowed the hundreds of thousands of refugees fleeing from
Kampuchea to seek a haven within Thailand. Yet fearful of Vietnamese–
Kampuchean retaliation, the Thais made it clear that it was harbouring
'economic migrants' and not refugees. The distinction was important. The term
'refugee' was redolent with political symbolism. It would be regarded as a
diplomatic dagger thrust at the legitimacy of the Vietnamese-backed regime in
Kampuchea. 'Economic migrant' was safer, less condemnatory. It was a term
which in theory would allow the West to assist the Kampucheans who took
shelter along the Thai border without at the same time alienating Thailand's
neighbours.

It was within this political maelstrom that the international community sought
to assist the millions of victims faced by two of the most severe natural and man-
made disasters of modern times. Hundreds of private voluntary relief agencies
established operations in the Thai border area to deal with the refugees; several
finally gained permission from the suspicious and extremely defensive
authorities in Phnom Penh to work inside Kampuchea amongst the famine
victims. Governments from the Eastern as well as the Western bloc provided
massive amounts of relief equipment and supplies: the former concentrating
upon the famine, and the latter, in terms of bilateral assistance, dealing with the
Thai border.

And heaped upon this relief imbroglio was the United Nations. From the
Secretary-General of the United Nations to logistics experts from the UN's
World Food Programme, a bevy of participants from the extensive United
Nations family sought in theory to add coherence and direction to the complex
relief operations taking place inside and along the Thai border of Kampuchea.
The UN system had been mobilised to stem what many observers felt would be
nothing less than 'a holocaust'.[3]

The UN's role in disaster relief

The UN Secretariat's role in disaster relief has always suffered from a degree
of ambivalence. Until the early 1970s, the Secretary-General could rightly maintain that disasters, no matter how tragic, did not really fall within the sphere of
his responsibilities. The UN Secretariat had of necessity to be concerned with
the 'greater issues' of the day, principally those involving global security and
stability. To the extent that the United Nations could or should be involved in
disaster relief, that was the responsibility of those Specialised Agencies which
form part of the UN family.

The idea of a UN family is about as ambivalent as the Secretary-General's
view of his role in disaster relief. The founders of the United Nations, concerned
that the functional work of the UN should not be disrupted by the highly political
activities of the General Assembly and the Security Council, sought to make a
clear distinction between the political institutions of the United Nations and
those ostensibly non-political components such as the Food and Agricultural
Organisation. These functional agencies were endowed with a considerable
degree of autonomy, each, in the words of Sir Robert Jackson, a kind of

independent barony which fought to protect its respective sphere of interest.[4]

As long as the Secretariat remained focused upon global security issues, the arms-length relations between the Secretary-General and the Specialised Agencies proved a convenient stance for both. However, when the bumbling and chaotic responses of the UN agencies to disasters in East Pakistan, Peru and Biafra became apparent in the late 1960s and early 1970s, member governments felt obliged to reassess the role of the Secretary-General in disaster relief. The office of the UN's Secretary-General appeared a suitable place to instil the necessary degree of coordination in times of serious disaster emergencies.

As early as 1968, there were a host of proposals designed to enhance the coordinating role of the Secretariat. Yet, as one official directly involved in these efforts was later to confess, no one took these proposals very seriously.[5] Nevertheless, by 1972, given pressure from the increasingly disaster-prone developing countries and the persistent failures of the UN agencies to harmonise their disaster relief activities, member states agreed to create a United Nations Disaster Relief Organisation.[6] UNDRO was designed to give the United Nations family a focal point, directly under the Secretary-General, to mobilise and coordinate UN involvement in disaster relief.

From the very outset, UNDRO ran up against the entrenched positions of the Specialised Agencies of the United Nations: 'The barons will never surrender power.'[7] They were unwilling to accept the role of UNDRO, and treated the new organisation as an irrelevant upstart; and while a series of inter-agency agreements established some semblance of working relations between the new agency and its more established sister organisations, UNDRO has evolved as just another agency within the system.[8] Its purported coordinating and directing responsibilities in times of disaster have been reduced principally to one of providing information to the international community at large.

UNDRO's eroded status, however, did not mean that the Secretary-General's emerging involvement in disaster relief was to be commensurately reduced. On the contrary, over the past decade, as more and more disasters were brought to the world's attention, the authority of the Secretary-General has been enhanced, but with a good dose of practical realism. Rather than any single UN body attempting to coordinate the family of agencies, the theme of the 1980s is to build and encourage 'plural capabilities'.[9] In other words, rather than have any single agency attempt to direct and coordinate the efforts of the independent agencies, greater emphasis would be placed on the need to promote inter-agency cooperation in times of disaster. The Secretary-General would promote such harmonisation in times of serious disaster either by appointing a 'lead agency' or by appointing an *ad hoc* coordinator.

The idea underlying a lead agency is, in principle, sound. It assumes that there are certain types of disaster, for example, famine, in which one agency would by the very nature of its particular expertise have a predominant interest (for example, the United Nations Children's Fund) and that its efforts could be supported by subcontracting to other agencies such as the World Health Organisation, where supplementary assistance was required. Of course, the principle has merits and can work effectively as long as two conditions exist. The first was that the disaster, *per se*, has to reflect the clear interests and capabilities of the lead single agency; the second is that the Secretary-General's assumptions about the clarity of the disaster requirements and appropriate expertise of the agency he appoints are shared by other agencies. Only too often, however, such common perceptions are not easy to foster.

Nor is the idea of an *ad hoc* coordinator easy to implement. While in theory the selection of a coordinator to direct the relief efforts of the UN agencies bears the moral weight of the Secretary-General of the United Nations, in practice it takes more than moral weight to keep the agencies in line. If the coordinator has access to resources — 'the power of the purse' — to induce agency cooperation, then the designated coordinator's authority is clear. Yet without such carrots, there is little to persuade the agencies to cooperate.

Resources available to the Secretary-General to put at the disposal of a relief operation have never surpassed a meagre $30,000 per disaster. For amounts beyond that, the Secretary-General has had to rely on special emergency appeals principally to government donors. However, governments have rarely shown an interest in supporting such special initiatives to any great extent. They continue to fund preferred UN agencies or funnel relief resources bilaterally or through private voluntary agency partners. Their general reluctance to support on a significant scale an appeal from the Secretary-General reveals in so many instances the very nature of the problem which surrounds a major disaster relief operation.

The nature of the problem

'Don't let anybody tell me that nobody knew what was going on in Kampuchea. Waldheim [UN Secretary-General in 1979] was asked to take the lead, but the Carters [US President Jimmy Carter] were the trigger.' Sir Robert Jackson whom Waldheim had appointed as the UN Special Relief Coordinator in Kampuchea recalled with a degree of bitterness his efforts in November 1979 to persuade the US administration to use the mechanisms of the United Nations to coordinate the international relief effort in Kampuchea. Jackson knew that it was crucial to gain the backing of the United States for a UN coordinated effort; for the United States, as in most emergency operations, provided between 40 and 50 per cent of all international assistance, and its attitude would in turn influence the majority of other major governmental donors.

The US administration showed little inclination to comply with Sir Robert's request. The Kampuchean crisis was both too political and already too publicised. The government of the United States was not going to relinquish its own political interests to some internationalised effort. It was not going to be caught by its domestic opponents assisting the Vietnamese-backed Heng Samrin regime. Nor was it going to lose the opportunity of scoring political points by immersing totally its own contributions to the Thai refugee operation in some general pool of international assistance.

For the US administration, the Kampuchean crisis had also become too publicised. The administration had already begun to feel the hot breath of private voluntary agencies and congressional criticism down its neck. It was anxious to show that the government was responding to the plight of Kampuchea, and that once again the United States was demonstrating its humanitarian concern. At best, the UN would play a parallel role with donor governments. The former would be able to coordinate but, at the same time, it would not be able to interfere with the bilateral programmes over which the US government would maintain control.

Jackson's inability to persuade the United States to focus the entire relief effort under one single UN umbrella pointed to some of the more fundamental aspects of the nature of disaster relief. First, disasters themselves are 'complex'; they are rarely divisible into clear-cut man-made or natural components. Increasingly, they concern profound structural, sociological, economic and political problems; and relief, *per se*, more often than not becomes a statement about the very legitimacy of authority within a disaster afflicted area. Secondly, while many practitioners deny that disaster relief, *per se*, is political[10], the reality is that 'humanitarian assistance' is redolent with political symbolism. Thirdly, despite the media impression that disasters are obvious and their solutions blatantly apparent, that is anything but the case. Disasters only too often lack any sense of clarity at all. Numbers of afflicted, the cause of the disaster, the needs of the affected are all extremely complicated, requiring a sensitive understanding about when and where relief should be injected as well as the more obvious difficulties of appropriate supplies and logistic support.

Traditionally, it has been assumed that disasters could be simply divided into clear categories. Natural disasters, such as earthquakes, floods, cyclones, are supposed 'acts of God'. They are divorced from any man-made intervention. Yet, this comfortable assumption is belied by an ever more apparent reality. If one takes a look at the impact of what are purported to be natural disasters, the evidence only too clearly reflects the fact that natural disasters principally affect those who are impoverished and structurally deprived. It is not the flood or the earthquake — the agents of disasters — which cause death or injury; it is the fact that the victims have been forced to live in inadequate housing or in disaster-vulnerable locations which accounts for the loss of life and the mayhem.[11]

Disasters and the relief process expose vulnerabilities which go to the very root of established societies. They are indeed 'complex' because the impact of the vast majority of natural disasters reflects the weaknesses of the society as a whole. For this very reason, external intervention, as the relief process is often described, rarely fails to underscore the man-made components of a disaster, the inequalities, the economic deprivation and the extremes of social stratifications.

Even those with experience at the sharp end of political intrigue and calculation frequently maintain that 'humanitarian assistance' has to be distinguished from long-term development assistance.[12] The former, many maintain, is essentially apolitical while the latter is but a further weapon in the donor's diplomatic arsenal. Time and again, however, that impression is denied by the complicated political factors which such supposed humanitarian aid engenders. Governments respond with greater alacrity where the government of the afflicted has close links with the donor. More often than not, donor governments will respond in ways that accord with specific domestic pulls and pushes. Donor governments want to be seen to be doing good for reasons which often have little to do with the plight of the afflicted.

For the government of the afflicted, particularly in resource-poor countries, a disaster is always political. The discrepancies which external assistance can create between those benefiting from relief, and those not, can, ironically create serious internal tensions. Governments of the afflicted frequently feel that the ways they handle a disaster will be regarded as a test of their effectiveness and, therefore, are often extremely sensitive to the possible implications of international assistance. Well-intentioned international assistance can still fuel domestic opposition, can embarrass their own undertrained and resource deficient attempts at self-help, and ultimately can lead to the very collapse of governments, themselves.[13]

What compounds the political difficulties inherent in disasters and disaster relief is the very nature of a disaster. The media tend to render a disaster so obvious, the needs of victims so apparent. Yet disasters are not readily apparent nor are they so amenable to easy solutions. For example, perhaps one of the greatest difficulties at the onset of any relief situation is that of determining the numbers requiring assistance. Even in the relatively confined 1985 Colombian volcano disaster, precise figures of the afflicted could not be accurately determined for at least a fortnight.[14] Without greater accuracy and precision, some of the more fundamental aspects of a relief operation remain in the realm of the unknown, for example, how many people one is actually attempting to assist. The greater the ambiguity, however, the greater is the propensity for individual relief organisations to respond in ways that each feels is appropriate. The fallacy in such an approach is that donors — multilateral and bilateral — begin to urge their assistance upon recipient governments with anything but perfect knowledge or figures. The need to be seen to become involved often outpaces the need to promulgate effective and appropriate assistance to an identified afflicted group. Relief seiges are too often the result, with aid clogging limited air and seaport facilities with all sorts of material assumed to be, though not necessarily, useful.

The stories of inappropriate and chaotic relief operations are legion: tins of pork sent to Muslim victims of disaster, stiletto-healed shoes sent to monsoon-soaked village communities. Such stories are part of disaster relief folklore, and generally speaking represent bygone eras. Nevertheless, this folklore emphasises two things. The first is how little one had known until quite recently about effective disaster relief. The second is that disaster relief is complicated, requiring sensitivity to local conditions, innovative capabilities and a multiplicity of diverse skills.

In the final analysis the complexities involved in disaster relief demand that organisations which become involved in relief operations be innovative, well organised and able to provide appropriate and timely assistance. If there is a disparity in the types of aid which different organisations provide to disaster victims, a relief operation can disintegrate into a chaotic bazaar. If relief agencies cannot agree on when to give and when to discontinue aid, local economies may be added to the list of disaster casualties. If relief organisations are unable to work together, duplication and ineffective use of transport and distribution facilities are the inevitable result. Yet all these practical realities have to be understood in terms of the complexity and ambiguity inherent in all disasters, and it is in this uncertain realm that the United Nations family must work in times of disasters.

The United Nations family in action

The United Nations Children's Fund was the first UN agency that attempted to become involved on both sides of the Kampuchean border. Since its mandate did not require it to seek the approval of member governments in order to intervene, it took the initiative. UN Secretary-General Waldheim, therefore, designated UNICEF as the 'lead agency'. However, given the complexities of the operation and the probability that other UN agencies would become involved, Waldheim subsequently appointed Sir Robert Jackson as special relief coordinator to oversee the entire operation. Waldheim, though, soon to be facing the prospect of his re-election, felt that bringing other nationals into the operation would ultimately broaden his own support base; hence he added yet another special coordinator, Ilter Turkman, a Turk who was UN Assistant Secretary-General, to serve alongside Jackson.

If the operation ultimately was to deal with feeding famine victims inside Kampuchea as well as the refugees along the Thai border, the World Food Programme would have to become involved. However, for WFP to become involved it required the direct approval of the director of the UN Food and Agricultural Organisation. But the highly centralised institution of the FAO was reluctant to authorise the emergency programme, for many member states — principally those from Africa — were vociferously complaining that there already had been an overconcentration on the problems of Asia at the expense of Africa.

And then, of course there was the United Nations High Commissioner for Refugees who would have principal responsibility for the refugees. With the prospect of possibly the largest influx of refugees since the East Pakistan crisis almost eight years before, UNHCR would be an obvious participant in the border relief operation. However, UNHCR, perhaps surprisingly, had been wary of becoming involved. According to the government in Bangkok, those on the borders were not refugees. They were 'economic migrants', and strictly speaking UNHCR did not have the mandate to assist those who were not refugees.

The United Nations Disaster Relief Organisation had been squeezed out of the affair. The scale was too vast and the animosity of its sister agencies towards it too intense for UNDRO to serve any useful role. The other agencies maintained that UNDRO really had no relevant role to play, and UNDRO, attempting to mend fences with its more established counterparts kept itself at a distance.

Bilateral donors were either providing direct assistance to Bangkok (and in the case of France and the Scandinavian countries to Phnom Penh) or to UN agencies with which they wished to work. Private voluntary agencies, as in the case of Oxfam–UK, were introducing their own resources into Kampuchea, while numerous private agencies spent the millions of dollars donated by a sympathetic public to assist the border areas. Some voluntary agencies became the operational partners of UNICEF; others did everything they could to avoid such entangling alliances. Governments on occasion funded private voluntary organisations directly and at other times 'earmarked' multi-agency funds to go to specific private voluntary organisation relief work.

In observing the evolution of the massive relief operation on both sides of the border, it was difficult to say who was actually in charge. Governments were individually organising their own bilateral aid programmes with either Bangkok or Phnom Penh. They were contributing massively to UN agencies, but frequently dictating — 'earmarking' — how their individual contributions were to be used. Private voluntary agencies sought involvement in ways and in areas where they could best demonstrate their effectiveness to their own distant donors. Individually they established links with departments within the governments of recipient nations in order to promote their own particular programmes. It was indeed 'pluralism run riot'.

The situation did not lend itself to any clearly coordinated effort. The UN coordinator in practical terms lacked the authority and the resources to constrain, let alone guide, the relief attempts of the multiplicity of participants who were descending upon the affected countries. He even had little control over the UN agencies that were becoming involved. The FAO, after long delays, finally gave the WFP permission to provide emergency relief. UNICEF, the lead agency, found its own efforts constantly thwarted by recipient governments and constantly challenged by the UN High Commissioner for Refugees. And UNHCR, finally convinced that it had to become involved in the crisis, did so in ways that were regarded as 'prudent'. It distanced itself from any involvement that might be regarded as an infringement of its mandate, and in so doing, made only the most cursory effort to coordinate through UNICEF or the special relief coordinator.

In times of disaster, there are at least sixteen UN agencies which in one way or another can become involved in disaster-related activities. They range from the World Meteorological Organisation and the World Health Organisation to the International Labour Organisation and the United Nations Development Programme. To this list special offices such as the UN Office for Emergency Operations in Africa have been added recently to give special focus to acute problem areas.[15] For the most part, each of these agencies and special offices have significant degrees of autonomy sustained not merely by their individual constitutions but also by support bases within the government departments of members states.

'To make the UN family truly effective', suggested a long-serving member of the Secretariat, 'one would have to tear it down and start again.' Yet, given this practical impossibility, he went on to suggest that there was an increasingly urgent need for member states at least to coordinate their own intra-governmental approaches to UN bodies. 'Every meeting of ECOSOC (the United Nations Economic and Social Council) seems to have 3,000 different voices!'[16]

In part, the difficulty of coordinating the efforts of the United Nations family stems from the inability of governments to deal with the institutions of the UN themselves in a consistent and coherent manner. This is ultimately reflected in the uncertain mandates of many UN agencies and indeed in the inconsistent uses of those agencies by governments. In turn, uncertain mandates and inconsistency influence the organisational behaviour of the agencies, affect the ways that the expertise of such agencies are employed, and ultimately generate conditions for intense inter-organisational rivalries within the UN family.

As the United Nations family attempts to gear itself up for a major international relief effort, there are persistent and enduring problems which mar its way. There follows an attempt to describe some of these difficulties.

Uncertain mandates

In one way or another, no UN agency really has adequate authority to intervene in the types of complex disasters which, increasingly, are faced by the international community. The cautious approach which UNHCR took towards the Kampuchean crisis is but one case in point. Confronted by growing numbers of peoples seeking food, shelter and security across international borders, the international system has been unwilling to create any effective international mechanism to relieve their plight. 'Mass distressed migrants' — numerically one of the greatest social problems confronting the international community[17] — fall outside the strict mandate of UNHCR. UNHCR generally must work within a framework which is no longer appropriate to meet the types of 'refugee problems' witnessed in Kampuchea and elsewhere. Where a government refuses to accept that mass distressed migrants are broadly speaking refugees, UNHCR is severely handicapped. They can only be assisted when member states deem it convenient to provide an *ad hoc* and informal extension of its mandate.

Throughout the UN system, one is confronted time and again with mandated authority inadequate to meet the crises of disaster victims. The World Food Programme is constrained in the provision of relief in at least three ways. To undertake emergency relief it requires the authority of another UN agency, one which on more than a few occasions has found itself at odds with the WFP. For actual relief supplies on any large scale, it depends upon the inclinations of donors represented on its Council of Food Aid. And for any disaster of long duration, for example, refugees, its assistance is restricted to a maximum of two years. With such restrictions, even WFP attempts to plan in advance runs aground on constitutional restrictions. Even the United Nations Children's Fund, perhaps the most flexible of all the UN agencies, lacks a mandate to intervene in the first stages of disasters.

The lack of effective mandates to deal with problems arising out of disasters reflects two fundamental issues: the first concerns the development of the UN family in general; the second involves the inherent tensions between state sovereignty and an effective international system. Only too often the answer to global or international problems is made by creating yet another intergovernmental organisation. Over the past forty years, agencies have been heaped upon the system, often with little regard for overlap in responsibilities and certainly with only minimal concern for how the effort of one agency might affect the work of another. Compounding this higgledy-piggledy growth of intergovernmental organisations has been the often sloppy, or, politically convenient, imprecision of many agency mandates. Lack of clarity, overlapping responsibilities and a general disregard for the effect of a new agency upon the IGO network as a whole have created an arena of ambiguity which promulgates inter-agency rivalries and complicates even the most basic attempts to coordinate.

Given the ambiguity of their mandates, the agencies themselves are often uncertain how best to interpret their roles. More often than not, their objectives are determined not by their prescribed constitutions but rather by what they feel member states will tolerate. The components of the UN family must contend constantly with the inherent conflict between states' interpretations of sovereignty and their own mandated authority. UNHCR will extend its 'good offices' to assist non-statutory refugees when it feels that governments will accept such non-mandated involvement. Yet should governments show any inclination that UNHCR might be overstepping the mark, the organisation will retreat into the most conservative and most prudent approach to fulfilling its responsibilities.

The case of UNDRO's mandate is particularly relevant. Resolution 2816, establishing the Office of the UN Disaster Relief Coordinator, made clear that UNDRO was to mobilise, direct and coordinate the relief activities of the various organisations of the UN system. Yet this ostensibly clear mandate was replete with imprecision and ambiguity. Was UNDRO designed to be operational, in other words, to organise relief operations on the ground? Was UNDRO to become involved in man-made disasters; and, if so, how would such a role impact upon that of UNHCR? What actually did 'to direct, mobilise and coordinate' mean? Would UNDRO really be able to tell established agencies when, how and where to respond?

The reality during UNDRO's birth was that those member states that sponsored the creation of UNDRO just found it too impolitic to address these basic issues. There was a hue and cry by many throughout the developed and developing world that the UN should become more involved in disaster work, and to that extent UNDRO was a convenient response. However, the complications and political sensitivities which a truly clear, let alone effective, UNDRO role would introduce made it more convenient to obfuscate the basic issues. Rather than clarify the mandate, ambiguity was the preferred option.[18]

Inconsistent use of UN agencies

'There is a fundamental contradiction in the role of all UN agencies,' said an official from the US Agency for International Development, 'You can't tell governments whom you depend upon for your funds what to do.'[19] While in part this self-evident truth explains one aspect of the dilemma faced by the UN agencies, it by no means encapsulates the more subtle interplay between governments and intergovernmental organisations. There are constant trade-offs between the two. Often governments do not wish to suffer international opprobrium by failing to comply with an agency's request to assist afflicted peoples. In support of a particular objective, agencies have not been unwilling to play one political grouping against another: 'You've got to play the blocs even within the Western bloc,' suggested a former senior UNHCR official.[20] Conversely, intergovernmental organisations must also play the game; they, too, undertake activities which in certain instances have questionable legality or at least circumvent the normal interpretation of their mandates.

Yet, broadly speaking, it is not the issue of funding, *per se*, nor the dubious trade-offs which most complicate the roles of intergovernmental organisations. Of far greater consequence is the inconsistency with which UN bodies in general are used by governments of member states. This inconsistency affects not only the way that intergovernmental organisations give priorities to their objectives, but also the resources at hand to deal with emergencies.

Even if the Secretary-General of the United Nations launches a major international appeal for an emergency, member states might well ignore his pleas. Jacques Beaumont, in charge of emergency relief for UNICEF, recalled that

ten days after a major international appeal was launched by the Secretary General in September 1984 for the Lebanon there was no response. We in UNICEF decided not to approach anyone independently for funds, but nevertheless the US State Department just called to ask what we were doing about drugs for the Lebanon. The official at the State Department said that he didn't want to go through the Secretary General's special fund; he wanted the money to go through UNICEF.[21]

Member governments pick and choose how and when they wish to use intergovernmental organisations. In Honduras, the United States wanted UNHCR to undertake a repatriation programme to return refugees from El Salvador. When in desperation local UNHCR officials had to admit that none of the refugees was willing to be repatriated the US government refused to accept UNHCR's findings and turned to another intergovernmental organisation, the International Committee on Migration to take on the task.

The World Food Programme, like all other UN agencies, feels compelled to respond to the diktats of its donors. Despite the fact that WFP normally has very few people on the ground, food donors have besieged WFP increasingly to fulfil requests which it has neither the resources nor the manpower to do. Monitoring of individual food donations by the EEC, Canada or Australia, and purchasing of transport for relief operations inside Ethiopia are but two examples of undertakings imposed upon the WFP. Yet, from the organisation's perspective, it cannot assume that such demands will continue. It cannot request increased funding nor seek to ensure an appropriate structure to enable it to undertake such tasks when, in fact, it can never be sure that governments will continue to use it in that way in the future.

Whether they are concerned with technical issues or those affecting broader policies, intergovernmental organisations live in a world made unpredictable by the inconsistent ways that they are used. This fact has significant consequences upon the very structure and behaviour of these organisations.

Organisational behaviour

Uncertain mandates and the inconsistent use of international organisations go a long way to explain the overcentralised and ponderous decision-making structures which bedevil the vast majority of UN agencies. These same factors also explain only too often why there is a wide gulf between the formal objectives of such organisations and their preoccupations with what might be termed 'organisational health'.

The greater the institutional insecurity, the less control it may have over its agenda and resource base, and the greater will be the propensity to define organisational objectives in terms of the organisation's survival. Organisational survival under such conditions is reflected in what one observer described as 'prudence'. Prudence or caution is reflected in certain basic organisation characteristics. There is a tendency to restrict activities to pre-established standard operating procedures, programmes and repertoires. Individual initiatives are frowned upon as institutionally disruptive. Formalism marks the implementation of such preprogrammed operational activities, and employees respect relatively rigid lines of communication, with relatively little cross-fertilisation of ideas and information. Priorities are determined in terms of what the organisation should be doing: means, not ends, provide the focal points for resolving problems.

The spectrum of UN agencies is broad. Some, such as UNICEF with its wide network of voluntary support groups and more flexible mandate, are far less rigid than an organisation such as UNHCR. For UNHCR, prudence pervades throughout the organisation's structure. Those within it view acceptable performance as complying with fixed routines rather than testing initiatives. They become immersed in what might be described as 'lower task management', for example, the compilation of reports and budgets rather than with the anticipation of new problems and new ways of dealing with them. Prudence and security demand that formal approval is given at each stage of the organisation's hierarchy, and this process in turn means that ultimately all decisions of any consequence must filter up through and be sanctioned by the central authority of the organisation.

If one matches such organisational tendencies against the need for initiatives and flexibility so often demanded by disaster relief operations, there is little doubt that the rigidly hierarchical structures of the majority of UN agencies are unsuitable to deal with the plight of emergency victims. As one emergency officer for UNHCR admitted, UN agencies 'just lack the flexibility to deal with emergencies'.[22] 'Prudence', explained an old UN hand, 'is not as much a question of individual courage, etc., as much as it is perhaps due to the perception of individuals' roles from an organisational perspective. Prudence concerns the reluctance of individuals to push the organisation's response beyond what those within it feel will be accepted.'[23] UNHCR, in Kampuchea, turned its back on some of the most blatant violations of refugee rights because UNHCR officials felt that to protest would be regarded by headquarters as not in the interest of the organisation.

All relief situations are redolent with ambiguity, and ambiguity is abhorrent to all organisations, particularly those which are predisposed to rely heavily on preprogrammed procedures and high degrees of formalism. The greater the ambiguity for rigidly hierarchical structures, the greater is the tendency of those 'below' to depend upon instructions from the 'top'. Yet where the top is uncertain about its own authority and not in control of resources, it resolves such ambiguity by guiding the organisation towards a minimalist position: that which the organisation can do safely. 'With an organisation such as UNHCR, one does not use a criterion of success or failure — merely what one can do; the more tangible aspects of such a minimum centres around donors' pressures being reflected from the organisation's headquarters.'[24]

The gulf between the ambiguity of organisational objectives and the preoccupation with institutional health is often bridged by focusing upon the priorities implicit in money. Funding slices through ambiguity and provides a concrete basis upon which to determine priorities. It is not irrelevant that all too often those who have attempted to coordinate the efforts of intergovernmental agencies in emergencies speak of 'the power of the purse'. The availability of funds — the means — frequently determines the priority which emergencies — the ends — actually receive. Such attention to means, of course, also reflects organisational concerns with survival. The accumulation and expenditure of resources are concrete and identifiable standards of performance. They reflect both donor approval and organisational continuity.

When, however, an emergency situation lacks ambiguity and when donors' reactions are judged to be sympathetic and host governments are cooperative, the relief machinery of the UN agencies can work in relative harmony.[25] Yet, in the world of disasters, ambiguity is generally the norm and the social and political complexities which they entail are never far from the surface. More often than not, those UN bodies involved in emergency relief cope with ambiguity and complexity by resorting to caution, by relying on well-established and rigid organisational routines and communication channels which ultimately ensure organisational health and define 'acceptable performance'.

The expertise dilemma

Like the over-bureaucratised structures of most intergovernmental organisations, the personnel policies of IGOs offer an easy target for criticism. Appointments based on criteria of quotas and patronage, lack of expertise, a general disinclination to abide by the standards of international civil servants are all readily apparent failings of the intergovernmental world. Yet these criticisms are obvious. They ignore the complexities, the trade-offs, which UN agencies have to face and they re-emphasise the inherent insecurities which are generated by uncertain mandates and inconsistent behaviour of their intergovernmental constituents.

Even in instances where agencies, for example, UNICEF, UNHCR, are not bound by the principle that recruitment be based on equitable geographic distribution, there are subtle and not so subtle pressures placed on agency administrators by governments to place their own nationals. It is interesting to note 'the consternation of US mission officials [in Geneva]' when UNHCR filled two headquarters appointments in 1980 directly without reference to the US Office of Humanitarian Affairs. US officials, according to a US House of Representatives study, 'consider such appointments to be a form of patronage'; and the report went on to query why the US contingent on UNHCR's staff should represent only 11 per cent of the total when the United States contributes 'more than one-quarter of the UNHCR budget'.[26]

Staffing represents part of the trade-offs which IGOs have to make to earn a modicum of flexibility and, more important, survival. Yet personnel policies based upon the sensitivities of national governments ultimately result in international administrations which, in the words of an early UNESCO report, 'n'est que la projection de l'administration nationale sur un plan élevé, avec des plus vastes proportions'.[27] Paradoxically, UN agencies justify such coteries of national interest by maintaining that national links ensure an IGO direct access to national negotiating tables. However, the reality is that 'officials are often considered representatives of the world community for purposes of bureaucratic bargaining at the national level, but these same persons in the daily activities of international institutions usually represent a particular national or ideological point of view'.[28]

Not only does this reality undercut the very conception of the role of the international civil servant, but it also means that on occasion even the most urgent issues such as disaster relief operations find their way into the maelstrom of contending national approaches and prejudices. In a world in which a major disaster strikes on average three times a week, the inclination for those within the intergovernmental agencies to measure their responses in terms of what would be acceptable to their own individual governments is a complicating component in the calculation of who receives assistance when and where.

Patronage also leads to inappropriately trained officials assuming responsibilities for which they are not prepared. While the level of understanding about the approaches to disasters and disaster relief has gained in sophistication over the past decade, the level of needed expertise within the agencies to deal with disasters has not made a commensurate adjustment. In part this is due to the very conservative approaches which the agencies take to their own involvements in relief. In part it is due to their preoccupations with donor requests which only too often drown the potential expert in a sea of donor-oriented paperwork. In part it reflects the very real problem that agency personnel policies and the garnering of experts do not often coincide.

Despite these hazards, more and more specialists in disaster management are being introduced into various UN agencies. They are brought in either on permanent or temporary bases. Yet, on whatever bases they serve, the expert must contend with certain inescapable realities. In theory, the expert's responsibilities should be focused upon the plight of the disaster victim. The reality, however, is that he or she must constantly deal with two more pervasive pressures. Governments of the afflicted impose a variety of constraints upon the expert. A government might be concerned that external assistance will inflate the living standards of the afflicted in relation to the non-afflicted. It might view a full-blown relief effort as undermining the government's own authority.

These sorts of hazards are compounded by the demands placed upon the expert by his or her own agency. Field representatives of agencies must constantly balance the wishes of the governments to whom they are accredited with the wishes of their agency headquarters. These tensions are passed on to the expert in a variety of ways, and tend to distort the effectiveness of the expert.

Field representatives may inculcate the expert with the need for the latter to approach his or her task in a way that would not be embarrassing to the government. This tends to ensnare the expert in a way of thinking that reflects less the requirements of the disaster victim and more the requirements of the agency and the host government. Less subtly, the field representative may use his authority over relief allocations to control the expert. He may withdraw the resources available to the expert or may force the expert to comply with management procedures which delay or frustrate the expert's task.

Such professional insecurities and unknowns for the disaster management expert exist because the agency with which he or she works abounds with these very same unknowns and insecurities, only on a larger scale. They effect not only the competence of the expert, but also the very relations which the agencies have with each other.

Inter-agency relations

Uncertain mandates, the inconsistency with which agencies are used by government constituents, and the hazards placed in the way of experts all spark the mechanisms of agency self-protection. Some call it inter-agency rivalry.

To be seen . . .

The more publicity a disaster receives, the greater is the need for an agency to be seen to be involved. It would be wrong to conclude that intergovernmental organisations are unconcerned about the distress of disaster victims; but, on the other hand, it would be right to conclude that organisational efforts on behalf of victims are undertaken with an eye to those organisations' support bases.

What governments, donors or recipients, think about the efforts of intergovernmental bodies becomes a criterion in determining what organisations are inclined to do. Where governments are inclined to provide agencies with considerable financial support, the agencies see this as a cue to concentrate their own efforts. Where governments are not so inclined, the agencies' sense of priorities are commensurately affected. Not only does one have to be where the action is, one also has to be seen by supporters to be where the action is.

Thus territorial claims in the world of relief become a major organisational preoccupation. The right to demonstrate one's authority and to justify one's organisational role represent a high stake in the game. The game, however, becomes a bit more difficult when that right is unclear, when ambiguity blurs the boundaries of which agency should be doing what and where.

Where ambiguity reigns. . .

The greater the overlap in mandated authority, the less clear-cut the roles of the relevant agencies, and the greater is the propensity to fight for stakes. The more complex the disasters, the more ambiguity reigns.

In a situation in which victims of natural disasters also become victims of man-made disasters, there is all too often a breakdown in the regulated responsibilities of the agencies. At what stage can UNHCR intervene, and if UNHCR does not feel that a particular situation falls within its own competence, does this leave the way open for another agency? Would the intervention of another agency set a precedent which ultimately would reduce the authority of UNHCR?

If one reflects back on the Kampuchean operation, UNHCR was initially reluctant to become involved on the Thai border because 'economic migrants' did not fall within the competence of the organisation. Technically, there was no international agency which had the competence to respond to these distressed migrants until UNICEF entered on the scene. UNICEF, normally restricted to assisting children and lactating mothers, justified its involvement by declaring that in helping all such mass distressed peoples, it was 'preventing the creation of orphans'. UNHCR clearly began to realise soon after UNICEF's intervention that, despite the former's initially conservative interpretation of its mandate, UNICEF might well be encroaching upon an area in which UNHCR should be involved. The clashes between the two in Kampuchea became legion, ultimately with UNHCR attempting 'to make a bid for the whole show'.[29]

The relations between the two were marked by significant degrees of lack of cooperation, of independent initiatives and of a general unwillingness to harmonise efforts — all at the expense of the victims of those who crossed the border in such despair.

And the power of the purse. . .

Earlier in this discussion, the often mentioned influence of the 'power of the purse' was described as having an important value for the organisation since it reflected a tangible criterion of acceptable performance. While indeed the purse plays this role, it also has an even more obvious function.

The purse is a cake to be fought over, for resources are a major factor in the security of an organisation. Where there is money on the table, agencies show little restraint in gorging what they can. Each will seek to justify a greater portion by proposing operational initiatives which in a less competitive environment would be recognised as falling into the competence of another. The smaller the cake, normally the less the competition; but if the cake is large, then the energies of the agencies are bent towards getting and justifying whatever they can grab.

In emergency operations, where funds may flow fast but time to plan is limited, the pressure to partake of the feast is particularly great. Appropriate needs and relevant and coordinated approaches give way to the sorts of independent initiatives which will consume funds, and these pressures, in turn, pit one agency against another.

A suitable place for disasters?

'Why did the Secretary General just heap one relief coordinator on top of another during the Kampuchean relief operation? Why wasn't there greater overall coordination?' John Saunders, a former UN Assistant Secretary-General who was brought out of retirement to run the UN operation from Bangkok, pondered the questions for a moment.

You know, the UN in New York and governments never think about organisation. Everything is measured in terms of political interests. Until the Kampuchean crisis began to gain a lot of publicity, nobody did anything. When the crisis broke, everybody wanted the credit. Nobody was about to put money into a common pot and certainly the Secretary General was not going to be allowed to hold the pot.[30]

Diego Cordovez, UN Under-Secretary-General for Special Political Affairs, reflected for a moment. 'You see the real problem endemic in the relationship between the agencies and the Secretariat is a sense of grievance. We [the agencies] do the hard work and you [the Secretariat] get all the credit. You don't give importance to the real problems such as Kampuchea.'

'I've never been convinced that the UN should have a disaster relief function,' said a former UN Assistant Secretary for Administration. 'The Red Cross should be there instead. The intergovernmental's role is really marginal . . . It was never really intended that the UN system should become responsible for dealing with disasters. If there was a role perhaps it was accepted grudgingly.'[31]

As presently structured, the United Nations family is by no means a suitable place for responding to the plight of disaster victims. Yet, the relative ineffectiveness of the UN system underscores a far more profound problem: that the international system as a whole is both unprepared and unwilling to meet the increased complexity and scale of disasters.

Yet as long as donor governments feel compelled to weigh their responses in terms of international and domestic interests, as long as international assistance looms as a potential threat to governments of the afflicted, and as long as the full and enduring dimensions of disasters are not recognised, the disaster relief system will continue to remain inadequate. In so saying, the UN family, too, will continue to prove only marginally effective in disaster relief.

However, the fact remains that, with all the failings of the present approach to disaster relief, the United Nations family still serves as the only consistent intergovernmental network there is to respond to disasters. One is consigned to a world of what in the introduction to this chapter was referred to as 'marginal systems'. It would be difficult to imagine that the UN would, in the foreseeable future, ever be restructured in such a way as to make it a truly effective mechanism of relief. However, one might gnaw at the periphery of some of the problems which constrain its efforts and, in so doing, marginally enhance this 'marginal system'.

Clarification of mandates: There is an obvious need to make the mandates of the agencies of the United Nations clearer. Too much overlap, too much imprecision and restrictions hamper the present roles of the agencies in the field of disaster relief.

Early warnings: If disasters were given a more ostensible platform, if they were brought to the attention of the international community sooner, governments and non-governmental organisations would be 'embarrassed' into responding with greater alacrity. The United Nations Secretariat should be made responsible for alerting the international community to the present 'state of disasters'. It should be held accountable by the international community for announcing when and where disasters of all kinds occur.

Independent experts: A permanent group of independent experts should regularly report on the work of UN agencies in the field of disaster relief.

Such reports would be intended to make known to the international community where and when, through lack of cooperation, or whatever, individual UN agencies have hampered UN attempts at relief efforts.

Non-voluntary funding: Most UN agencies depend upon non-budgeted, voluntary funds from donors for disaster relief operations. The organisational problems which this poses for the agencies should be eliminated by increasing the size of agencies' emergency funds. These funds should not be earmarked by donors. They should be left to the discretion of the agencies to apply where they deem best.

Plural capabilities: Member states should insist that the Secretary General be required to contract with the agencies where and how the latter would organise their various expertise in times of disasters. Such contracts would be a matter of record, and would serve as criteria for performance to be judged by the independent panel of experts mentioned above.

Strengthening disaster-prone governments: Ultimately, it is the government of the afflicted that must bear the burden of disaster relief. Governments' disaster relief capabilities should be significantly strengthened. Development assistance should be married with disaster prevention and preparedness programmes. Governments should have pre-disaster agreements with UN agencies about the best ways to integrate the efforts of the latter with the mechanisms of the former. These governments at the same time must be assisted in developing their own disaster relief institutions. Such institutions would include non-governmental as well as governmental institutions.

To some extent, the above suggestions would enhance the relief capabilities of the United Nations as well as the overall response to disasters. They do not and cannot address the full range of political and institutional problems which hamper the potential effectiveness of the United Nations family in disaster relief. Yet, in a world still uncommitted to an effective international relief system, the UN remains a marginally more suitable place to concentrate efforts than elsewhere. As presently structured, the UN is not particularly suitable for disaster relief but, then again, is there a viable alternative?

Notes

1. Interview with Victor Palmieri, 23 September 1983, New York City.
2. At the time of writing, the civil war continues in Kampuchea and refugees from Kampuchea still flock to the Thai border. The period, 1979–82, refers to that period when Kampuchea was in the forefront of the world's attention.
3. See William Shawcross, 1984, *The Quality of Mercy: Cambodia, Holocaust and Modern Conscience*, London, André Deutsch.
4. Interview with Sir Robert Jackson, London, 5 January 1981.
5. Interview with Erik Jensen, London, 27 June 1985.
6. General Assembly Resolution 2816 (XXVI).
7. Interview with Sir Robert Jackson, New York City, 26 September 1983.
8. An important example of such UNDRO inter-agency agreements is that announced by Bradford Morse, Administrator of the United Nations Development Programme, on 12 October 1983.

9. See UN Report on Special Economic, Humanitarian and Disaster Relief Assistance (E/1981/16–9 March 1981) prepared by George F. Davidson.
10. For example, Maurice Williams, formerly Deputy Administrator, United States Agency for International Development, and at present Director, World Food Council, stated in an interview in New York, September 1983, that 'disaster relief is not political'.
11. See *Prevention Better Than Cure*, Report on Human and Environmental Disasters, published by the Swedish Red Cross, Stockholm, 1984.
12. Interview with Joseph J. Sisco, Washington, DC, 12 September 1983.
13. This was certainly the case in the wake of the international relief effort to help victims of the 1970 cyclone disaster in what was then East Pakistan.
14. For two weeks after the disaster, no Colombian or international authority could give precise figures of the numbers of people who had died.
15. Despite the large numbers of UN agencies that in one way or another are involved in disaster relief, the main agencies are: United Nations Children's Fund, the World Food Programme, United Nations Disaster Relief Organisation, United Nations Development Programme, United Nations High Commissioner for Refugees, and the World Health Organisation.
16. Interview with Diego Cordovez, Under-Secretary-General for Special Political Affairs, New York, 17 December 1981.
17. See Robert Chambers, 1985, 'Mass distress migration and rural developments in Sub-Saharan Africa', evidence given before the Foreign Affairs Committee, 30 January 1985 in House of Commons Second Report on the Famine in Africa, HMSO, 24 April.
18. Steven Tripp, former Relief Coordinator for the US Office for Foreign Disaster Assistance, recalled in an interview on 15 September 1983 attempts he made to persuade the US Representative to the UN, George Bush, to have the proposed UNDRO mandate clarified. Bush's reaction was reported to be 'I couldn't give a damn'.
19. Interview with Hunter Farnham, in charge of Refugees, Emergencies, Disaster Food Aid in Africa, US AID 15 September 1983.
20. Interview with Zia Rizvi, former Special Assistant to the UN High Commissioner for Refugees, Geneva, 23 March 1984.
21. Interview with Jacques Beaumont, Emergency Officer, UNICEF, 27 September 1983.
22. Interview with Philip Sargisson, Chief, Emergency Unit, UNHCR, Geneva, 20 March 1984.
23. Interview with Zia Rizvi, op.cit.
24. ibid.
25. The drought emergency operation in Chad in 1984, led by an UNDRO team, was a demonstration that the UN agencies can work effectively together when the right conditions exist.
26. Committee on Foreign Affairs, US House of Representatives, 1981, *Reports on Refugee Aid*, Washington, DC, USGPO, p. 33.
27. *L'Administration Nationale et les Organisations Internationales*, UNESCO II AS, Parish, 1951, p. 8.
28. T.G. Weiss, 1986, *International Bureaucracy: An Analysis of the Operations of Functional and Global International Secretariats*, Lexington, Mass., Lexington Books, p. 59.
29. Interview with John Saunders, a former Assistant Secretary-General of the United Nations, Brighton, 17 December 1985.

30. ibid.
31. Interview with George Davidson, former UN Under-Secretary-General for Administration and Management, 22 September 1983.

Recommended reading

B. Harrell-Bond, 1986, *Imposing Aid: Emergency Assistance to Refugees*, Oxford, Oxford University Press.

P. Gill, 1986, *A Year in the Death of Africa*, London, Paladin.

K. Jansson, M. Harris and A. Penrose, 1987, *The Ethiopian Famine*, London, Zed Books.

R. Kent, 1987, *Anatomy of Disaster Relief: The International Network in Action*, London, Frances Pinter.

P. Lawrence (ed.), 1986, *World Recession and the Food Crisis in Africa*, London, James Currey.

D. Williams, 1987, *The Specialized Agencies and the United Nations*, London, C. Hurst and Co.

9 International institutions and the common heritage of mankind: sea, space and polar regions*

Mark Imber

Introduction

The international institutions described and analysed in this volume have as their common basis the provision of services to citizens in circumstances where the state alone is unable to furnish these needs. The seventeenth-century creation of the sovereign state is in these respects inadequate to provide for twentieth-century needs in the fields of development, security and rights. The scope of this chapter is to examine the principles and operations of those international regimes and institutions whose tasks extend *beyond* the frontiers of states to those until recently unexplored and hence unclaimed territories of the oceans, space and the polar regions. The two competing principles which may be seen in contention are on the one hand 'creeping territoriality', that is, the extension of traditional claims of sovereignty over these newly winnable domains and resources, and on the other hand the principle of the 'common heritage', that is, to draw an analogy with the 'commons' of English law, the view that that which belongs to no one individual is owned in trust by all and, therefore, that any benefit that may be derived from its exploitation should accrue to the community at large, either by collective enterprise, or by taxation of the profit of private ventures.[1] The term 'creeping territoriality' is chosen by this author and may be seen in operation in such actions as the extension of claims to territorial waters beyond the centuries-old tradition of three miles, to new claims of twelve or even two hundred miles and the extension of sovereignty over the continental shelf, legitimised in the 1958 Geneva Conventions on the Law of the Sea, by which the United Kingdom and other North Sea states have taken exclusive sovereignty over the oil reserves of the sub-soil beyond the limit of territorial waters, without effecting the status of these waters as the high seas and with freedom for all to navigate upon them.

The term 'the common heritage of mankind' is the creation of Arvid Pardo, formerly the Foreign Minister of Malta. In a speech to the UN General Assembly in 1968 Pardo addressed the problem of the potential exploration of the deep ocean bed and, in a resolution adopted by the General Assembly on 17 December 1970 by 108 in favour, none against and fourteen abstentions, called upon the members to recognize that 'the sea-bed and ocean floor and the sub-soil thereof, beyond the limits of national jurisdiction, as well as the resources of the area are the common heritage of mankind'.[2]

The adoption of this resolution signalled the opening of a twelve-year process of negotiation among almost the entire membership of the UN and resulted in the

* This work is based on research funded by the Economic and Research Council, reference no. E00232141.

opening for signature at Montego Bay, Jamaica on 10 December 1982 of the United Nations Convention on the Law of the Sea.[3]

The twelve years of sometimes deeply contentious negotiation over the law of the sea coincided with, and affected attitudes to, the other common heritage issues, namely space exploration, the uses of inner space for both peaceful and potentially military purposes, and the future of Antarctica, in which, under the provisions of the 1959 treaty, all territorial claims were frozen and the continent secured for exclusively peaceful scientific research.

Before turning to each of these contexts in which creeping territoriality has come to confront the common heritage approach it is useful to consider the common factors which underlie these newly exploitable domains, and with them the general principles which set the parameters of choice between the different regulatory regimes available to the international community.

General principles of the common heritage

New concepts of territory

As noted the commons extend beyond the conventional definitions of the boundaries of the sovereign, territorial state. In the case of the oceans the contest between the extension of territorial waters beyond three miles and securing the wealth of the high seas for the common heritage encroaches upon what since Grotian times has been considered the *res nullius* of the high seas. In the case of Antarctica the territory involved is an uninhabited continent which, although subject to territorial claims since the turn of the century by the pioneering polar exploring nations, has never been subject to any *permanent* human colonisation or settlement in the way that ordinarily claims to territory would be established. Given that the first orbiting satellite was launched in 1959 and the achievement of the first lunar landing made in 1968, it is not surprising that this has created a situation in which human achievement has rapidly outstripped the evolution of international law governing the uses of inner and outer space.

The first requirement of any international regulation of the commons must therefore be to define the territorial and spatial limits over which any new regime is intended to have jurisdiction and, by a simple corollary, limit the extension and encroachment of creeping territoriality represented by the claims of states.

Technological innovation

Each of the commons discussed here have in some sense lain dormant, not so much awaiting discovery as the means and incentive to initiate its exploitation. The technology of offshore oil extraction and the deep-sea mining of ores and heavy-metal 'nodules' has developed very rapidly since the 1950s. Pre-war exploitation of oil reserves in the shallow and calm waters off California and the Gulf coast of Louisiana demonstrated the feasibility of offshore recovery, but only after major changes in the knowledge of oil-platform design did it become possible to undertake the drilling of reserves in the deeper and stormier conditions of the North Sea. Despite nearly a century of scientific endeavour in

Antarctica the nature and extent of the continent's mineral reserves has only very recently become understood, and the means of establishing permanent human settlements for their exploration remains untested.

Therefore, the second requirement of international regulation is that the inevitability of technological innovation is recognised. Its control should be designed in such a way which is sufficiently flexible to permit the application of new technologies possibly unheralded at the time of creating the regime. Only in this way can the problem of institutional 'lag' behind the pace of technical change be contained.

Economic motives

A feature of the three commons is that changes in prices and markets for the materials or services associated with each of them has brought some previously known resources into demand, and some existing demand into scarcity. For example, the post-1973 raising of oil prices has brought large sectors of North Sea production into profitability which would have otherwise remained unexploited. The shortage of certain rare metals, widely forecast in the early 1970s, lay behind the stimulation of interest in the recovery of these ores from the sea-bed of the high seas. The difficulties encountered by both the United States 'Spaceshuttle' and the European 'Ariane' launches have created a scarcity of launching opportunities for geostationary satellites. More controversially, the implications for closed or fragile political systems of direct broadcast television from these orbiting satellites create a political demand for their control by governments afraid of the consequences of such exposure. Management of this aspect of the commons must therefore provide for surges in demand for the resources and services in question, and for the disruptive effects that violent fluctuations in prices might have on what are, inevitably, long-term, high-value and high-risk investments. Although anathema to advocates of free-market regulation in these fields, the risks involved create a situation in which some degree of regulation may be necessary to *tempt* speculative capital investment into action.

Natural monopolies

Although, as noted above, subject to great competitive pressures, a further justification for the promotion of orderly, that is, internationally regulated, exploitation of the commons is that elements of natural monopoly attach to the likely technology employed. As with such land-based projects as pipelines and trunk roads, there are numerous advantages to be gained from the provision of large single facilities deriving the full benefit or economies of scale, so with such technologies as communications satellites, deep sea-bed mining or Antarctic mineral exploration.

To satisfy the demands of both efficient operation and fair pricing, monopolies, when adopted as the preferred form of activity, require regulation. In the context of international institutions this implies the need for a broad-based participation of the membership. The risk always exists, as will be shown in the Antarctic case, that when the most active contribution is seen to come from a small minority of the membership the claims of the passive beneficiaries come into conflict with the active risk-bearers.

Potential military uses of the commons

In the absence of a territorial regime for the commons, the ease with which states can gain access to them creates a strong potential for their use for military purposes. Historically the United Kingdom favoured the restrictive three-mile limit for territorial waters because, assured of naval supremacy, British diplomacy could be carried to within sight of the enemy's beaches. In other words, for the well-armed maritime state 'freedom of the seas' maximised the potential for the threat and use of force. In more modern times the extension of territorial waters to twelve miles and the requirement under the 1958 conventions that submarines should navigate on the surface when transiting another states' territorial waters have presented problems for the secrecy of movements of the submarine-based strategic deterrents of the superpowers. In outer space the earliest measures taken to secure an international regime for outer space rested on the anxieties of the 1960s that orbiting weapons systems or lunar colonisation would give one side the decisive advantage in the acquisition of first-strike nuclear technologies. Although more difficult to conceive of the military uses of Antarctica, the existence of so many competing territorial claims in the area and its immediately adjacent territories such as the Falklands and South Georgia present the opportunity for disputes between the claimants unless the territorial claims of the many parties can be permanently resolved.

In the earliest deliberations of the UN Atomic Energy Commission in 1945 an interesting, parallel commitment to 'peaceful uses' was enunciated. An ambitious proposal for the international ownership of the world's nuclear materials and their 'leaseback' to member states was proposed but not adopted. However, when in 1957 the International Atomic Energy Agency was established it was charged with the responsibility of 'safeguarding' the use of certain sensitive, that is, potentially military materials. The IAEA responsibilities were later greatly expanded in the provisions of the Treaty on the Non-Proliferation of Nuclear Weapons (NPT) of 1968. Under this treaty over 120 countries have accepted the principle and practice of on-site verification of their compliance with the peaceful uses terms of the NPT. Thus although for the superpowers objections remain to the idea of on-site inspection, the great majority of the world's states have accepted it. The application of IAEA-type safeguards to the Antarctic context is straightforward. Similarly international inspection of payloads would render the secret introduction of military hardware into space more difficult. The application of this idea to the emplacement of weapons on the sea-bed is logistically more daunting.[4]

The ecological dimension

The ecology of the commons is largely unknown. The partial knowledge that we have concerning the condition of the shallow inshore seas provides ample evidence of over-zealous exploitation during the last century; palaeogic fish species, whales, white fish stocks and the contamination of especially vulnerable shellfish species, all attest to an unconcerned assault on the wealth of the seas by one predatory land mammal, namely man. The consequences for those dwindling inshore stocks, as heavy-metal dumping, radioactive waste discharge and overfishing continue, are unknown. In approaching the ecology of the deep oceans, good grounds exist to doubt the wisdom of an unregulated assault on its wealth. The parallel lessons for atmospheric nuclear testing were partly responsible for the negotiating of the Partial Test Ban Treaty in 1963. Antarctica has thus far needed no protector, but the proved existence of substantial mineral reserves under the ice-caps and protein-rich 'krill' stocks in the South Atlantic waters adjacent to the continent raises the spectre of environmental damage in very sensitive locations.

The requirement is therefore clear that any regime for the commons must first calculate and then charge to the developer the full social and environmental cost of any activity, and furthermore enact standards and monitor and punish violations of any absolute prohibitions on some activities. When calculating the acceptable limits of exploitation, be it for background radiation from nuclear waste or 'replacement rates' of fish stocks, experience would suggest the need to err at all opportunities on the side of caution, on the side of fish!

Summary

The cumulative impact of the considerations discussed above is to establish the principle that the commons cannot be considered simply as unexplored and unclaimed territories suitable for expropriation and exploitation on a first-come-first-served basis as applied to the world's land surface. The analogy with 'common grazing rights' extends beyond the simple legal matter of title to the territories concerned. There is the notion of trusteeship whereby the bounty of the commons is regarded in some sense as being the property of future generations as well as the one living now, and that its wealth, great but not inexhaustible, must be carefully husbanded. Those who seek to take wealth from the commons are thus welcome to pursue legitimate peaceful activities with due regard to environmental constraints and respect for the regulatory principles outlined above. More problematic is the issue of those who, due to poverty, or in the case of the oceans, those who are landlocked, cannot participate directly in any economic activities in the commons. (No amount of common land was of any use to those peasants who did not own a pig to let loose upon it.)

If the common heritage means what it says, then the wealth of the oceans is as much the property of the citizens of landlocked Mongolia as it is of island states such as the UK or Indonesia. As will be demonstrated, the practical problems of extending this concept to those unable to use it featured most saliently in the law of the sea negotiations.

The seas

International customary law has long upheld the right of coastal states to extend their jurisdiction and absolute sovereign control over some part of the sea. Traditionally, these territorial waters have been restricted to an extent of three miles beyond the shoreline of the state, reflecting what is called the 'cannon-shot' rule, the principle that no state should claim jurisdiction over what, in practice, it cannot control. Within this customary tradition the only sort of interference in the rights of any vessel to use the high seas without impediment has centred on the right of all naval vessels to act in suppression of piracy and, more latterly, slavery. In other words, custom has placed no constraint on the conduct of legitimate trade, fishing or transit beyond the territorial sea. Indeed the customary right of 'innocent passage' permits peaceful, lawful transit of a country's territorial waters without interference.

The twentieth century, however, has witnessed several new developments in military practice, fishing, oil exploration and mining technologies which have strained the simplicity of a simple division between that part of the sea reserved exclusively for the sovereignty of the state and that part, literally, free for all. The First World War witnessed the extension of 'stop and search' on the high seas by the allied navies seeking to maintain the blockade of Germany, whilst the Germans themselves extended their submarine warfare against the allies to the point of unrestricted submarine warfare against even neutral shipping suspected of trading with the allies. The Lusitania was the most famous victim of this policy. In furtherance of the blockade the allies resorted to widespread mining of international waters in the North Sea and English Channel, effectively denying these waters to the passage of genuinely neutral shipping transiting them. New technologies in the fishing industry such as sonar detection, purse-seine netting and the formation of floating 'factory ships' have led to a doubling of the world's fishing catch over the period 1950–69 to 67 millions tonnes.[5] The impact on certain species such as the herring has been to reduce their stocks below replaceable levels. The discovery, first of natural gas off the coast of eastern England, and then of commercially recoverable deposits of oil off the north-eastern coast of Scotland and the east coast of Norway, has created a situation in the North Sea whereby in the oil-glutted summer of 1986 the United Kingdom was ranked as the world's fourth largest oil-exporter, although ironically dependent upon maintaining a high-price regime to sustain profitability in the deep, stormy and thus expensive conditions of the North Sea.

These new uses of the comparatively shallow, marginal seas has created a direct conflict between the desire of states to extend their jurisdiction, unilaterally, over larger expanses of water, and the older customary constraint of the three-mile limit. Although some states adopted a partial solution through claiming a twelve-mile limit, and in the extreme case of Chile, 200 miles, the limitation of this apparent answer lies in the fact that it is neither sovereignty nor the water surface that is principally involved.

In the case of pressures on fish stocks the most productive grounds are frequently located well beyond any reasonable extension of territorial waters, whilst fishing from these waters does not necessarily imply any need to exercise *sovereignty* over all its aspects. Similarly, in establishing a claim to the continental shelf, as unilaterally proclaimed by US President Truman in 1945, it is the *sub-soil* not the surface or body of water that was claimed for national jurisdiction.[6]

Out of consideration for this piecemeal assault on the customary regime, the United Nations convened its First Conference on the Law of the Sea (UNCLOS I) in Geneva in 1958. This conference and UNCLOS II of 1960 addressed a number of issues that were codified into four Conventions. These established a formal regime for:

(i)   The Territorial Sea and Contiguous Zone;
(ii)   The High Seas;
(iii) Fisheries and the Conservation of Living Resources;
(iv)   The Continental Shelf.

In part the Conventions codified existing custom, in part they established new concepts, most obviously in relation to the continental shelf. They were, however, curiously *imprecise* in some very sensitive matters, most obviously in refraining from setting any outer limit for the territorial sea, or continental shelf.[7] The major positive achievements of the Territorial Sea and Contiguous Zone Convention lay in its formal definition of sovereignty and innocent passage (Article 14), and in the formulation of the straight baselines method of defining the line from which the territorial sea claim could be projected. States with deeply indented or island-fringed coast were permitted to draw straight lines following the *trend* of the coastline within certain closely defined circumstances (Article 4). The contiguous zone was defined as an area beyond territorial waters in which a state may nonetheless exercise certain controls for the sake of customs, fiscal, immigration or sanitary regulation (Article 24). Although the Convention made no attempt to fix a limit for the breadth of the territorial sea (in other words parties to it were still free to claim variously three, twelve or more miles), the contiguous zone was expressly limited to a maximum of twelve miles from the baselines from which the territorial sea is measured. Thus a state claiming a twelve-mile territorial limit would not be able to claim a contiguous zone beyond that.

The High Seas Convention established four freedoms, namely those of navigation, fishing, the laying of pipelines and cables, and the right of overflight by aircraft (Article 2). Significantly the Convention also established the right of land-locked states to maintain and operate merchant and fishing fleets, and to enjoy transit rights over the neighbouring territory to implement this right (Article 3). In establishing the provisions for the prevention of pollution from ships or pipelines, the Convention refers to pollution resulting from the exploration and exploitation of the sea-bed. This, evidently within the freedom of the seas approach, clearly established, as late as 1960, the right of individual states to pursue this activity on the sea-bed and its sub-soil. As will be shown, not until 1970 did the first suggestion of the common heritage, or *res publicae* suggest an alternative to the free for all or *res nullius* of long tradition.

The third Convention concerning fishing rights defined conservation of fish stocks in terms of the 'Optimum sustainable yield'. The Convention set out a procedure whereby coastal states might take unilateral measures for the proclamation of the conservation regime. Unilateral measures can only be taken if after a six-month period of negotiation no agreement has been established with the affected parties. Conservation measures adopted under the convention cannot discriminate against foreigners, in other words, the coastal state proclaiming the ban or limit is bound by its terms as well. In the event of disputes, the conventional provides for a five-member arbitration procedure involving the FAO and ICJ (Articles 8 and 9). Despite establishing important details of conduct the Convention declined to establish the actual extent of any exclusive fishery zone for coastal states. This was therefore of little help in resolving disputes such as the so-called 'cod war' between Iceland and the United Kingdom in 1971 which centred on Iceland's claims to a fifty-mile exclusive fisheries zone.

The fourth Convention to be negotiated by UNCLOS I and II concerned claims to the continental shelf. The most striking feature of this Convention is that it enshrined the principle of creeping territoriality with regard to the oil and mineral wealth of the continental shelf. Rather than defining the shelf in terms of its established geology the shelf was defined quite arbitrarily as:

the seabed and subsoil of the submarine areas adjacent to the coast but outside the area of the territorial sea, to a depth of 200 metres or *beyond the limit to where the depth of the superadjacent waters admits of the exploitation of the natural resources of the said areas* [Article 1; emphases added]

The only limit to the extent of claims is the limit of what is technically feasible or, as in the case of the North Sea, where claims by states on the opposite shores of closed waters or concave coastlines require a median line to distinguish their claims.

The Convention was, however, explicit in stating that the right to exploit the sea-bed and sub-soil of the shelf carried with it no rights over the surface water, or the rights to fish within the *body* of that water. The only exception to this was the right to proclaim a 500-metre safety zone around each rig or production plat-form. The method chosen for determining the boundaries of claims by opposite or adjacent states was, essentially, the median principle for the former and the projection of a line perpendicular to the trend-line of the coast for the latter. This system is prejudicial to 'shelf-locked' states with concave coastlines such as West Germany. In this case an agreement between the Federal Republic, Denmark and Norway accommodated the German desire for a larger 'slice'.

The four Geneva Conventions represented a mixture of codification of custom and innovation. In many significant respects the Conventions evaded crucial difficulties. A noted commentator observed

in order to effect the compromises necessary to reach agreement on a convention which would be sufficiently widely accepted to be effective, the states concerned either left many definitions open-ended or used vague and ambiguous terminology.

Birnie continues by observing that for the newly independent countries,

many of the new states joining the international community after 1958 were poor and developing, including a large number of landlocked states. Most of these did not find the regime of loosely regulated freedom laid down in the Geneva conventions, especially the freedoms of navigation and fishing met their interests as technologically deprived states. Nor did they approve of the extensive and unlimited rights over continental shelves conceded to coastal states.[8]

Not only were many less developed countries unhappy with aspects of the Geneva regime; the ambiguities within it left many developed countries in an uncertain position. The creeping territoriality permitted by the regime confronted the great maritime nations with the possibility of numerous international straits becoming entirely subject to twelve-mile territorial claims, notable among these being Malacca, Hormuz, Bab-el-mendeb, Sunda and Bali-Lombok. Although innocent passage would, of course, still be permitted, a number of oil-pollution accidents in the 1970s raised the legitimate question as to how 'innocent' is the passage of a quarter-million-tonne tanker close inshore with possibly a less than fully serviceable radar or a less than fully sober captain? The permissive terms of the continental shelf Convention were to prove of little assistance in reconciling competing claims by Greece and Turkey to parts of the Aegean, UK-Irish claims to Rockall Bank, the numerous claimants to the Spratleys, and were to feature in Argentine claims to the Falklands and South Georgia in 1982.

It was therefore to a receptive audience that Malta's Foreign Minister, Arvid Pardo, made his 'common heritage' speech in the United Nations in 1967, which led to the creation of the Committee of Peaceful Uses of the Sea-Bed and Ocean Floor beyond Limits of National Jurisdiction. The three-year deliberations of the Committee led, in 1970, to the adoption by the UN General Assembly of Resolution 2749 (XXV) which enshrined the principles that were to form the basis for deliberation in the UNCLOS III negotiations. The resolution was adopted by 108 votes in favour, none against, with fourteen abstentions. Central to the resolution was the affirmation that 'the existing legal regime for the high seas does not provide substantive rules for regulating the exploration of the . . . area and the exploitation of its resources'. The resolution continued by declaring 'The sea-bed and ocean floor, and the subsoil thereof, beyond the limits of national jurisdiction as well as the resources of the area are the common heritage of mankind' (Paragraph 1). Other clauses affirmed the reservation of the area concerned for 'exclusively peaceful purposes', and that its resources be used 'for the benefit of mankind as a whole' (Preamble).[9]

For the implementation of this pledge the resolution also provided for the creation of the *appropriate international machinery*. . . as soon as possible'. In other words, the resolution called for the creation of a new international institution with jurisdiction over the resources of the area concerned. The task of the organisation is described as the

. . .orderly and safe development and rational management of the area and its resources and for expanding opportunities in the use thereof, and ensure the *equitable sharing by States* in the benefits derived therefrom, taking into *particular consideration* the interests and needs of the *developing countries whether landlocked or coastal* [Paragraph 9; emphases added].

The principles outlined in this part of the resolution concerned the implicit right of some future international organisation to supervise the terms upon which the potential wealth of the sea-bed would be realised *and distributed* among the states of the world. In view of the fact that the majority of the world's states were without the slightest chance of acquiring that wealth by their own endeavours, the redistributive implications of the regime came to dominate negotiation within the UNCLOS III. Later this was to feature prominently in the declared reasons for some Western states to decline to sign the 1982 UN Convention which embodied these principles, and established the basis for the International Sea-Bed Authority. The Committee on Peaceful Uses of the Sea-Bed continued its deliberations for a further two years, producing a six-volume report as the basis for the UNCLOS III sessions. The first session of this conference was held at New York in 1973 and proceeded to its first deliberative session in Caracas the next year. Superficially the decade over which the deliberations of the conference was to be extended appears protracted. However, when the enormity of the task before it is considered in the context of seeking to codify three centuries of customary international law, create new concepts of property, *and* create a new international organisation for the execution of the regime, a more generous view can be taken.

UNCLOS III revealed an unusual division of the participants, more subtle and sometimes conflicting with the more conventional political alignments of East and West, or the more nebulous North and South. The participants certainly caucused in their conventional regional groups, but also formed interest groups more appropriate to the specific issues under discussion. There was, for instance, a group of Land-Locked and Geographically Disadvantaged States (LLGDS) comprising the twenty-nine land-locked states and certain others with concave, or very limited coastlines. Thus Zaïre, Iraq, Mali and Mongolia caucused in the same group with Luxemburg, Belgium and West Germany. This group, claiming over fifty members, was to have a crucial role in advancing common heritage concepts.

Since the common heritage can only apply to resources beyond the limits of national jurisdiction, the LLGDS were, in effect, in competition with the Coastal States group who sought to legitimate creeping territoriality by larger claims, both to a standardised twelve-mile limit, territorial sea and the mooted Exclusive Economic Zone (EEZ). The Coastal States group came to number over ninety members with the Latin American states taking a prominent role in the promotion of the EEZ concept. Smaller groups emerged around such specific issues as archipelagic interests, pollution control, and nuclear-weapons-testing in the South Pacific. States with substantial shipping interests such as Greece and Panama and a dominant share of the world's merchant tonnage had a particular interest in innocent passage and marine anti-dumping proposals.

A second major feature which distinguished the conduct of the UNCLOS III negotiations was the adoption of consensus decision-making and the deliberate avoidance of voting, through the conduct of the negotiations until the resolution on the adoption of the final draft convention in 1982. Although this method of proceeding undoubtedly prolonged the negotiations, it is an example of making haste slowly so as to ensure support at all stages of the process. The text that eventually emerged from the UNCLOS III process was the UN Convention of the Law of the Sea. Dissent, especially on the part of the Western powers, has focused upon the issue of mining rights on the floor of the high seas, and upon the structure and powers of the International Sea-Bed Authority.

The Convention standardises the limit of the territorial sea at twelve miles, and that of the contiguous zone at twenty-four miles. The Convention regularises the procedures for deriving the straight baselines from which these limits are calculated, a system generally favourable to island-fringed and/or deeply indented coastlines and archipelagic states (Article 7).

Although the Convention upholds the right of innocent passage in territorial waters, a new concept of transit passage is created which places more rigorous constraints on the passage of ships through those straits used for international navigation. These obligations include tighter controls on pollution, traffic separation, trans-shipment of goods and customs control (Articles 38, 39).

The traditional basis of innocent passage is also more restrictively regulated: Article 19 establishes twelve specific prohibitions, including weapons practice, collecting information to the prejudice of the security of the coastal state, trans-shipment of goods, pollution and fishing. The open-ended definition of the limit of the continental shelf contained in the Geneva Convention No. 4 was part of the ambiguous and permissive package bequeathed to UNCLOS III. The Convention sets a complex formula for the calculation of the outer limit of the shelf on geological criteria of slope and thickness of sedimentary rocks. However, a definitive limit is created beyond which no claims can be entertained, namely 350 miles from the baselines, or 100 miles beyond the 2,500-metre isobath or undersea contour (Article 76). In return for this extended definition of the continental shelf the coastal states are required to share some part of the value of resources recovered from that part of the shelf beyond the 200-mile limit. Five years after the commencement of exploitation the coastal state is required to pay a 1 per cent levy to the ISA. This rises annually by 1 per cent to a figure of 7 per cent by the twelfth year (Article 82).

It is in the regime for the EEZ that an element of compromise emerges between the territorialist and common-heritage claims. Superficially the EEZ can be represented as another triumph for the coastal states, further whittling away at the expanse of the high seas. It is certainly true that the coastal states are granted full sovereignty over the resources of this area (Article 55). However, the Convention requires that the coastal states set fishing limits in terms of a maximum allowable catch and give other states access to the surplus over and above that amount (Article 70). This right to participate in the surplus fishing capacity of the EEZ extends to the land-locked and geographically disadvantaged states in accordance with principles expressed elsewhere in the Convention. The constraints on this right of access can be limited for reasons of conservation, and in the case of 'overwhelming dependence' on the part of the coastal state concerned (Article 71). The aspects of the Convention's provisions that have proved the most controversial concern the rights of the ISA in respect of deep sea-bed mining. This is the stated reason for the continuing US policy of non-signature.

The argument is hypothetical to the extent that, as the Convention is as yet unratified, the provisions for the creation of the ISA have not yet been activated. The powers that are described in the Convention are therefore unused. In its projected structure the ISA will resemble the conventional form of a specialised agency. Provision exists for the creation of an Assembly of all the members, a

Council of thirty-six members, some selected on grounds of competence and interest in the maritime field and the remainder reflecting the principle of equitable geographical representation (Article 161). In addition there will be a Secretariat with permanent headquarters at Kingston, Jamaica, and an International Tribunal for the law of the sea at Hamburg. The most controversial aspect, however, concerns the creation of the Enterprise, established as an organ of the ISA (Article 186).

Under the terms of the Convention the Enterprise is to be the sole or joint developer of sea-bed mining activities (Article 153). Production quotas for nickel are set, and a guaranteed minimum production of 38,000 tonnes assured for the Enterprise (Article 151). It was objections to this system of exploitation and regulation, combined with provisions for the mandatory transfer of technology, that is technical expertise, to the Enterprise which precipitated the US decision to withhold signature of the Convention. In an attempt to secure US collaboration the concept of 'pioneer rights', which the Americans colloquially termed 'grandfather rights', was pursued in the period 1981–2. Attached to the Convention in the form of a Resolution[10] adopted by the Conference is a formula designed to protect the pioneer investors and so secure US and British compliance. The resolution extended preferential rights to the four pioneer countries which had signed the Convention (France, Japan, India and the USSR), these being defined as countries which had to this time expended $30 million in exploration of the area. In addition, the resolution extended to the non-signatories the offer that four entities (corporations or state trading companies) of the non-signatories (United States, United Kingdom), could also share in these preferential rights on condition that those states sign the convention before January 1983. Neither the United States nor the United Kingdom took up this offer. The principle of the common heritage of mankind and its translation into a *practical* commercial regime for the redistribution of revenues derived from the exploitation of the deep sea-bed would therefore appear to have become stalled. Not only stalled on the question of the non-compliance of the most significant commercial actor in the field whose competence may be exaggerated, but perhaps more fundamentally stalled by the recession in primary product prices which has indefinitely postponed any practical interest in offshore recovery of heavy-metal minerals.

Despite the enthusiastic endorsement of the Convention as evidenced by the 117 states who signed on the day the treaty was formally opened for signature, a disturbing and disappointingly small number of those signatories have in fact ratified the Convention. By 1986 only fourteen states had done so and a minimum of sixty were required for it to enter into force.

Ironically, therefore, the UNCLOS III process and the Convention it has produced *may* come to be interpreted as having done more to legitimise creeping territoriality over those aspects of maritime affairs within the practicable range of exploitation by coastal states than to secure the common heritage for the benefit of all mankind.

Antarctica

In recent years some countries have asserted the claim that Antarctica should be considered a territory to which the common-heritage principle be applied. This is based upon the argument that although the present territorial regime in the continent is unorthodox, to the extent that the several claims to the territory are effectively frozen under the terms of the Antarctic Treaty of 1959, the system established by the treaty is, however, exclusive and prejudicial to the interests of the developing countries.

Antarctica is governed by the terms of the 1959 Antarctic Treaty, to which thirty-two countries are party, and under which sixteen states, the 'consulting parties' make policy by consensus in a biennial conference. These sixteen comprise the original twelve parties to the International Geophysical Year with the recent addition of four others.[11] The distinction between the consulting parties and the others is based upon their record of scientific exploration of the continent established during the period until 1969 in the case of the twelve, and since then for the other four. Under the treaty all territorial claims in Antarctica, below the 60° parallel, are frozen indefinitely, and the continent is reserved exclusively for peaceful purposes. What might at first appear to be a regime of exemplary functional principles has become liable to criticism. The obscurity and remoteness of Antarctica, which clearly assisted the undisturbed development of the two-tier system of regulation has been undermined by several factors. The continent is some 14 million sq. km. in extent and has substantial reserves of mineral resources, most obviously in oil, iron, coal and copper. Its seas are a rich reserve of both fish stocks and the unique shrimp-like krill which have attracted the attention of Eastern bloc and Japanese fishing fleets.

The UNCLOS III regime requires that *some* authority take responsibility for the notional Antarctic EEZ and related issues; lastly, the Falklands War of 1982 highlighted the potential for conflict which exists in the territorial claims of two 'consulting parties' in the waters adjacent to Antarctica above the 60° line. These pressures have added to the underlying tension between the functional elite of the consulting parties and the spokesmen of the developing countries, the great majority of which have only gained their independence since the creation of the 1959 regime. For these states, decolonisation and the more congenial possibilities of a larger UN role in Antarctica have prompted calls to link the administration of the continent to the common-heritage concept.

A third organisational model does exist, however, as an alternative to both. The environmental organisation Greenpeace has advocated that Antarctica should serve as the prototype for the creation of a world park, in which *all* human economic activities would be required to take second place to the conservation of the unique and vulnerable *natural* heritage.

Under the regime of the 1959 treaty, Conventions have been concluded safeguarding the fauna of the continent, and the marine life of its waters.[12] Quite separately from the treaty but of considerable significance to Antarctica is the moratorium on hunting, agreed under the auspices of the International Whaling Convention. The coordination of scientific research between sixteen consulting parties has been largely handled by the non-governmental Scientific Committee on Antarctic Research, a part of UNESCO.

Malaysia has been in the forefront of attempts to have the status of Antarctica placed on the agenda of the UN for the purpose of seeking reforms to the treaty regime. Addressing the 1982 General Assembly, the Malaysian Prime Minister said:

Like the seas and seabeds these uninhabited lands belong to the international community. The countries presently claiming them must give them up so that either the United Nations administer these lands or the present occupants act as trustees for the nations of the world.[13]

In reaction to these criticisms the sixteen consulting parties have taken extensive measures since 1983 to liberalise the flow of information, access to meetings and invitations to the *non*-consulting parties to attend the biennial sessions of the consulting parties. Throughout, the sixteen have insisted that their competence, expertise and cohesion have had positive advantages for the administration of Antarctica, the implication being that the balance of interests contained within the hybrid assembly of sixteen pioneer exploring nations is of greater benefit to Antarctica than the artificial importation into the continent of the political disputes of the General Assembly. Already, South Africa's status as a consulting party has been challenged on anti-apartheid grounds.[14]

Outer space

Outer space is the largest and least developed 'domain' to which the common-heritage approach has been linked. It is subject to the regulation of the 'Treaty on the Principles Governing the Activities of States in the Exploration and Use of Outer Space, including the Moon and Other Celestial Bodies', a UN-sponsored treaty usually known simply as the Outer Space Treaty of 1967.[15]

The Treaty was the product of nearly a decade of intermittent discussion in the Committee on the Peaceful Uses of Outer Space established after the question was first raised in the General Assembly in 1958. As in the case of pressures for the reform of the law of the sea which stemmed from growing commercial and military innovations in the use of the sea, so it was that the first successful launch of an earth-orbiting satellite, the Soviet Sputnik vehicle, galvanised the international community into consideration of a regime for space. The major practical provisions of the 1967 Treaty concern arms control, the prohibition of the placing of nuclear weapons or other weapons of mass destruction into earth orbit, or their emplacement on the moon (Article IV).

The Treaty is explicit in establishing the common title to space:

Outer space, including the moon and other celestial bodies is not subject to national appropriation by claim of sovereignty, by means of use or occupation, or by any other means. [Article II]

The Treaty is also explicit about the use and exploration of the area; it shall be

Carried out for the benefit and in the interest of all countries, irrespective of their degree
of economic or scientific development, and shall be the province of all mankind.
[Article I]

Subsequently more specific conventions have been negotiated concerning the
registration of objects launched into space, liability for damage resulting from
their unscheduled return and for the rescue and return of astronauts.[16]

Of more immediate application in the lives of the public is the developing
regulatory framework for the launching and operation of communication
satellites, by which modern telephone, radio and direct-broadcast television are
sustained. This is the task of the oldest of the UN specialised agencies, the International Telecommunication Union, originally established in 1865 as the International Telegraph Union. The ITU subsidiary organ, the International
Frequency Registration Board has, since 1906, operated a regime for the allocation of radio frequencies between its members so as to minimise the problems
of interference and standardise procedure for emergency services and distress
frequencies.

The advent of the geostationary orbiting satellite, in equatorial orbit at an
'altitude' of approximately 36,000 km. offers greatly increased opportunities for
broadcasting and radio-telephone communication. The regulatory problem, and
opportunity, stems from the fact that as one such satellite can receive and
transmit signals from an area of 42 per cent of the world's surface only a very
limited number of these satellites are needed. It is in other words a natural, new
monopoly. Some system of consortium ownership, leasing and/or renting of
satellite time would therefore appear a highly attractive alternative to *national*
ownership of satellites for the great majority of the world's states. This is
especially so for large developing countries for which satellite transmissions are
a more economic form of data transfer than land lines and their associated
infrastructure.

Conclusion

Each of the domains considered in this chapter has been made subject to a
sophisticated regime of *potential* regulation. For the most part human
knowledge, exploration and use of these commons remains in its infancy except
for the intensive exploitation of shallow inshore waters. Each regime has
fulfilled the first requirement identified in the introduction, namely defining the
scope and extent of these territories and distinguishing that part of them to which
conventional territorial rules apply, and that part to which more innovative rules
may be applied. The Convention on the Law of the Sea makes extensive and
detailed plans for the control of technological innovation, issues which the
Antarctic Treaty parties and the IFR are now addressing. The principal
constraint on activating the various provisions for economic exploitation appears
to be the ready availability of cheap and reliable onshore reserves of each of the

major minerals that may prove to be recoverable from the sea-bed or Antarctica.

Each regime reserves the commons for exclusively peaceful uses with the sole exception that the submarine-based nuclear deterrent of some states relies upon freedom of navigation in the waters of the high seas for their undetected operations. As in all measures of arms control, verification remains an obstacle to confidence building. In this regard an IAEA-type inspectorate for upholding the 1971 Sea-Bed Treaty, and payload inspection of spacelaunches would offer a radical challenge to self-policing by sovereign states.

The ecology of the commons remains in need of the closest possible study and protection. It would appear obvious that a prominent voice and role be granted to those non-governmental organisations such as 'Greenpeace' whose actions have done so much to dramatise the potential ecological tragedy of the commons.

However, the underlying question remains as to how to reconcile the interests of the technically proficient minority in deep-sea exploration, Antarctic research and space exploration with the claims of the passive majority to their share of what is nominally proclaimed as the common heritage. The compromises offered on the matter of 'pioneer rights' would appear reasonable, and it implies that some recognition of the 'consulting parties' status in Antarctica is valid. The economics of manned space flight will ensure for the foreseeable future that this domain remains, practically, only within the grasp of the few.

David Mitrany suggested in 1943 that the problem lay in seeking

an arrangement which would show a measurable and acceptable relation between authority and responsibility, which would exclude no participant arbitrarily from a share in authority, while bringing that share into relation not to sheer power but to the weight of responsibility carried by the several members.[17]

In other words, and perhaps unfashionably, efficient administration cannot always be reconciled with universal participation in decision-making. The successful administration of the commons requires that imaginative answers be found to Mitrany's problem.

Notes

1. For a fuller discussion of the legal implications and terms, see C. Pinto, 1980, 'Toward a regime governing international public property', in A.J. Dolman (ed.), *Global Planning and Resource Management*, Oxford, Pergamon. In particular Pinto discusses the distinction between *res nullius* and *res publicae*.
2. UN General Assembly Resolution 2749 (XXV). For the text and discussion of this resolution, see UN *Yearbook 1970*.
3. *United Nations Convention on the Law of the Sea*, UN New York 1983. The full text of the treaty including the Final Act of the Conference and related appendices appears in this volume. See R.P. Barston, 1983, 'The Law of the Sea', *Journal of World Law*, vol. 17, no. 3.
4. For fuller discussion of the IAEA system, see M.F. Imber, 1983, 'The special case of I.A.E.A. special inspections' *Arms Control*, vol. 3, no. 3.

5. R.P. Barston and P. W. Birnie, 1980, *The Maritime Dimension*, London, Allen and Unwin, p. 1.
6. Presidential Proclamation No. 2667, 28 September 1945. Birnie discusses the implications of the Proclamation in Barston and Birnie, op.cit., pp. 10–13.
7. The texts of all four Conventions are reproduced in D. Bowett, 1967, *Law of the Sea*, Manchester, Manchester University Press.
8. R.P. Barston and P.W. Birnie, op.cit., p. 24.
9. With regard to the commitment to reserve the sea-bed for peaceful purposes, an important achievement was the completion in 1970 of the Treaty on the Prohibition of the Emplacement of Nuclear Weapons and other Weapons of Mass Destruction on the Sea-Bed and the Ocean Floor and the Subsoil Thereof, usually abbreviated to The Sea-Bed Treaty.
10. Resolution II, 'Governing Preparatory Investment in Pioneer Activities relating to Polymetallic Nodules', *supra*, Note 3, pp. 177–82.
11. The twelve original signatories are Argentina, Australia, Belgium, Chile, France, Japan, New Zealand, Norway, South Africa, the USSR, the United Kingdom and the United States. The four other consulting parties are Poland, Federal Republic Germany, Brazil and India. The other sixteen signatories with the status of 'non-consulting parties' are Bulgaria, Cuba, China, Czechoslovakia, Denmark, Finland, German Democratic Republic, Hungary, Italy, The Netherlands, Papua-New Guinea, Peru, Romania, Spain, Sweden and Uruguay.
12. The Conventions adopted are the 1972 Convention for the Conservation of Antarctic Seals and the 1980 Convention for the Conservation of Antarctic Marine Living Resources.
13. Records of the 37th General Assembly, 29 September 1982; UN Document A/37/PV.10 (1982), pp. 17–18.
14. At the 38th Session of the UN General Assembly both the delegates of Antigua and Barbuda and Sierra Leone called for the expulsion of South Africa from the treaty.
15. The full text of the Treaty and four subsequent Conventions and Agreements is reproduced in *The United Nations Treaties on Outer Space*, New York, 1984.
16. These are the Agreement on the Rescue of Astronauts, the Return of the Astronaunts and the Return of Objects Launched into Outer Space, the Convention on International Liability for Damage Caused by Space Objects, the Convention on Registration of Objects Launched into Space, and the Agreement Governing the Activities of States on the Moon and Other Celestial Bodies.
17. D. Mitrany, 1966, *A Working Peace System*, Chicago, Quadrangle, p. 64.

Recommended reading

Peter Beck, 1986, *The International Politics of Antarctica*, London, Croom Helm.
J.R.V. Prescott, 1985, *The Maritime Political Boundaries of the World*, London, Methuen.
Clive Sanger, 1986, *Ordering the Oceans*, London, Zed.
SIPRI, 1982, *Outer Space, a New Dimension in the Arms Race*, Stockholm, SIPRI.
United Nations, 1983, *The Law of the Sea, Official Text of the United Nations Convention on the Law of the Sea with Annexes and Index*.

10 The International Telecommunication Union

George A. Codding, Jr

Telecommunication is essential to the health and well-being of the modern nation-state. Domestically, an efficient telecommunication system is a necessary element in education, entertainment, security, and even nation-building. Internationally, it is the lifeblood of trade, commerce and effective diplomacy. Because of the nature of the technology involved, a certain degree of international cooperative action is necessary in order for the global telecommunication system to function satisfactorily.

The International Telecommunication Union (ITU) is the primary instrument that makes this cooperative action possible. The ITU has several features that set it apart from the vast majority of international organizations, among them its large membership, its modest cost, and its federal structure. One of the most interesting aspects of the ITU, however, is its longevity. The ITU is the direct descendant of the International Telegraph Union, which was founded in Paris in 1865, making it not only one of the oldest international organizations in existence, but also one of the hardiest. The ITU has survived two major wars, a number of lesser wars, and a disastrous world-wide depression.

The purpose of this chapter is to provide the reader with an overview of this intriguing international organization, with particular emphasis on its three major tasks, setting standards that permit new technologies and uses of telecommunications to be employed in the international telecommunication system, framing procedures for the determination of legal rights of administrations in certain types of disputes over the use of the system, and providing technical assistance to developing countries to help them better enjoy the advantages of the system.[1] Each of these functions, it should be noted, caters to the interests of a different configuration of the ITU's membership. The success with which the ITU carries out these three functions may, therefore, provide some clues to the ITU's continued vitality.

This chapter will begin with a short history of the ITU and the highlights of its involvement with the constantly evolving technology of telecommunications, followed by a brief description of the major elements of the ITU's structure. The bulk of the chapter will be devoted to the three functions that we have identified as being of possible significance as regards the ITU's continuing effectiveness.

Before proceeding, a definition of telecommunication is in order. According to the ITU's own charter, the term 'telecommunication' includes 'Any transmission, emission or reception of signs, signals, writing, images and sounds or intelligence of any nature by wire, radio, optical or other electromagnetic systems'.[2] However, with the move towards digitalization and as a result of the merger with computer technology, the term 'telecommunication' has taken on an even broader meaning. The ITU is in the process of trying to find a better definition; one suggestion is to call it simply 'information transfer'.

The ITU and the evolving technology

The history of the International Telecommunication Union is almost as extensive as that of the technology itself. The electric telegraph came into practical use in 1837 when it was used to link Birmingham with London. By the early 1850s, most of the major countries of Europe had initiated domestic telegraph systems and were beginning to explore the possibility of linking their systems with those of their neighbours.[3] Since these early contacts were carried out through the normal bilateral diplomatic procedures available at the time, there soon arose a confusion of rules, regulations and rates that threatened to negate the advantages of this otherwise rapid and efficient method of communication.

It was this situation that led Napoleon III to convene a telegraph conference in Paris in 1865 to which he invited representatives of twenty European countries which either already had or were contemplating the creation of domestic telegraph systems. Out of this conference came an International Telegraph Convention and Telegraph Regulation containing the rules and regulations considered necessary by the participants to create a workable European telegraph network. The 1865 conference also produced the International Telegraph Union, the immediate predecessor to the International Telecommunication Union, when it decided that the representatives of interested telegraph administrations should meet at regular intervals to revise the Convention and Regulations as demanded by the evolving technology of the telegraph. The fledgeling union quickly took on a more universal character as more states created their own telegraph systems and connected them to the European network.

The telephone also came under the purview of the International Telegraph Union in 1885, soon after it was invented. The Telegraph Union's involvement in regulating this new method of rapid, long-distance communication did not in the beginning take on the same intensity as it had for the telegraph, however, because of a number of technical and non-technical concerns, including the fact that administrations considered the telephone to be an adjunct to the telegraph rather than a method of rapid, long-distance communication in its own right. Nevertheless, from 1885 on, it was the Telegraph Union which supplied all of the telephone rules and regulations that the member administrations agreed were necessary for their purposes.

Radio was a temporary exception. The United States had refused to become a member of the Telegraph Union on the basis that since telegraph and telephone services in the United States were provided by private enterprise rather than government, the United States could not be a party to any international agreement that would place restrictions on what those entities could do and what they could charge for their services. Radio was different because it did not respect national boundaries. In order to include the United States, in its earlier stages radio was regulated by a governmental consortium known informally as the International Radiotelegraph Union. Since in most countries the telegraph, telephone and radio services were regulated by the same governmental entities, with the exception of the United States and one or two others, the participants in the two groups were almost identical. As evidence of the redundancy involved in the situation, the radiotelegraph group utilized the facilities of the International Telegraph Union's International Bureau rather than create its own secretariat.

This illogical situation was finally ended in 1934 when the two groups merged and adopted the name International Telecommunication Union, bringing all three methods of telecommunication for the first time under one roof.[4]

The increased use of radio just prior to and during the Second World War and the need to bring the ITU into relationship with the new United Nations Organization brought about the next step in the evolution of the regulation of international telecommunications. At an ITU conference called by the United States in 1947 an attempt was made to revise the manner in which an administration obtained a right to use a radio frequency free from harmful interference by radio stations from other countries. An International Frequency Registration Board was added to the ITU's structure to assume an essential role in the process. In addition, an Administrative Council was created, and the International Bureau was transformed into a secretariat and internationalized.

Two events have occurred since 1947 which have had a profound impact on the ITU and its work — the evolution of a new developing country majority and the incorporation of satellites into the telecommunication network. As we shall see, both have made new demands on the ITU system that are still far from being satisfactorily resolved. In addition, the ITU is becoming increasingly involved in the challenging technical problems involved in the digitalization of telecommunications and the concurrent issue of finding a workable interface between telecommunications and the computer.

Structure

The ITU has three principal elements in its structure which are involved in the functions we shall be investigating: conferences, international consultative committees, and the International Frequency Registration Board.[5] There are three different types of ITU conferences: the plenipotentiary, world and regional administrative conferences. The plenipotentiary conference is the ITU's supreme organ and meets, in principle, once every five years; all members have the right to send delegates. The plenipotentiary has the power to revise the International Telecommunication Convention, the ITU's basis treaty. The Convention is primarily concerned with overall policy and the ITU's structure, but does include some of the basic rules such as the obligation to interconnect domestic telecommunication networks, a prohibition on harmful interference between radio stations, and a priority for messages concerning the safety of life.[6]

A world administrative conference has jurisdiction over telecommunication matters of a world-wide nature including the revision of all or part of the Radio

Regulations, the Telegraph Regulations or the Telephone Regulations. Regional administrative conferences deal with specific telecommunications questions of a regional nature. As a result of a decision in 1973 to transform most of the telegraph and telephone regulations into non-binding recommendations produced by the International Telegraph and Telephone Consultative Committee (CCITT), the vast majority of administrative conferences are now devoted to the regulation of communication by radio.[7]

The ITU has two consultative committees, the International Radio Consultative Committee (CCIR) and the International Telegraph and Telephone Consultative Committee (CCITT), which study technical and operating questions and issue non-binding recommendations. The consultative committees are made up of representatives of interested administrations and recognized private operating agencies and carry out their tasks by means of a plenary assembly and numerous study groups and working parties. Each committee has an elected director and a specialized secretariat.

The third organ is the International Frequency Registration Board (IFRB). It is the task of the five-member, elected Board to supervise the process by which requests for radio frequencies and satellite communication systems, including geostationary satellite orbital positions, are incorporated into the Master Frequency List, an action which vests in them certain legal rights. The Board also has the task of informing the members of the ITU on ways to utilize the radio frequency spectrum and the geostationary satellite orbit in the most economical manner. The Board is made up of five individuals, 'thoroughly qualified by technical training in the field of radio', elected by the plenipotentiary conference. The Board elects its own chairman and vice-chairman and has its own specialized secretariat.[8]

Establishing standards

Establishing standards for equipment to be used in the international telecommunications network is the oldest of the functions carried out by the ITU for its constituents and the one that the developed countries now find the most important to their needs. Because of the consistently high quality of these standards, which take the form of non-binding recommendations on the part of the CCIR and the CCITT, they are usually adopted quickly and become the norm for the world's telecommunications industries.

One of the primary reasons for the creation of the International Telegraph Union in 1865 was to adopt standards that would permit the evolution of a true European telegraph network. In addition to creating the International Telegraph Union, that conference succeeded in adopting standard operating procedures, common technical standards, a common code — the international Morse code — and began to bring about some order into the European international rate structure.[9]

The conference method of establishing telecommunication standards proved to be adequate until the 1920s when technical developments — especially for radio and telephone — become so rapid that it proved difficult to carry out all of the necessary studies during the limited time available at conferences. The solution was to create semi-autonomous working groups to meet between conferences made up of representatives of interested administrations and recognized private operating agencies. The first such group, the International Telephone Consultative Committee (CCIF), was rapidly followed by the International Telegraph Consultative Committee (CCIT) and the International Radio Consultative Committee (CCIR). The ITU's 1947 Atlantic City Telecommunication Conference brought the consultative committees into closer relationship with the ITU and, because of an increasing overlap in functions, the CCIF and CCIT were merged in 1956 into the present-day International Telegraph and Telephone Consultative Committee (CCITT).

The CCIR has as its mandate 'to study technical and operating questions relating specifically to radiocommunication . . . and issue recommendations on them'.[10] The CCITT has a similar mandate, but it also includes tariff questions. The consultative committees have as their members interested administrations and recognized private operating agencies in the field of telecommunications and function through plenary assemblies which meet every four years; study groups; and semi-permanent working groups. Questions to be studied by the CCIs can be suggested by a plenipotentiary or administrative conference, the other CCI, the IFRB, or delegates to a committee's plenary assembly. A question accepted by a plenary assembly for investigation is assigned to one of the study groups, which prepares a 'study programme' on the subject and sends this to administrations for comment. The comments are considered at a meeting of the whole group. A report is drafted, and possibly a recommendation, which are submitted to all members of the ITU and the next plenary assembly. The plenary assembly has the power to accept, reject or modify the proposed recommendation.

The range of the questions studied by a consultative committee is apparent from the following list of study groups activated by the CCITT for the period 1984–8:[11]

Study Group	Title
I	Definition, operation, and quality of service aspects of telegraph, data transmission, and telematic services (facsimile, Teletex, Videotex, etc.).
II	Operation of telephone network and ISDN (Integrated Services Digital Networking).
III	General tariff principles, including accounting.
IV	Transmission maintenance of international lines, circuits and chains of circuits; maintenance of automatic and semi-automatic networks.
V	Protection against dangers and disturbances of electromagnetic origin.
VI	Outside plant.
VII	Data communication networks.
VIII	Terminal equipment for telematic services (facsimile, Teletex, Videotex, etc.).
IX	Telegraph networks and terminal equipment.
X	Languages and methods for telecommunications applications.

XI   ISDN and telephone network switching and signalling.
XII   Transmission performance of telephone networks and terminals.
XIII   (Not activated 1984–8)
XIV   (Not activated 1984–8)
XV   Transmission systems.
XVI   (Not activated 1985–8)
XVII   Data transmission over the telephone network.
XVIII   Digital networks, including ISDN.

While in the past the CCIs have concentrated their efforts on developing standards for particular new telecommunications technologies or uses of telecommunication technologies, the integration of computers and telecommunications has forced the CCIT, at least, to think in much broader terms. Theoretically, with a move towards all digital communication and the employment of computers, there is a possibility of achieving a global Integrated Services Digital Network (ISDN) whereby a whole range of telecommunications — voice, data, picture, teletex, etc. — can be carried on the same system. The protocols necessary to achieve a universal ISDN has forced the CCITT to think and work in much broader terms than in the past. Five of the CCITT's present fifteen study groups deal in some way with ISDN.[12]

Over the years, the consultative committees have tended to be dominated by the developed countries. The 1984 plenary assembly of the CCITT, for instance, was attended by representatives of ninety-four of the 160 members of the ITU and twenty-one recognized private operating agencies. All of the missing delegations were from developing countries. The discrepancy is even more important in the study groups. In 1985 only fifty-seven of the ITU's 160 administrations participated in even one of the CCITT's fifteen study groups. The vast majority of those that did attend, especially those that attended more than a few, were from the developed countries.[13] The record is similar for the CCIR.

Frequency management

One function carried out by the ITU which is of great importance for both its developed and developing country clients is the establishment of the procedures by which a telecommunications administration obtains protection for its radio stations and satellite communications systems against harmful interference from stations and systems of other administrations. As we shall see, however, the proper method of achieving this goal has become a serious bone of contention in recent years.

This aspect of the work of the ITU has three components: the protection of specific telecommunication services, such as broadcasting, maritime mobile and satellite broadcasting; the protection of individual radio stations; and the protection of geostationary satellite communication systems.

The oldest in time is the assignment of certain portions of the usable radio-frequency spectrum to the various radio services. This is accomplished, sometimes with great difficulty, in administrative radio conferences and is enshrined in the Table of Frequency Allocations contained in the ITU's Radio Regulations. The present Table of Frequency Allocations embraces the radio-frequency spectrum from 9 kHz to 400 GHz and involves thirty-eight different radio services.[14] Since the Radio Regulations are an appendage of the ITU's International Telecommunication Convention, the Table of Frequency Allocations is binding on all of the members of the ITU. Nevertheless, as with any formal compact of this kind it is possible for parties to make reservations that will permit them to engage in deviant usage. Although the Table of Frequency Allocations has numerous such reservations, 'footnotes' in ITU terminology, it nevertheless provides a highly useful and necessary guideline for the world's telecommunication administrations.

The second is the system by which administrations obtain rights to use particular frequencies, or frequency bands, without harmful interference from radio stations in other countries. The main actor in this process is the ITU's five-man International Frequency Registration Board (IFRB).

Administrations must notify the IFRB of any frequency assignment: (1) that is capable of causing harmful interference to a radio station of another country; (2) that is to be used for international communication; or (3) for which an administration desires 'to obtain international recognition of the use of the frequency'.[15] The IFRB examines the notification for conformity with the International Telecommunication Convention and Radio Regulations to determine whether it will cause harmful interference with a station that has already been recorded by the IFRB in the Master International Frequency Register. If the findings are satisfactory, the Board enters the frequency in the Master Register and the date of registration determines the rights of that administration to protect its frequency from harmful interference from others.[16]

While the notification and registration procedure has been deemed adequate for determining rights for most terrestrial radio communications, in certain frequency bands where there has been overcrowding an alternative procedure has been adopted. This procedure, which has been given the name 'a priori rights-vesting' as opposed to the older 'first-come, first-served rights-vesting' procedure, involves first the making of an inventory of the existing and projected usage, and then the allotment of the available frequencies in the frequency band under question to each participating country according to a prearranged formula. The rights of a country to use a frequency without harmful interference under this procedure depends not on the date of registration, but rather on whether it has been allotted to that country in a formal, agreed plan.

The first use occurred in Europe in the 1920s when interference between the broadcasting stations of different countries became so acute as to make the proper reception of signals extremely difficult. With the help of the International Broadcasting Union a European broadcasting allotment plan was created based on such considerations as existing services, size of country, and population density. The ITU later become responsible for the European plan and extended the a priori approach to several other radio service bands such as the aeronautical and maritime mobile services.[17]

The most recent development involves geostationary satellite communications. When this type of communication was in its infancy, a variation of the first-come, first-served method was adopted. Administrations considering plans to initiate a geostationary satellite communication system were requested to send the IFRB the characteristics of the system, including the geostationary satellite orbit, for registration in the Master Frequency Register. By 1971, however, a concern had arisen in many administrations that there might not be enough appropriate geostationary satellite orbital positions and related radio frequencies by the time they were in a position to take advantage of satellite communication. As a result, a series of conferences was called by the ITU to investigate methods whereby all countries would be assured access to these space resources when the time came that they could use them.

Two different approaches to the problem evolved in these conferences. On one side there was the United States, at first all alone but later joined by certain other developed countries including the United Kingdom, which argued for a continuation of the first-come, first-served approach. The essence of this approach was that new technological advances and new ways of using those technologies would always make adequate space resources available for all countries that could possibly use them. Anything more rigid than the notification and registration approach, or a variation thereon, would make that unlikely if not impossible. The opposing side, which was made up of almost all of the developing countries and many of the developed ones, took the position that they were not willing to rely on the older approach. The only method that would guarantee them access to space resources was the a priori method or a variation on that method.[18]

The votes, as it turned out, were on the side of the proponents of the a priori approach. The 1977 ITU Broadcasting Satellite conference succeeded in drawing up an allotment plan for the geostationary satellite broadcasting service for Regions 1 and 3[19] in which each participating administration was allotted geostationary orbital positions in the arc between 37° West and 170° East and associated frequencies in the 12 GHz radio frequency band on the basis of various agreed criteria including the size of the population, number of languages, and the size of the country in question. The USSR received the largest share. The countries in Region 1 (the Americas) also drafted an a priori plan for their region six years later. This second international broadcasting satellite conference allotted the forty-eight geostationary orbital positions and 2,114 frequency channels at their disposal, with the United States receiving the largest single share.[20]

The desirability of the two methods of rights-vesting was debated again at the 1985 ITU World Administrative Radio Conference on the Use of the Geostationary Satellite Orbit. The 1985 conference was the first of two conferences which had been convened by the ITU to look at the other communication services using geostationary satellites to determine what should be done to guarantee in practice 'equitable access' of all administrations to space communication resources. The United States repeated its arguments that the modified notification and registration procedure adopted in 1971 was superior because it was flexible and thus would tend to make more resources available for all concerned.[21] Although the United States had picked up support by 1985, in the end the conference agreed to recommend to the second session to be held in 1988 that it draft an a priori allotment plan for those portions of the radio-frequency spectrum used by the fixed geostationary satellite service where there was evidence of a relatively high utilization intensity. In other areas, the second conference would devise improved planning procedures.[22]

The results of the 1985 Space conference, combined with those of the 1977 and 1983 Space conferences, seem without doubt to have validated the a priori planning method as a legitimate ITU approach to frequency management in satellite communications in cases where there is overcrowding or a fear of over-crowding, just as it had in the past for terrestrial radio communication.

Development assistance

The third and newest major function provided by the ITU for its constituents is development assistance. While agreement on standards for new technology is of primary importance to the developed countries, and frequency management to both the developed and the developing countries, development assistance is of primary importance to the developing country members of the ITU. Despite the fact that the developing countries make up the vast majority of the ITU's membership, however, the ITU thus far has been less successful in providing development assistance than it has in developing satisfactory telecommunications standards or providing for mutually agreeable procedures for frequency management.

Prior to the establishment of the United Nations technical assistance programme, the major thrust of the ITU was the maintenance of a rapid and efficient international telecommunication network for those countries that could afford to participate in it. Although the ITU performed many services for its members that would help upgrade their telecommunication services, including the providing of information, the ITU was not overly concerned with the state of the domestic communication networks of its members as long as their major cities were connected to the system.

Except for a brief period of initial hesitation, the ITU has always been a participant in the United Nations technical assistance programme. As a participant, it carries out studies, selects experts to help administrations of developing countries improve their facilities, screens applications for study abroad, and gives advice on equipment for field projects that have been requested by a developing country and approved by the United Nations Development Programme (UNDP). It receives compensation for these services from the UNDP, as do other participating international organizations. Because of the nature of the UNDP, the ITU itself has little to say as regards how the UN funds are used or the amount that is allotted to telecommunications. As to funding, the ITU has always been the junior partner in the UNDP.[23]

As the developing countries have become more and more prominent in ITU activities, they have attempted to involve the ITU organs more directly in programmes that will help them to improve their telecommunications services. The directions taken indicate three different but interrelated purposes: (1) to make the provision of technical assistance a major function of the ITU as reflected in its Convention; (2) to increase the actual involvement of the organs of the ITU in technical assistance as part of their regular duties; and (3) to create an independent ITU technical assistance fund from ITU sources.

The first of these objectives has been the easiest to achieve. As far back as the ITU Plenipotentiary of 1959, the ITU Convention was amended by adding to the ITU's list of specific functions the duty to

foster the creation, development, and improvement of telecommunications equipment and networks in new or developing countries by every means at its disposal, especially participation in the appropriate programs of the United Nations.[24]

In 1982 the developing country majority made development assistance the major function of the ITU when the following was adopted as the first overall function of the ITU:

to maintain and extend international cooperation between all members of the Union for the improvement and rational use of telecommunications of all kinds, as well as to promote and to offer technical assistance to developing countries in the field of telecommunications.[25]

The developing countries have had some success in their second objective, achieving a greater involvement of the organs of the ITU in the provision of technical assistance. In 1959 the developing countries were able to require the Consultative Committees to

pay due attention to the study of questions and to the formulation of recommendations directly connected with the establishment, development, and improvement of telecommunication in new or developing countries in both regional and international fields.[26]

This led the consultative committees to create a number of Special Autonomous Groups (GAS) which have produced publications aimed directly at the needs of the developing countries.

In the 1965 plenipotentiary, by which time they were in the majority, the developing countries were highly critical of both the ITU's and the UNDP's record in development assistance, and they offered a number of wide-ranging proposals to change the situation. The two major ones were to create a new ITU technical assistance organ along the lines of the consultative committees, with its own elected director, and a number of regional ITU offices in less developed areas of the world to assist local telecommunication administrations with their problems.[27] While the developing countries were unable to achieve either of these specific goals, they were successful in enacting a number of resolutions on that subject. One directed all of the ITU permanent organs to increase the amount of technical information of special interest to the developing countries in their publications. Another authorized the Secretary-General to investigate methods of training personnel from the developing countries and to recruit four telecommunication engineers for the secretariat to help the developing countries with 'difficult, specific national problems in telecommunication development'. . . [28]

The pressure of the developing countries for help was strong at the 1973 plenipotentiary in Malaga-Torremolinos. Almost two dozen proposals were submitted which dealt in one fashion or another with development assistance. Some were simply additions to, or updates of, decisions made in 1965, but a number were new. The 1973 plenipotentiary added a provision to the section of the Convention requiring the Administrative Council to

promote international cooperation for the provision of technical cooperation to the developing countries by every means at its disposal, especially through the participation of the Union in the appropriate programme of the United Nations, in accordance with the purposes of the Union, one of which is to promote by all possible means the development of telecommunications.[29]

In addition, the 1973 plenipotentiary passed ten resolutions and one opinion, all of which are classified as relating to technical cooperation.[30]

Both the regional offices proposal and the proposal to create a new International Consultative Committee for Technical Cooperation were raised again in 1973. The latter received so little support that it was not brought to a vote and the regional offices proposal was defeated in a secret ballot in a plenary meeting by forty-five in favour, sixty-eight opposed, and four abstentions.[31]

The developing country requests to involve the ITU organs in technical assistance matters reached a high point at the 1982 Nairobi plenipotentiary. The conference added a new section to the duties of the Administrative Council, requiring it to 'determine each year the policy of technical assistance, in accordance with the objectives of the Union', and two sections dealing with the IFRB. The IFRB, for instance, was required by the new Convention to take into account 'the specific needs of developing countries' when furnishing advice to members concerning the best use of radio frequencies and geostationary satellite orbits and to provide assistance to developing countries in their preparation for future radio conferences.[32]

The developing countries were also successful in gaining a majority to approve the principle of an ITU regional presence in the developing world and the creation of the new Centre for Telecommunication Development, which will be treated later. By means of Resolution 26 the Nairobi plenipotentiary asked the Secretary-General to report to the Administrative Council the cost and benefits of achieving 'a strengthened regional presence which will be as economical as possible and at the same time improve the effectiveness of the Union's activities'.[33] The Administrative Council was instructed, on the basis of the report and consultations with member administrations, to take the necessary steps to provide the stronger regional ITU presence. In all, the 1982 plenipotentiary passed eighteen resolutions and one opinion dealing with the matter of technical assistance. It should be noted, however, that the 1982 plenipotentiary at the same time placed a strict limit on how much the expenses of the ITU would be allowed to increase in the period prior to the next plenipotentiary scheduled for 1989.[34]

The third objective, to create an ITU development assistance fund from ITU-based resources, has been the most difficult to achieve. It is one thing to issue instructions to ITU organs to carry out studies and even to provide some assistance to developing countries, but it is another to convince those countries with the necessary finances to fund an independent ITU development assistance programme.

As mentioned earlier, the discontent of the developing countries with the level of development assistance that had been available from the UNDP prompted a proposal at the 1965 plenipotentiary to create a completely separate ITU development assistance fund. Although defeated decisively in 1965, it was raised again at the 1973 plenipotentiary along with a provision that it be financed through the regular ITU budget. Although the 1973 proposal had the backing of a great majority of the delegates, a number of developed countries, including those from the communist group, were successful in eliminating the provision that the fund be financed from the regular budget and substituting a provision that the new fund be financed through voluntary contributions.[35] Although the ITU initiated the new programme, entitled the Special Fund for Technical Cooperation, the contributions that were received were never of any great consequence.[36]

The subject of funding an ITU development assistance effort was one of the major subjects discussed at the 1982 plenipotentiary in Nairobi, and the developing countries achieved victories the benefits of which are still to be determined. In the first place they were successful in creating a successor to the ill-fated Special Fund. The new effort was entitled the Special Voluntary Programme for Technical Cooperation, and its resource base was enlarged from contributions 'in any currency or in some other form' to 'contributions in currency, training services, or in any other form'.[37] The second victory, which was achieved primarily at the initiative of the Algerian delegation, was the formal inclusion in the primary objectives of the ITU of the offering of technical assistance to developing countries in the field of telecommunications as mentioned earlier. On the basis of this change, the Nairobi plenipotentiary passed a resolution requesting the Secretary-General and the Administrative Council to investigate methods of reinforcing 'the operational capacity of the Union to provide technical assistance for the benefit of the developing countries', funding for which would come from the regular ITU budget.[38]

The third victory was the decision in Committee 6 to direct the Secretary-General to establish an International Commission for World-Wide Telecommunication Development, made up of

representatives of the highest decision-makers from administrations, operating agencies, and industry in the developing and developed countries as well as the major financial institutions [to examine] the totality of existing and possible future relationships between countries in the field of telecommunications involving technical cooperation and a transfer of resources in order to identify the most successful methods of such transfer.[39]

The committee, made up of seventeen distinguished representatives of governments and industry, mostly telecommunications-related, was established in May 1983, and Sir Donald Maitland of the United Kingdom was chosen as its chairman. The committee's report, entitled *The Missing Link*, was submitted in December 1984. As might be expected, the committee came to the conclusion that although communications infrastructure are an essential element in the economic and social development of all countries, in much of the developing world telecommunications services 'are poor or indifferent', and in many remote areas 'there is no service at all'. To bring telecommunications in the developing countries up to the standards that the Commission considers necessary, a 'total investment of US$12 billion a year will be needed across the board'.[40]

The Commission made three major recommendations. First, developing countries should give a higher priority to improving their telecommunications infrastructures. Second, an effort should be made to make 'existing networks in developing countries more effective and progressively self-reliant and to exploit the benefits of the new technologies'.[41] The third recommendation was for a greater effort to find the funds necessary for the enhancement of telecommunications in developing countries. Among the steps that the Commission felt should be taken to achieve the latter recommendation were for countries and international agencies providing developing assistance programmes to give a higher priority to telecommunications, for those who provide international satellite systems to finance earth segments and terrestrial facilities, and for developed countries to provide insurance cover for suppliers of telecommunications equipment to developing countries. The Commission also recommended that 'member states of the ITU consider setting aside a small proportion of revenues from calls between developing countries and industrialized countries to be devoted to telecommunications in developing countries'.[42]

For longer-term financing the Commission recommended: (1) that governments of developed countries investigate their financing institutions in order to ensure that they can meet the requirements of developing countries; (2) that members of the ITU and international financing agencies study the possibility of creating 'a revolving fund and . . . telecommunications investment trusts as methods of raising funds for investment in telecommunications'; and (3) that the Secretary-General study a proposal 'for an organization to coordinate the development of telecommunications world-wide (WORLDTEL)' and submit his conclusions to the next plenipotentiary conference.[43]

The proposals of the Commission are far-reaching and, if carried out with any real amount of enthusiasm, would certainly result in giving telecommunication development a greater degree of visibility in the ITU than it has had in the past and might even stimulate the upgrading of telecommunication facilities in developing countries. However, in view of the magnitude of the problem as identified by the Commission and the record of the ITU in finding additional funds for technical assistance, the process will be a long one indeed.

Conclusions

That the ITU has been able to survive for more than 120 years testifies to the fact that it has done a good job in meeting the changing needs of its heterogeneous clientele in the past. For the first hundred years that task consisted mainly in providing an arena in which the participating telecommunication administrations were able to establish the rules necessary for an efficient international telecommunication network. Two major aspects of this phase of the ITU's work included making standards to enable new technologies to be used in the international network and establishing a system whereby the rights of states to use radio frequencies could be used without harmful interference from the radio stations of other countries. At a time when the countries involved were of a similar stature as far as development was concerned and the technology was advancing at a moderate pace, this was adequate to meet the needs of most of the members, and the Union continued to grow and prosper.

However, our survey of the ITU's three major functions reveals some hard evidence that the new developing country majority is becoming increasingly dissatisfied with the manner in which the ITU is carrying out its responsibilities.

Of the two older functions, the one that both groups seem to agree is in their best interest is frequency management. Communication by radio continues to be important to all countries, old or new, developed or developing, and its success depends on operation free from harmful interference. However, even here we have seen some important differences of opinion arise as to the best method of extending the rights-vesting aspects of frequency management to space resources.

The standards-making function continues to have a high priority in the plans of administrations from the developed country members of the ITU as dramatic developments continue to occur in telecommunications technology. The developing countries, however tend not to see any immediate benefits to themselves from these activities and few, if any, long-range benefits as evidenced in the failure to participate in the work of the ITU's consultative committees.

Of major importance is the difference in the value placed on development assistance activities. The developing countries have been sold on the idea that telecommunications are essential to their ability to compete in a highly competitive world and thus place high priority on improving their domestic telecommunications networks. Many of the developed countries, however, fail to see any immediate benefits to themselves from the ITU's engagement in such activities and few, if any, long-term benefits. As a result they have tended to oppose any increases in the ITU's development assistance functions and, when they are overruled, have failed to provide the finances necessary to make it successful.

No international organization can maintain its vitality if it fails to maintain a proper balance of interest and benefits for its members. The present situation, therefore, is a potentially serious one for the ITU and should be addressed in the near future if the ITU is to continue to serve the telecommunication needs of the world as it has in the past.

Notes

1. The ITU also performs an important informational function to its client states which

will not be treated to any great extent in this chapter. For further reading on the information function, see George A. Codding, Jr and Anthony M. Rutkowski, 1982, *The International Telecommunication Union in a Changing World*, Dedham, Mass., Artech House, Chapter 13.

2. See ITU, 1983, *International Telecommunications Convention, Nairobi, 1982*, Geneva, Annex 2, para. 2015.

3. For many years the structure of the International Telegraph Union was restricted to periodic conferences and a small secretariat located in Berne, Switzerland, staffed and directed by the Swiss government. For the early history of the ITU, consult the author's *The International Telecommunication Union: An Experiment in International Cooperation*, 1952, Leiden, E.J. Brill, (reprinted 1972), New York, Arno Press.

4. To make it possible for the US to participate in the new organisation, it was decided that in addition to ratifying the basic treaty it was necessary to accept only one of the three administrative regulations, the one for telegraph, telephone or radio.

5. The ITU also has an Administrative Council, a forty-one member body which meets in Geneva once a year to oversee the work of the ITU and to act as a liaison with the UN and the General Secretariat.

6. See *International Telecommunication Convention, Nairobi, 1982*.

7. The change was made because it was felt that the CCITT was a better form than the cumbersome international conference for keeping abreast of the rapidly changing telegraph and telephone technologies.

8. Article 10, *International Telecommunications Convention, Nairobi, 1982*.

9. See George A. Codding, Jr., *The International Telecommunication Union: An Experiment . . .* Chapter 1. For a history of the ITU since 1952 consult George A. Codding Jr. and A.M. Rutkowski, *The ITU in a Changing World*, op. cit.

10. See *International Telecommunication Convention, Nairobi, 1982*, Article 11, para. 1.

11. See ITU, CCITT, 1985 *Red Book*, vol. 1, Geneva, pp. 3–4.

12. For further information on the developing ISDN, see A.M. Rutkowski, 1985, *Integrated Services Digital Networks*, Dedham, Artech House.

13. See ITU, *Report on the Activities of the International Telecommunication Union, 1984*, Geneva, pp. 96–100; and *Report on the Activities of the International Telecommunication Union, 1985*, Geneva, pp. 113–15.

14. See ITU, *Radio Regulations, Edition of 1982*, Article 8.

15. Ibid, Article 12, para. 1.

16. If there should be an unfavourable finding, there are a number of procedures by which an administration can obtain an eventual entry of that notification in the Master register with full or partial rights.

17. See George A. Codding Jr. and A.M. Rutkowski, op. cit., pp. 267–68. In view of the stand taken by the United States in regard to the use of the a priori approach for geostationary satellite communications, which will be discussed next, it is interesting to note that in 1947 the United States proposed, unsuccessfully as it turned out, that the a priori system be used for practically all of the terrestrial radio service bands where there was intensive use.

18. See for instance, Donna A. Demac, George A. Codding Jr., Heather Hudson and Ram. S. Jakhu, *Equity in Orbit: The 1985 ITU Space WARC*, London, International Institute of Communications, Chapter 4.

19. For frequency management purposes the ITU divides the world into three regions: Region 1, including Europe, Africa and the USSR; Region 2, the Western Hemisphere; and Region 3, Asia and Australasia.

20. See ITU, *Final Acts of the World Administrative Radio Conference for the Planning of the Broadcasting Satellite Service in Frequency Bands 11.7–12.2 GHz (in regions 2 and 3) and 11.7–12.5 GHz (in Region 1)*, Geneva, 1977; and ITU, 1983, *Final Acts of the Regional Administrative Radio for the Planning of the Broadcast Satellite Service in Region 1*, Geneva.

21. See for instance the United States, Department of State, Bureau of International Communications and Information Policy, 1986, *Report of the United States Delegation to the First Session of the ITU World Administrative Radio Conference on the Planning of the Geostationary Satellite Orbit and the Space Services Utilizing It, Geneva, Switzerland, August 8–September 16, 1985*, Washington D.C., pp. 2–5.

22. See ITU, *World Administrative Radio Conference on the Use of the Geostationary Satellite Orbit and the Space Services Utilizing It, First Session, Geneva, 1985, Report to the Second Session of the Conference* and *Addendum to the Report to the Second Session of the Conference*, Geneva.

23. In 1984, for instance, the UNDP allocated only $19,057,140 to telecommunication projects, of which $4,664,627 was used for Africa, $3,128,433 for the Americas, $5,540,458 for Asia and the Pacific, $1,276,159 for Europe, $4,447,563 for the Middle East. See ITU, 1985, *Report on the Activities of the International Telecommunications Union in 1984*, Geneva, pp. 161, 208.

24. ITU, 1960, *International Telecommunication Convention, Geneva, 1959*, Geneva, Article 4, para. 2.d.

25. ITU, 1982, *International Telecommunication Convention, Nairobi, 1982*, Geneva, Article 4, para. 1.a.

26. *International Telecommunication Convention, Geneva, 1959*, Article 13, para. 1.3.

27. The developing countries also sought the creation of a special ITU development assistance fund. This will be discussed later in this section.

28. See ITU, *International Telecommunication Convention, Montreux, 1965*, Geneva, Resolution No. 29.

29. *International Telecommunication Convention, Malaga-Torremolinos, 1973*, Article 8, para. 4(4).

30. *ibid.*, Resolutions 16–25 and Opinion No. 2.

31. The proposal to create regional ITU offices was defeated in committee by a vote of thirty-six for to thirty-six against (with four abstentions), but passed in the same committee in a secret ballot by forty-seven to forty-one (with one abstention) before it was presented to the plenary meeting. See United States Department of State, Office of Telecommunications, *Report of the United States Delegation to the Plenipotentiary Conference of the International Telecommunication Union, Malaga-Torremolinos, Spain, September 14–October 25, 1973*, TD Serial No. 43, Washington DC (mimeo), pp. 40–1, 44–5.

32. See *International Telecommunication Convention, Nairobi, 1982*, Article 8, para. 4(2) and Article 10, para. 4c) and e).

33. *ibid.*, Resolution No. 26.

34. For a discussion of the problem of expenses, see United States Department of State, *Report of the United States Delegation to the Plenipotentiary Conference of the International Telecommunication Union, Nairobi, Kenya, September 28–November 6, 1982*, Washington DC, pp. 8–10.

35. See *International Telecommunication Convention, Malaga-Torremolinos, 1973*, Resolution No. 21.

36. In 1980, for instance, the fund contained the grand total of 34,250 Swiss francs. See ITU, 1981, *Report on the Activities of the International Telecommunication Union in 1980*, Geneva, p. 103.

37. *International Telecommunication Convention, Nairobi, 1982*, Resolution No. 19.

38. *ibid.*, Resolution No. 18.

39. *ibid.*, Resolution No. 20.

40. See ITU, 1985, *The Missing Link*, Report of the Independent Commission for World-Wide Telecommunications Development, Geneva, pp. 1, 57, 65.

41. *ibid.*, p. 66.
42. *ibid.*, p. 68. The ITU took the first concrete step towards achieving its goals when at its 1986 meeting the ITU Administrative Council created an ITU Centre for Telecommunications Development. *Report on the Activities of the International Telecommunication Union in 1985*, pp. 140–1.
43. *ibid.*

Recommended reading

Annual Reports of the International Telecommunication Union.
George A. Codding, Jr and Anthony M. Rutkowski, 1982, *The International Telecommunication Union in a Changing World*, Dedham, Mass., Artech House, Inc.
Michigan Yearbook of International Legal Studies, 1984, *Regulation of Transnational Communications*, New York, NY, Clark Boardman Company, Ltd.
Robert J. Saunders, Jeremy J. Warford and Bjorn Welleius, 1983, *Telecommunications and Economic Development*, Baltimore, Md, John Hopkins Press.

11 The Commonwealth: a bond that held

A.J.R. Groom

The largest meetings of heads of governments on a regular basis occur not, as might frequently be thought, in the annual meetings of the UN General Assembly, but in the biennial meetings of Commonwealth heads of government (CHOGMs) and the triennial meetings of non-aligned heads of government. To gather together, and keep together, something like fifty leaders in the CHOGM for a week or so is no mean feat, and success in which is a great tribute to the continuing relevance of the Commonwealth.

Prime Minister Nehru of India had the foresight and intuition to realise that the Commonwealth was capable of developing a 'healing touch' in so many ways that make it unusual among international institutions. Nehru's particular contribution to the evolution of the contemporary Commonwealth was an important one: he kept India in the Commonwealth on a basis of unfettered independence as a republic, while at the same time acknowledging the British monarch as 'Head of the Commonwealth' — a titular symbolic status. By so doing he made it possible for the Commonwealth to evolve into a multilateral, egalitarian, transregional association the usefulness of which, in its modest way but in a multitude of domains, often comes as a refreshing and delightful surprise. Without Nehru the Commonwealth might well have closed ranks as a club of increasingly cantankerous British 'cousins' (such as Britain, Australia, Canada, and New Zealand and perhaps South Africa) of infrequent and limited relevance. But Nehru was not alone in seeing virtue in a continuing Commonwealth connection — if the terms were right, so did Gandhi himself — like generations of political leaders in many former British possessions during the last forty years. What, however, is the current state of the Commonwealth?

The contemporary Commonwealth reached its present form in the early 1970s.[1] The Secretariat had established itself as an independent actor following its baptism of fire in the Anglo-African confrontation over Southern Africa. The parties to that conflict had acknowledged damage-limitation procedures, Britain had joined the European Community, but a significant number of leading members from all continents had decided that the association was worth keeping. The Commonwealth then began to play its new, modest but efficient role in world affairs — economic, political, technical and social — buttressed, as ever, by its network of non-governmental ties. Despite its nebulous character which defies definition, the Commonwealth is real, significant and relevant. It encompasses a network of ties, governmental and non-governmental, in virtually every domain known to man: it has grown out of and facilitates an impressive movement of goods, services, ideas and people in a remarkably non-coercive framework. This informality and diversity of relationships is aided by the lack of a constitution but it is guided and moulded by a set of formal principles and the evolution of habits rooted in established and acceptable practice.[2]

The Commonwealth is a voluntary association of governments and NGOs which share a historic British connection and wish to work together to further their individual and common interests. They have a surprising but real sense of fraternity which comes through in the behaviour of the most hard-nosed participants and which has survived many buffetings of considerable political import. This sense of fraternity has two elements: the first is a 'distant cousin syndrome', and the second is a sense of common interest. The distant cousin analogy suggests that Commonwealth governments and peoples react to each other in new circumstances in a different way from non-Commonwealth governments and peoples. Just as on meeting a distant cousin for the first time a person will observe the rules of family ties and behaviour by sharing information and affording help in an open relationship in a manner that would not be accorded to a total stranger, so Commonwealth 'distant cousins' do not approach each other negatively, but positively, and in a cooperative and friendly manner. There is sense of 'we feeling' that pervades Commonwealth relations which includes a notion of Commonwealth interest, and even international community interest, over and above the pursuit of self-interest. Even where disputes arise between Commonwealth members the aim is, at the very least, for the Commonwealth to discuss issues in an independent and catalytic manner if this will help and if it is desired. It is to be supportive of the parties rather than to be partisan.

The generally supportive nature of the Commonwealth is illustrated by the decision-making process. The Commonwealth can only recommend; it cannot command or coerce. Its informality in negotiation is exemplified by the seminar-like heads of government meetings with their frequent interjections, the general avoidance of set speeches and the usually friendly, even 'matey' atmosphere which, although sometimes interrupted by tension, nevertheless permits the frank discussion of delicate issues. Heads of government can let themselves go with a peer group without fear that advantage will be taken. This is a situation rare in their experience to which they attach sufficient importance to devote a week or more of their time every other year. There is often no specific end in view but any decisions, if decisions are required and desired, will be taken by consensus and in private. And they usually return home having found the meeting fertile in ideas.

New member states, new governments and new leaders are socialised into the ways of the Commonwealth in a variety of ways. Heads of government meetings set and reflect the tone at other levels. The Secretariat and its activities have an important inductive role for new members and new governments, and the existence of non-governmental ties, which often precede independence, even at that time instil into participants the informal, frank and consensual way of doing business. Indeed, the Commonwealth is not only about the business that it does, but also about the way in which it does business.

The informality, frankness and a cooperative spirit, even when in dispute, are aided substantially by a common working language and compatible administrative practice. The role of English is important because language constitutes a paradigm which is shared and which has a subtle but pervasive influence that facilitates bridge-building. With the use of English and compatible administrative procedures 'progress' is given a head-start. Yet to participate in this process is in no sense to deny participation in other organisations. Although the Commonwealth commands loyalty, it does not command exclusive loyalty. Indeed, one of its virtues is its diversity, and practically all Commonwealth countries also have strong regional or other extra-Commonwealth ties.

A prime, indeed a necessary characteristic of the contemporary Commonwealth is its lack of Anglo-centricity, especially at the intergovernmental level. There is no British leadership and there could be no such leadership. The Secretariat plays a central role and is a driving force, while from time to time a Commonwealth 'leader' emerges on an issue or group of issues. Trudeau, Nyerere, Fraser, Lee Kuan Yew, Kaunda and Mrs Gandhi, among others, have played, and in some cases, continue to play such a role. The British government has been in many instances a reluctant participant which, while it may have been good for the Commonwealth in forcing it to establish its new identity, has been bad for Britain in its continuing search for a new role and identity in the contemporary world. However, the situation is somewhat different at the NGO level where there is a greater Anglo-centricity. Nevertheless, this is changing with the growth of Commonwealth regional and Pan-Commonwealth ties of many Anglo-centric NGOs to broaden and diversify their range of participants and their transnational base. The work of the Commonwealth Foundation has also greatly facilitated movement in this direction with the establishment of centres for the use of professional associations in developing countries and NGO liaison units.

The Commonwealth is not one thing: it is different things in different areas and for different members. Its diversity and flexibility, and yet continued relevance, allow all to join in to the extent, where and how they wish to do so. It is used by all its members, but it is held dearest by those who have few other avenues into the world. In particular, it enables small countries to act on a world-wide stage in a familiar and supportive setting without the encumbering and overwhelming framework, formality, intrigues and bureaucracy of the United Nations and its agencies. Even in questions of high politics in the Commonwealth there is a welcome element of fraternity. It is a political and functional forum in which governments can try out ideas, test policies and get feedback on their standing in a world-wide context and in a friendly and frank fashion that is available virtually nowhere else. Commonwealth heads of government particularly value their meetings for those purposes. For small countries the Commonwealth is an invaluable and flexible source of trustworthy and relevant information, help and research, whether from other members or from the Secretariat, to the extent that many would be lost without it; whereas for medium powers, such as Australia or Canada, it is a manageable forum for a world-wide policy and an invaluable entrée into global politics. Above all, the Commonwealth is a North–South bridge, and one of the few acceptable bridges for all parties, which has already been crossed in an attempt to ameliorate North–South problems with some degree of success. As Secretary-General Ramphal has suggested, 'the Commonwealth cannot negotiate for the world; but it can help the world to negotiate'.[3]

The Commonwealth is part of the nervous system of world society. It is not particularly salient but it usually manages to be a haven of relative sanity in a difficult and dangerous world. The world could survive without it, but not as well. It leads to a modest exchange of people, ideas, goods and services transregionally as well as between North and South on a basis more acceptable to the participants than many other institutions. Moreover, it is capable of genuine discussion of differences and even of their resolution. It is not overtly coercive and its structures are not oppressive. It brings a sense of community into the struggle to control coercion and dismantle oppressive world structures. In short, it is an unusual, but legitimised, part of the institutional structure of contemporary world society. It is a bond that has changed but it is also one that has held.

The actual and potential usefulness of the Commonwealth is often ignored or denigrated by those who ought to know better. Academics in the Western World have tended to discuss it with a passing slight and practitioners, while availing themselves of its services, have not always made a due acknowledgement. British prime ministers have provided some cases in point. Moreover, defenders and protagonists have sometimes exaggerated virtues and not sufficiently taken into account difficulties. This balance sheet therefore attempts to point to successes and failures in the conviction that the Commonwealth has a role to play in the betterment of mankind's lot, especially in North–South relations. Without it our frail ability to manage a range of global problems which threaten to up-end contemporary world society in a catastrophic manner would be further diminished. Change is inevitable and desirable, but catastrophic change is not. The Commonwealth has within it the possibility of lessening the danger of catastrophic change and enchancing and facilitating the likelihood of creative change. It is in no way a panacea but we can ill-afford to do without its potential even if, should we not have it, we would hardly think of inventing it.

The Commonwealth has a supreme virtue and ideology — that of bridge-building. It is not used for the purpose of disassociation from or coercion of third parties, except in the case of South Africa, and then principally with the ruling political elite. It is concerned with the promotion of the individual self-interest of member-states within the organisation, their mutual interests in the outside world and that of the world community as a whole. It is the conscious admission and pursuance of the latter which is of unusual value. Such efforts have attracted the attention of the cynics and make for easy game but, whatever the failings in motivation or execution, the occasional successes in bridge-building in a dangerous world, whether political or economic, are a hope for humanity.

A strength of the Commonwealth is in the North–South dimension since it contains both Northern and Southern members and a Secretary-General and Secretariat well versed on the issue. Moreover, it has been successful in easing some of the problems in NIEO, in the ACP–EC relationship and in individual cases such as the negotiations between Papua New Guinea and Rio Tinto Zinc. It is happily ironic that a former imperial structure has gone through a metamorphosis such that on the question of decolonisation its building activities are evident, as in the final process of bringing Southern Rhodesia to independence as Zimbabwe. Commonwealth efforts at bridge-building have demonstrated the flexibility and informality of the institutional settings, a supportive non-partisan approach to the parties and a strong notion of community interest mixed with self-interest in promoting a process the end-result of which is to create a 'win-win' situation not a 'win-lose' situation.

Being blessed with the absence of a constitution has given the Commonwealth an uncommon flexibility and diminishes the likelihood that members will play political games with the constitution. It also encourages the membership to operate on a consensual basis, there being no truck with majority voting of a divisive nature. However, the Commonwealth does have a firm idea of what it is about and, as we have seen, this has been codified into a set of principles and, more important, into working habits and methods of doing business.

The Commonwealth is also unusual in that it does not have a 'general assembly' functioning on a continuing basis which has the possibility of 'parliamentary diplomacy'. Rather, there are heads of government meetings periodically interspersed with meetings of senior officials whose function is to prepare the summit meetings and deal with 'matters arising' from previous summits or intervening events. Other ministers and their officials also meet regularly as do the more than 200 Commonwealth bodies of a governmental or non-governmental character. The heads of government and ministerial meetings are firmly in the tradition of intergovernmental cooperation: there is no sense of any form of supra-national integration and this is reflected in the decision-making process. Only recommendations on a basis of consensus can be made. However, the Commonwealth has a large number of action programmes in the technical and assistance domains, both governmentally and non-governmentally, in practically every conceivable field. Sovereignty, however, is not prejudiced. Indeed, the Commonwealth adheres rather strictly to the injunction not to discuss or intervene in the domestic affairs of member-states without their consent. There are occasional exceptions and, after the intervention in and discussion of Uganda's affairs during Idi Amin's time, Commonwealth Secretary-General Ramphal put it well:

There will be times in the affairs of the Commonwealth when one member's conduct will provoke the wrath of others beyond the limits of silence. Any other relationships would be so sterile as to be effete. What we must work for is an ethic which constrains meddling but which also inhibits excesses of the kind that demand and justify protest from without.

There never will be unanimity that criticism or complaint is legitimate comment, not improper interference. But the truth is that, although the line may be indefinable, all the world will know when it is crossed.[4]

The Commonwealth is hampered in its search for consensus by its heterogeneity. However, a significant consensus on a substantive issue does thereby achieve greater weight even if its achievement is difficult. Moreover, the Commonwealth has been able to develop effective intra-organisational regional frameworks which have helped in partial and pan-organisational consensus building. Examples of this are CARICOM and the Asia–Pacific regional CHOGRMSs. But heterogeneity is also an asset. The Commonwealth is a transregional organisation — one of the very few and therefore all the more precious. The Commonwealth links together developed Western countries and developing countries from all continents. This makes the North-South trans-regionalism of the Commonwealth in a polarising world all the more important. There are few such acceptable ties. Moreover, transregionalism is important since the world is not conveniently organised at the universal, regional and national levels; it is far more complex and transregional associations enable us better to institutionalise that complexity.

Transregionality can, however, lead to a degree of duplication of organisa-tional frameworks that may involve a costly redundancy, particularly for hard-pressed Third World countries. It is clear that there is overlapping membership and activity but these are, for the most part, beneficial because they are the points of linkage for the coordination of other organisations. They are also, frequently, points of growth and creativity. Nevertheless, despite its trans-regionalism the Commonwealth does have an element of exclusiveness. The Commonwealth is restricted to members with a past British connection, although the membership of Mozambique remains a possibility. However, not all such territories have been invited to join or would have wished to do so, for example, those of the Arab world, and Commonwealth membership and institutionalised racism are incompatible, as the case of South Africa already illustrated.

Any organisation must, in order to survive, be able to perform four functions to a minimum level: to adapt to the social and physical environment as a coherent unit, to integrate its sub-units, to develop a sense of identity and to have enough self-knowledge to enable goals to be set. The structures and processes through which these functions are performed can vary enormously but the func-tions themselves are a *sine qua non* of survival. The Commonwealth has demonstrated a manifest ability to adapt, but the Commonwealth has only been able to adapt at the price of a significant decline in its ability to integrate its sub-units. For most members the Commonwealth tie is only one of many and not usually the most salient one. Moreover, the strength of numbers hinders integra-tion and ultimately saps its effectiveness of action. While the price of survival is a loss of cohesion, nevertheless the Commonwealth has a surprising sense of common identity. The degree of effective commitment is heartening. But commitment for what? The Commonwealth has found its niche. It knows what it can do, and how, and it is now in the business of getting on with the job. It has an identity. The Commonwealth may be small beer but it is a good local brew.

If one factor can be said to have made the contemporary Commonwealth it is the establishment of the Secretariat and the appointment of two different, but excellent, Secretaries-General. Arnold Smith in many ways got the British off the hook of an Anglo-Centric Commonwealth despite themselves, and Shridath Ramphal has hooked the Third World membership on the Commonwealth and helped to develop the institution as a bridge in the North–South dimension. The Commonwealth Secretariat that these men have led is small but good. It has developed services and programmes that fill a need: small, client-orientated, fast and efficient. Its resources are limited, but used to great effect. It is an exemplar for others.

The Commonwealth is an association not only of governments but also of peoples. This is no empty rhetoric. It is fact and exemplified by the 'unofficial' Commonwealth of more than 200 Commonwealth organisations most of which are NGOs. The Commonwealth is firmly rooted in grassroots ties which expand and contract from area to area but which, collectively, provide a propitious climate for intergovernmental cooperation particularly as they lose their Anglo-centricity and become less skewed towards the developed Commonwealth countries. In a sense a sort of Commonwealth would survive for a while without, or even despite, governments.

For the present the Commonwealth has reached its cruising speed and seems likely to be threatened only by a global catastrophe such as nuclear war or, perhaps, by the question of South Africa. In the meantime the bond holds as it adapts to a changing environment and it is fructuous. Peoples and governments the world over have good practical reason, in a myriad of ways, to cherish it.

Notes

1. For a detailed study of the Commonwealth, see A.J.R. Groom and Paul Taylor (eds), 1984, *The Commonwealth in the 1980s*, London, Macmillan.
2. See the 1971 CHOGM in Singapore's *Declaration of Commonwealth Principles*, the 1977 Gleneagles statement on *Apartheid in Sport*, and the 1979 *Lusaka Declaration of the Commonwealth on Racism and Racial Prejudice*.
3. Shridath Ramphal, 1979, *One World to Share*, London, Hutchinson, p. 123.
4. *Report of the Commonwealth Secretary-General*, 1977, London, Commonwealth Secretariat.

Recommended reading

John Chadwick, 1982, *The Unofficial Commonwealth*, London, Allen and Unwin.
A.J.R. Groom and Paul Taylor (eds), 1984, *The Commonwealth in the 1980s*, London, Macmillan.
Shridath Ramphal, 1979, *One World to Share*, London, Hutchinson.
Arnold Smith, 1981, *Stitches in Time*, London, Deutsch.

Part III

Assessment and reform

12 Some reflections on reform of the United Nations*

Maurice Bertrand

The notion and the feasibility of reform

The thesis to be propounded in this report is essentially as follows:

That forty years after the establishment of the United Nations, it is not only desirable today but entirely feasible to give serious thought to the reform of the United Nations and its system of organizations;
That these reflections must challenge the concepts underlying the institution;
That they must therefore focus, following the two unfinished experiments of the League of Nations and the United Nations, on a third-generation world organization genuinely in keeping with the needs of the modern world.

This thesis does not suggest that the present Organization has failed. On the contrary, the idea of reform is not only compatible with the acknowledgement of the historic role played by the United Nations, but it implies an affirmation of its importance and usefulness today. It merely postulates that it is possible to reflect on the establishment of a system that would be still more useful in the present political context.

Nor does the thesis mean that we can underrate the extreme difficulty of such an undertaking. It is perfectly true that attempts made so far to amend the Charter of the United Nations have been unsuccessful and that there is a tacit agreement among Governments not to try to resurrect them. On the other hand, those Member States which criticize the management of the organizations within the United Nations System[1] most strongly have not always shown themselves enthusiastic about supporting the various proposals for internal reform put before them.

It is a fact of life that getting amendments of any significance to structures, policies and methods accepted and applied in the United Nations and the specialized agencies is difficult. To achieve a consensus of the Member States on a technical recommendation is no easy matter, and even when resolutions deciding to change rules or the practices in force are adopted unanimously, resistance from the secretariats quite frequently succeed in draining the decisions of their content . . .

However, this situation is in the process of changing. First of all, criticisms

* This chapter consists of extracts from the full report made by the editors with the kind permission and advice of the author. Most footnotes in the original have been omitted.

alleging 'mismanagement' of the United Nations and some of the organizations of the United Nations System have reached the status of a political phenomenon. It arises both inside and outside the United Nations, mainly from the Governments of the wealthy Western or socialist countries, and over the last couple of years it has generally gone hand in hand with proposals for financial stringency or threats of withdrawal; while the countries members of the Group of 77 have raised the question, following the failure of the 'global negotiations', of ways and means of escaping from a cul-de-sac. It is as if North and South were both seeking a new type of dialogue and considering whether the management and the concept of the role of the world organizations could provide the opportunity.

At the same time, in a very large number of countries, rich and poor alike, a feeling of frustration is developing. The hope of seeing the world organizations contribute more to peace and to the reduction of armaments dies hard in the collective unconscious. Certain situations involving underdevelopment or violations of human rights seem more and more shocking to a better-informed public opinion. Criticisms of the 'ineffectiveness' of the United Nations are made in the light of an idealistic and sometimes naïve but in any event exigent view of the possible role of the Organization in its various fields of activity.

The logical conclusion of this type of frustration and criticism is of course the idea of reform. If public opinion felt that reform calculated to improve the performance of the Organization in relation to peace, development and human rights was feasible, the pressure it exerted on Governments would be such that they would abandon their present hesitation as to the possibility of change. What is more, that would be a very different exercise from past attempts at partial reform, proposed by particular countries merely to improve their own situation within the Organization . . .

No doubt to embark on any serious consideration of so radical a change would imply transformation of the political climate surrounding the problem. To pretend that the present crisis and the trend in public opinion could lead to the introduction of radical reforms may today seem utopian. Yet current criticisms show some awareness of the fact that the role played by the World Organizations is contradictory, uncertain and poorly adapted to present-day problems . . . The challenge to the very concept of the United Nations has already been issued. It arises not in the direction of an illusory 'strengthening' of the powers of the Organization but, on the contrary, in the direction of greater realism . . .

Managerial shortcomings or structural shortcomings

Extraordinary complexity

The causes of 'shortcomings' in the System are not methodological but structural. The question is not one of management but one of negotiation. The most obvious shortcoming, both for the outside observer and for those living and working within the System, is without any doubt the fragmentation of effort or the lack of a definition of priorities and of 'coordination'. It is easy to demonstrate that this situation is bound up with the very structures of the organizations. Before we can speak of coordination or priorities, we must recognize the extraordinary and unnecessary nature of institutional complexity. Familiarity with the phenomenon is such among those acquainted with the Organization that in the end they find the situation normal and regard the 'knowledge of the System' as a sort of palpable professional skill . . . The lack of coordination and definition of priorities is due to the extraordinary complexity of the structures.

Extreme fragmentation

With regard to activities at the various headquarters, the most important aspect is the universal nature of the content of programmes. Nothing is outside its scope — in the economic, social and humanitarian fields we find all the questions dealt with by the national administration in the individual countries . . . The extraordinarily ambitious coverage results in an extreme fragmentation of the resources available. This is reflected in many instances in the secondment of one or two professional-level officers to the study and treatment, from various angles, of a given world problem . . . With regard to operational activities, the dispersal and fragmentation also derive, first and foremost, from the distribution among various independent bodies . . . This system of allocation of funds means that in a single country which is a recipient of aid, about fifteen different organizations . . . intervene simultaneously to organize their projects there . . . This dispersal is increased still further by the fact that all these bodies operate in the form of 'projects', most of them modest in size, whose main component is expert services. Thus the average amount of the projects financed by UNDP (about 1,000) in 1983 was $393,000. Since the average annual cost of employing an expert is about $100,000, the average project involves supplying two to three experts a year, plus a variable figure for equipment. The high degree of independence enjoyed by the proponents of a project, as regards design and method, thus leads to fragmentation of responsibilities.

The complexities of intergovernmental machinery and experts reflect the number of bodies and programmes. Moreover, because of the number of member states, the main committees, with a representative on each committee, cannot examine all problems in detail. This has led to the creation of smaller committees, specialized 'subsidiary organs', and a system of relationships has been established between them. Then a whole network of coordination machinery has been superimposed on this structure. The vagueness of the terms of reference, the similarity of jurisdiction between organs . . . and the number and repetition of 'general debates' preceding the examination of agenda items repeated in committee after committee whose relative status is not clearly defined, have created in the United Nations particularly a state of confusion which in spite of countless efforts it has been found difficult to remedy. The machinery of the specialized agencies, generally limited to an Executive Board and a General Assembly, is no doubt simpler, but its geographical spread does not facilitate the coordination either of methods or of programmes.

The interplay of influence and power

This situation involves in turn for each of the member states the obligation:

To organize a network of representation at the four headquarters of the United Nations and those of each of the agencies, as well as with the regional economic commissions (i.e. in some fifteen different cities);

To arrange for coordination of its representatives with each of these organizations or headquarters; to earmark for such missions staff varying in strength with the power of the States but invariably numerous and not necessarily all of very high grade.

Furthermore, the complexity and often the relative unimportance of the problems dealt with makes it impossible for a central administration to give instructions on all subjects, and the foreign ministries responsible for this coordination do not have all the powers they need to supervise the representatives of technical ministries. The result is that in a very large number of cases, in spite of considerable paperwork, the personality of the representatives has a greater impact on the official position taken up by Governments than the directives sent from the capitals themselves. In these circumstances it is hardly surprising that the representatives of one and the same Government may take different points of view, on administrative or financial problems, for example, according to the organizations to which they are accredited. The credibility of the entire representation and negotiation system clearly suffers somewhat from this.

Thus it is also not surprising that the problems of management and functioning of the System as a whole ultimately take up an undue proportion of the work schedule of delegations and secretariats. The way in which the mill operates becomes much more important than the quality of the flour it produces. In order to overcome the difficulties inherent in the complexity of the whole, delegations are forced not only to learn how the machinery conditions the interplay of influence, but also to follow closely the most trivial administrative matters.

But the impact of influence and power to initiate on the orientation of the various programmes is very different in the specialized agencies and major programmes . . . on the one hand and in the United Nations itself on the other. In the above-mentioned agencies and major Programmes, the role of the Director or Secretary-General of the organization and his team, if he has been able to set one up, may be considerable. His personal philosophy in relation to world problems, his attitude towards development, may have a direct impact on the decisions taken by its Executive Board or General Assembly. He may influence the definition of the objectives of the agency (since he is responsible for drawing up programming documents), the apportioning of financial resources to this or that programme, and finally the definition of priorities. The dictatorial power at his disposal in relation to staff and recruitment increases still further his scope for influence. In the United nations, on the other hand, delegations have organized a measure of parliamentary power which is exerted even in the administrative field. Most of the initiatives come from the delegations themselves, which actually leads to stagnation. Changes of direction in programmes are few and modest, and the creation of new 'programmes' is extremely rare. The consequence is that the heads of departments or divisions have the possibility of taking the initiative, at least indirectly, in the design of programmes and in the collection of voluntary funds, thus giving them greater influence in their particular field than the Secretary-General.

The guidelines given to the organizations at the time of their establishment, and the historical corpus of decisions which have gone to confirm or modify their spirit, have given each one of them an individual character. The philosophies of international action developed within these micro-climates are very different in the ILO, UNESCO, WHO, UNICEF and UNDP. The third world colouring of UNCTAD and UNIDO, the Western philosophy of the 'enlightenment' which continues to inspire UNESCO, the specifically tripartite nature of the ILO, and the diversity of the view of development which inspire the action of the agencies or the various Programmes of the United Nations, force delegations to take account of all these nuances if they are to have any effectiveness.

Impossibility of coordination

It is difficult to see how such a situation could be rectified by better management methods . . . It is certainly not for want of having provided a whole machinery for this purpose, both at headquarters and in the field . . . This extraordinary perseverance produced no results . . .

This useless effort at coordination has in fact over the last fifteen years gone hand in hand with a parallel effort towards planning, programming, monitoring of the implementation of programmes and evaluation. Progress has certainly been made on paper in these fields, since the principle of the establishment of a planning cycle has been approved in the United Nations and most of the agencies, and instruments to this end have been devised . . .

These formal exercises have made it possible — and this is by no means negligible — to provide a better description of activities. But they have not been used for the purposes for which they were initially intended, namely a better definition of priorities; definition of accessible objectives; examination of alternative solutions; concentration of means of action on a few prime objectives; better organization and better division of labour between executants; and utilization of the lessons to be drawn from failure and success with a view to establishing better programmes. There have been better descriptions of the existing activities, but there has been no improvement in either their design or their implementation.

Improvements in method have thus not succeeded in correcting the structural shortcomings . . .

Quality of the 'outputs' and level of qualifications of the staff

As regards the quality of the outputs, allegations of serious shortcomings can be based on precise sources: reports drawn up by the various secretariats or by outside experts, or opinions expressed by the delegations of the member states themselves in a large number of resolutions or in the regular reports of certain subsidiary organs . . . By taking as our base of reference the managerial methods applied in the best national civil services or in large private firms, we can establish a strict account without great danger of error.

In the case of operational projects, numerous studies highlight the fact that, in the main, they should be better planned, with objectives that are better defined and easier to evaluate, that the experts should be better qualified and better acquainted with the problems of the countries concerned, that they should be appointed within the periods scheduled. In the case of publications, the sales figures . . . are ridiculously low . . . and a perusal . . . easily explains why they command such little success . . . There are of course exceptions . . .

Unquestionably, the explanation for this situation lies in the average inadequacy of qualifications of the personnel. The situation in this field is in fact extremely bad, and far removed from the principles laid down in . . . the Charter. The average level of qualifications of staff in the Professional grades (staff engaged in programme design, management, research and drafting) bears no relation to their responsibilities. In the United Nations, for example, 25 per cent of these professionals have had no university training, and 10 per cent have had less than three years of university studies . . .

It is probably in the higher posts that this situation of unsuitability for the duties actually performed is most serious. In the Director grades (D-1 and D-2) the percentage of staff members who have had no university education is roughly the same. A sense of responsibility and managerial or analytical ability at the highest levels (Director, Assistant Secretary-General, Under-Secretary-General) are a matter of chance, depending on appointments which are often made without concern for qualifications or professional and administrative experience. The lack of a definition of the qualifications required for recruitment and promotion to higher grades, the indifference shown towards standards of work and competence, the absence of a system of in-service training, create a deplorable working environment in which the best staff members no longer find the motivation needed to dedicate themselves to their tasks.

The only way to reverse this situation would be by shaping and applying a staff policy aimed primarily at enhancing professional competence and a sense of responsibility . . . the laxness that prevails in this matter would seem to put a premium on mediocrity . . .

The main reason for this is that it is not certain that Governments want this in the light of the conception they have of the role of the Organization. The United Nations Secretariat, and to a rather lesser extent the secretariats of the main agencies and programmes, are regarded at present by the member States as areas over which they have to exert political influence so as to gain maximum control over operations and install the largest possible number of their nationals . . . Governments attach only secondary importance to the efficiency of the organizations. The mediocrity of the outputs does not strike them, in most cases, as a major concern, since the benefit they derive is negligible. In short, they do not have a clear picture of what purpose a World Organization could serve, even it it were better run . . .

The nature and the role of the World Organization

Intellectual confusion and smokescreens

The fact that no one has a clear idea what the United Nations and its System of organizations amounts to is a phenomenon which must be faced . . . A perusal of the texts, resolutions or documents can tell us virtually nothing about the real nature of the organization . . . In short, it is as if the System were all the time throwing out a smokescreen to conceal its true nature:

by defining its mandate in an unreal fashion;
by trying to give the impression that the outputs from its activities have a direct effect on the internal realities of states;
by maintaining a permanent state of confusion between the functions of negotiating or seeking greater consensus on the one hand, and the functions of management on the other.

Lack of realism and mere talk

Lack of realism and mere talk are not confined to the texts of Charters and Constitutions. They permanently play an essential role in the life of organizations. No doubt a certain amount of idealistic wording is necessary to the extent that a certain vagueness facilitates meetings between the representatives of opposing regimes or ideologies . . . Mere talk fulfils two distinct functions, both of them harmful to the image and to the effectiveness of the organization.

The first function is that it conceals the fact that no agreement has been reached, possibly because there were no real negotiations. 'Verbal consensus' thus replaces real discussion of the problems and the give-and-take of vested interests
. . .
The second function of verbosity is probably even more harmful: it is that of which numerous illustrations can be found in planning and programming documents. We read, for example, in the United Nations Medium-Term Plan for the period 1984–9 that the public administration objectives of the major programme in this field are 'to strengthen and enlarge mutual cooperation among developing countries at the subregional, regional and interregional levels, focusing on opportunities for mobilizing administrative and institutional resources available in developing countries' and 'to develop administrative infrastructure in the various development sectors in developing countries', 'to develop and improve the managerial and administrative capabilities of the developing countries to enhance the performance of their public managers'. A thorough study of this programme reveals that the 'outputs' corresponding to these ambitious tasks consists essentially of a few publications of no great consequence, which do not reach those for whom they are intended and are not sold to any public, of the odd meeting unrelated to the administrative problems of the countries concerned, or of the odd unpretentious and ineffective project. One may wonder, therefore, whether this type of programme has any relationship to the facts of life . . .

The degree of unreality varies with the programmes. Some render precise service. But in a general way, the world-wide scale of all these undertakings; the gulf between the ambitions and the means; the lack of a transmission belt between the offices at headquarters and the responsible national services within each country; the inability to define modest objectives accessible within the stated time limits, raise doubts whether in the long run most of the activities have any connection with reality . . .

It is all the more difficult to understand the nature of this System in that it has evolved considerably since it was established. It has been given many tasks to perform which were not foreseen at the outset; it has given a new interpretation to the ones that it did receive; it has become considerably more complex and diversified. At the same time an enormous number of other international organizations have been endowed with terms of reference comparable with its own. Finally, there is a tendency at all times for the specialist and the initiate to put forward partial views as if they represented the entire landscape . . .

Place of the World Organization in the system of international relations

The illusion that the United Nations still, in spite of its ineffectiveness, occupies a central and important position in the system of international relations dies hard. The criticism of its allegedly exorbitant cost, for example, could lead to the belief that it skims off a considerable proportion of the public revenue from each State, and the regret expressed to the effect that it is not more effective in the realm of peace, suggests that it might have real power. Actually, in the sphere of international relations, the United Nations and its System have very limited functions. The questions dealt with in the United Nations are only exceptionally dealt with at ministerial level, and the sum total of resources is extremely modest.

Bilateral diplomacy is still for essential issues — East–West relations, the strategic balance between the United States and the Soviet Union, economic and social relations among all countries, relations between the industrialized countries and the developing countries — the means most used to examine and solve concrete problems. At the same time, the vast network of intergovernmental international organizations, which has been considerably developed and strengthened over the last forty years, at geographical or ideological levels below the world level, is used by governments for purposes which are often very close to that of the United Nations System . . .

The relatively secondary place occupied by the United Nations System is also illustrated by the fact that the representatives of governments on intergovernmental bodies are essentially government officials — diplomats or representatives of technical ministries — but not members of Governments or Chiefs of State. In other international organizations, regular meetings at ministerial level are the rule . . . or there are at least annual meetings at this level . . .

A few figures may give an idea of the relative importance of the World Organization. The annual level of resources earmarked for the United Nations System, in the form of official and voluntary contributions is approximately $5.5 billion (in 1984), rather more than 52 per cent of this being devoted to operational activities, about 13 per cent to humanitarian expenditure on behalf of refugees, 30 per cent to economic, social, functional and technical activities, and only 4.4 per cent to political problems and peace ($243 million, including expenditure on the maintenance of peacekeeping forces). These resources may usefully be compared . . . with the budgets of other international organizations

(European Communities: $25 billion) or the budgets of cities or countries: New York, $7 billion; Federal budget of the United States, $800 billion.

Nature of the activities of the System and the notion of a 'world consensus'

But even more than to exaggerate its real importance, the most serious error in regard to the nature of the activities of the United Nations System is to regard it as involving managerial activities. The confusion — structural in some respects, or at any rate maintained obstinately — between negotiation and managerial functions derives no doubt from the illusion cherished by the founding fathers of the United Nations that the object of an intergovernmental organization was to enable its members to act together. But whatever its causes, they make it impossible to understand the real nature and role of the institution.

With the exception of a few specific domains (declarations of principle or drafting of conventions), where it is recognized that the role of the Organization is to facilitate negotiations between Member States, most of the activities described in the programmes of the various organizations are presented . . . as involving joint management in the particular fields. Yet clearly it is impossible to conceive of joint management except in the case of activities where there is agreement as to the objectives, the resources to be earmarked for it, and the method of implementation, and where it is known that there is some possibility of arriving at precise results. Such conditions are seldom forthcoming in regard to the whole body of activities presented as joint management activities within the United Nations System. Hence if we want to understand what the World Organization really is, it is essential to compare its activities with the type and level of consensus existing among the members of the international community. It is a mere cliché to say that the task of international organizations is easy in fields where the degree of consensus is high, and difficult and at times impossible in those where the degree of consensus is virtually nil. But this elementary fact is frequently forgotten in the analysis of world problems and the definition of the functions of the World Organization . . .

Thus people think, or pretend to think, that the main function of a world organization is to manage activities which would presuppose, if they were to be carried out properly, a level of consensus that is far from existing among the Member States. This basic and ongoing confusion has to be cleared up. It is simply not possible to manage jointly activities on which there is no consensus. *The normal function of a World Organization is thus essentially to work with extreme tenacity for a better consensus or a different type of consensus in order to enable some progress to be made in the direction of the distant goals laid down in the Charters and Constitutions.*

Management and the search for a consensus

We must keep this simple notion constantly in mind if we are to understand what we are trying to do, often in a very strange way, in the United Nations System . . . the World Organization we possess is actually an ensemble of four very different types of activity.

The first group is the only one really comprising managerial activities, namely the very limited fields in which there is consensus. These could include:

Humanitarian activities, especially those in favour of refugees, managed by
UNRWA in the case of Palestine refugees (management of educational, health
and social welfare or social security services), or by the Office of the High
Commissioner for Refugees in all countries (protection, reception, accommodation, health, assistance).
Statutory activities involving the compilation and distribution of information,
functional cooperation and technical standardization in the fields of transport,
telecommunications, meteorology, statistics, and certain aspects of health . . .
All the other activities of the World Organizations lie within areas where
consensus is at a very low level or even at variance with the tasks entrusted to
the Organization. These are essentially: the search for peace and security;
contributions to development; the organization of a forum for discussion,
research and negotiations concerning specific points (human rights, international
law, etc.).

We are no longer concerned here with 'management'. It is only in connection
with the last point that the Organization recognizes clearly that it is responsible
for negotiations. But the pursuit of the first two objectives — peace and development — is also nothing more than a difficult search for a common elucidation
of problems. In all three cases, analysis of the methods and structures used to
attain the objectives is the key to understanding why and how a basic revision
of the concepts on which the World Organization is founded is imperative.

The pursuit of the principal objectives

Examination of the three main objectives does not always lead to the same
conclusions. Each problem is *sui generis*, and the strategies adopted for resolving them have their own peculiarities. But in all three cases, the outworn and
obsolete nature of the institutions and their failure to adapt to the problems of
the modern world are not difficult to demonstrate . . . [The question of collective security and the search for peace is treated elsewhere in this volume: eds.]

Action in favour of development

The type of consensus that exists in the world in regard to development is more
complex in its definition than that in regard to security. As we all know, ideas
concerning development strategies are extremely diverse and are still in the
throes of confrontation and evolution . . . The very concept of development is
understood differently according to whether we look at it from the point of view
of general application of the Western model or concentrate on preserving and
enriching existing cultures.

But this great methodological debate which occupies the centre of the stage
must not conceal the political and sociological framework in which it takes place
and which determines the essence of the existing type of consensus. The two
basic elements are first of all the principle that each country is responsible for
its development, and second the political phenomenon of zones of influence.
These two phenomena, different and seemingly contradictory, complement each

other to create a situation which is hardly propitious for speeding up the development of the poorer parts of the world . . .

Zones of influence and fragmentation of bilateral aid

This situation in no way affects the maintenance of development of the zones of influence which have replaced the colonial empires, even though they do not· cover exactly the same geographical area . . . Aid systems tend first of all to create political dependence relationships between donor and recipient. Whether they consist of gifts in cash or in kind (supply of weapons, wheat, or payment of salaries of teachers or experts), low-interest loans or bank credits at market rates, aid is first and foremost a means of exerting influence . . . But these methods also have serious drawbacks from the economic point of view. Fragmentation and competition between bilateral aid schemes . . . create for the beneficiary countries difficult problems of coordinating the whole mass of external aid and project-by-project negotiations. The 'tied' nature of this aid brings with it unfavourable economic conditions because of the requirement that supplies or manpower must be purchased in the donor countries.

Even for the poorest countries — for example the twenty-five least developed countries identified by the United Nations — it has never been suggested that a coherent collective system of long-term aid should be set up which would enable them to draw up long-term plans and policies. The machinery of the Lomé Agreements between EEC and the ACP countries provides the only example of a trend in the direction of collective and institutional negotiation of aid . . .

Sectoral approach and doctrinal differences

In the face of such a situation, it might be thought that the role of the United Nations and its System should have concentrated first and foremost on problems of coordination. But what has happened is exactly the opposite: the United Nations System has developed a sectoral approach which has aggravated the fragmentation of aid and has added to the existing complexity. By so acting that . . . between fifteen and thirty additional bodies take a hand in the beneficiary countries, it has in almost every instance complicated the task of the developing countries instead of simplifying it.

Moreover this fragmentation of activities is not offset by any real coordination either at the intellectual level or at the methodological and institutional level. Each organization has not only its methods but also its theory on development and on the goals which should be pursued by the recipient countries. UNDP is the only exception . . .

Each agency tries to justify the importance of its sector, without any of these approaches forming part of an overall economic and financial analysis or suggesting criteria for determining priorities. Thus the industrialization goals of UNIDO, that of increasing agricultural production in FAO, the food strategies of the World Food Council or the World Food Programme, the ILO programmes on employment or the development of social security, and UNESCO's plans for the development of education, are not integrated into a coherent system of analysis.

The credibility of 'advice by remote control'

Differences in doctrinal approach, which have disastrous effects in regard to the selection of field projects, are perhaps even more sensitive at the level of 'headquarters activities'. They involve mostly studies and researches culminating in the drafting of documents, reports or publications. They deal sector by sector with the identification of problems, the definition of principles and criteria, the compilation and distribution of information, etc., and they are often difficult to separate from activities supporting field projects or discussions and negotiations. They represent the most important part of the work of the secretariats, and most of them are intended for intergovernmental or expert committees. Their 'outputs' are the background material for 'programmes' described in programme budgets or medium-term plans, where such exist . . .

What this actually means is that in offices situated in New York, Geneva, Vienna, Paris, Rome or certain other great capitals, two or three professional-level workers (whose levels of qualifications and competence are as a rule those described [above] . . . will draw up for each of these budget lines reports which will be distributed to an intergovernmental body, and in exceptional circumstances to a list of correspondents in the national public services concerned. Or else it means that they will organize sporadically one or two training courses for a few dozen individuals. In a few cases, these activities still help to prepare the ground for a large conference for which bulky documentation will be produced and which will be attended by representatives of national services.

In the absence of a precise system of evaluation, it is impossible to determine whether these thousands of sectoral activities of every kind exert any real influence on the harmonization of rules, the definition of policies of the Member States. The threshold of credibility of these undertakings is only crossed where certain conditions prevail, including the following: the degree of real and recognized competence of the administrative units in charge of the programmes; the sales figures for publications; the fact that the information distributed reaches the competent national circles responsible; the direct participation of the latter in intergovernmental operations; and the real interest which the Member States have in the problems under consideration. The degree of effectiveness depends, of course, also on the nature of the problems dealt with: advice on matters of social policy, recognition of the rights of workers or women, agrarian reform or population policy, has less chance of being genuinely taken into consideration than that relating to technical norms in forestry. In this connection, one of the most important factors is the functioning of the intergovernmental machinery itself. When, for example, in this or that Commission where experts representing the technical ministries should be sitting there are in actual fact members of delegations in New York or Geneva, obviously the impact on national policies will tend to decline, however vigorously the resolutions adopted have been formulated.

But as we have seen . . . there is no coordination here. This situation is all the more paradoxical in that while at the time when the specialized agencies were set up, they had as their essential goal the confrontation of methods, harmonization of viewpoints and definition of common standards in a given sector, the role given nowadays to this type of international cooperation has been gradually whittled down in favour of technical cooperation activities with the developing countries. It can be estimated that the bulk of the resources of the System, nearly 70 per cent, are today devoted to development.

The need to change the structures of the System

In short, it is the sectoralized, decentralized and fragmented structures of the System that are the reason for its failure to adapt to the solution of the development problems. The reason why in 1945 the United Nations System was given this sectoral structure was because it was felt at the time that problems of international cooperation would be solved better between technicians specializing in particular fields than by diplomats with instructions to deal with political problems. The idea was not a bad one, but it reflected a situation different from that of today. The question at the time was to achieve cooperation among about fifty Member States, some of them in charge of great colonial empires and intending themselves to deal with the problems of development and those empires. Today the problem is that of the development of more than 120 independent countries, representing three-quarters of the world's population, and of efforts to help them to overcome their historical handicap and close the gap between them and the countries of the North.

Development is an integrated problem. It means helping to solve in each country problems which often differ according to their size, their nature or their character, but which all have the following points in common:

They are tangible questions requiring a profound knowledge of local, national or regional situations and an interdisciplinary analysis of all their aspects.
They come up against the problem of inadequate resources of every kind and a multiplicity of needs and difficulties.
The countries concerned need a World Organization capable of facilitating syntheses, organizing coordination, helping to find long-term financial arrangements, and granting many-sided aid to solve the most urgent problems. What the United Nations System offers them is a series of divergent and contradictory recommendations, some thirty bodies whose action has to be coordinated with that of some twenty sources of bilateral aid, but it does not help them to solve their medium and long-term financial problems. Thus it seems evident that what we are obliged willy-nilly to reconsider today is the very structure of the United Nations System.

The world forum

The problems relating to the 'world forum' are different in nature from those of peace and development . . . The problem now is to examine whether the framework in which the Organization endeavours to broaden or to modify the nature of world consensus is indeed the right one . . . [The reply is] inevitably negative; the machinery of negotiation is not easily identifiable and separable from the rest of the activities under the various sectoral programmes and does not constitute a coherent system. The results achieved relate only to a few limited fields and do not represent solid progress in the direction of changing world consensus. This situation has its political reasons, which are well known, but they do not explain everything. Actually, it is the structure of negotiations offered by the World Organization that is ill adapted to solving the problems of the modern world.

No doubt it should be pointed out that any multilateral negotiations, and *a fortiori* negotiations at world level, have their own peculiarities and inherent constraints, and that in particular:

They almost inevitably put a premium on the ideological approach at the expense of a more technological approach. Since one of the functions of the 'world forum' is to enable the various 'world concepts' to confront each other and perhaps to begin to find common ground, this is not surprising. But the importance of this factor sometimes leads astray not only the lay observer but the negotiators themselves.

They call for considerable preliminary efforts to identify the problems which are susceptible to negotiation before any negotiations can begin. This work of identification is complex, and it comes up against difficulties of a cultural, technical, ideological and semantic kind; it can often only be concluded when a preliminary agreement is beginning to take shape on a given concept; so that it is no longer surprising that it implies attempt after attempt at formulation, often clumsily done, and that it is a source of endless talk.

Negotiation among 160 parties presents specific technical difficulties other than those of the size of the meeting chamber or the organization of simultaneous interpretation. It involves the definition of interest groups whose composition and dimensions vary according to the subject dealt with, and the method of representation of these groups . . .

Outline of what a 'world political space' could mean

The difficulties of devising a common view of world problems are bound up with those of establishing a 'world political space'. Yet the World Organization today furnishes the outline of a global system. The fact that the United Nations and its System has virtually attained universality tends to be underestimated nowadays precisely because this universality is being achieved at a time when the World Organization no longer deals with important problems . . . If we add to this achievement [of universality] . . . all the other positive achievements, even though entirely inadequate, already mentioned in the realms of peace, development or the institution of a forum for negotiation, we find ourselves faced with a political phenomenon which in the final analysis is more important than the sum of its constituent parts.

Universality; the existence of a political margin of action for the Organization in the realm of peace; the construction of an institutional and legal framework by means of decolonization and the development of international law; the exercise of moral constraint in the field of human rights; the institution of a debate taking into account, through the North–South dialogue, the interests of the poorer countries; the advent of new enlightenment in regard to certain important world problems, etc., constitute a genuine outline of a 'world political space'.

The debate which the framework thus constituted makes possible between the representation of the main political views of the world no doubt has its short-comings — ideological exaggeration, hypocrisy and inadequate information — and there is no question that it causes frustration. But these shortcomings are not more serious than those often found in political debates within democracies, within national political spaces which are nevertheless better structured . . .

The type of World Organization we possess today

The type of world organization we possess today can be defined as follows: it is an institution:

whose general goals — peace, development, human rights, search for a more satisfactory level of world consensus — fit in well with the notion one has of the mission of an organization of this type and are incidentally mobilizing public opinion;

whose overall achievements are far less negligible than is generally supposed, in that they have succeeded in building up the beginnings of a 'world political space' and outlining some elements of a 'world problématique';

whose structures and means of taking action are nevertheless ill adapted to the pursuit of the main goals, since they are conceived on the basis of three fallacies, which might be stated as follows:

Fallacy No. 1: that the 'maintenance of peace' can be brought about in the modern world through an institution;

Fallacy No. 2: that the development of the poorer zones in the world can be brought about by a sectoral and therefore non-integrated approach;

Fallacy No. 3: that negotiations to improve or alter world consensus can be conducted without prior definition of negotiation structures accepted by all the participants.

Thus reflections focusing on reform of the World Organization imply a challenge to the basic notions on which the present institution is founded and their replacement by notions more in keeping with reality.

The focus of reflections with a view to reform

The technical conditions that apply

If we accept the hypothesis that the conditions are now met for developing the notion of reform, it is all the more important to stress the difficulty of the under-taking. It is not simply a matter of covering over a few superficial defects. An inadequate analysis of the problem, even if it mustered a consensus, could well lead to failure. The experience gained some ten years ago through the work on 'restructuring' demonstrated clearly that the initiation and organization of a process of reflection on possible reform were tough technical problems which if poorly handled led to serious failure. Hence the technical difficulties arising can only be overcome if certain conditions are fulfilled.

The first of these is undoubtedly the recognition of the need to raise the issue of the very basic concepts and structures of the present System as a whole if we are to devise others and to construct a World Organization of an entirely new type. This first condition implies a second, namely that the process of reflection and comparative analysis will inevitably be a lengthy one. Assuming the reform of the World Organization is at least as important and as complex as that of the law of the sea, for example, it would not seem unreasonable to reckon that research, discussion and negotiation on this subject could take ten years. It would also make it easier to accept:

that a thorough-going preparatory effort, calculated to stimulate contributions from those best qualified to make them, must be organized;
that the task of devising machinery for a conspectus of analyses and the gradual achievement of a solution deserves special attention.

On the supposition that these conditions are met, I propose to devote this final section to the topics for reflection which I feel must be tackled. The first should be discussion of the very possibility of changing the type of world consensus on the basic concepts underlying the World Organization. This means examining not only the philosophical conflicts, but most of all the possible common ground. The second topic for reflection has to do with the structures which can be envisaged for seeking the main goal, which means exploring the possibility of innovation in a sphere which hitherto has remained extremely traditional and stereotyped. The third topic is that of the type of World Organization to which all these reflections could lead, implying the need to define both guidelines to provide a picture of what a third-generation World Organization might be and the transitional measures it is absolutely essential to envisage between what exists today and the Organization of tomorrow . . .

The search for common ground

. . . The contribution which the present World Organization has made has up to the present remained very slight, because of shortcomings which are both theoretical and structural. The fact that the Organization built up on the basis of already outmoded ideas of 'peace through law', 'general and complete disarmament' and sectoral development has not changed its views or its methods largely explains, as we have seen, the frustration of public opinion throughout the world in respect of it. Thus an effort to renew the basic concepts is particularly urgent in the direction of the search for common ground . . .
    The problem is essentially:

to define how it is possible to replace the direct search for peace, [which is] doomed to failure, . . . by indirect machinery for the gradual construction of peace, for example . . . through the development at world level of genuine joint action or joint ventures, however modest in scope, in which the commitment of Governments might demonstrate their will to peace much more surely to public opinion than speeches advocating disarmament;
systematically to explore ways and means of seeking complementarity between

national economic strategies, not merely between Western industrialized countries but between East and West or between North and South;
to see how it might be possible to crystallize institutionally, over and above
national sovereignties, the notion of human solidarity in the face of destitution,
and the right to food, education, social security and development;
to translate into more precise concepts the notion of an 'economic United
Nations' as a complement to the present notion of a 'political United Nations',
and to explore in greater depth the way in which public opinion, which has
grown used to the idea of a world institution entrusted with 'maintaining peace',
might adopt in a more realistic way the notion of a world organization which
ought to be more than anything else a centre for negotiations designed to identify
and develop zones of convergence.

Obviously this radical search is inseparable from a thorough-going revision of
ideas on the possible structures of the future World Organization.

The state of the art in regard to a World Organization

The definition of the structures of a World Organization in keeping with the
needs of the contemporary world raises a technical problem . . .

In 1945, the stock formula [of previous experiments such as the League of
Nations] continued to be used (Secretariat, Council, Assembly), complicated
somewhat in the light of five main considerations:

A desire for 'realism', reflected in the fact that the main responsibility for peace
and security was entrusted to the greatest and most powerful States through the
institution of the Security Council and the right of veto;
A 'sectoral functionalist' philosophy which consisted in deliberately and
systematically organizing cooperation at world level among specialists, sector
by sector — whence the integration in the System of the specialized agencies
which already existed and the creation of new agencies to cover the whole range
of national ministries (education, health, agriculture, etc.);
The concern in the economic and financial field to prevent a repetition of the
phenomena which had led to the Great Depression of the 1930s, and hence an
effort to organize world free trade, control of exchange fluctuations and credit
problems by setting up 'financial' institutions such as IMF, the World Bank and
GATT;
An attempt to define a whole series of common values for mankind as a whole,
rounded off with efforts to bring about economic and social cooperation;
Finally, the concern to maintain the cost of this series of organizations at a very
modest level . . .

The new techniques

Thus we find ourselves today in possession of an Organization which is largely
out of date and which has grown old without taking account of the progress made
over the last forty years in international organization 'technology'. But techniques have evolved. In response to new needs, types of structures have been

devised which are different from those we knew in 1945. It is therefore essential, when the time comes to reflect on a third generation type of World Organization, to give some thought to the present state of the art.

A new approach has come about mainly through the European Communities, which did not adopt the 'Assembly–Executive Board–Secretary-General' structure but a different system which might be referred to as the 'Council–Commission plus launching of joint ventures'. Under this formula, the Council of Ministers makes it possible to convene the incumbent ministers of each Government to discuss the views of each country and to defend their interests, while the Commission, composed of distinguished persons chosen by Governments on the basis of their competence, providing strong guarantees of independence and carrying out their functions in the interests of the organization, has the responsibility for seeking out the Community view, studying compromise solutions, making recommendations and executing the budget. Furthermore, either within the Community system (cf. the Common Agricultural Policy, European Development Fund) or outside it (CERN, Ariane Espace, Airbus Industry, Esprit, Eureka, etc.), joint ventures common to all the States' members of the Community or only to a few of them, and at times in association with non-member States, are launched more and more frequently, strengthening the Community's cohesion in respect of precise objectives.

Another international cooperation formula, much more flexible but embracing a larger geographical area, is that of the Western 'Summits' — a council without a permanent secretariat but holding regular meetings — which as we know was broadened on one occasion, that of the Cancun Summit Meeting, to include representation of the developing countries, thus covering both West and South.

There is no doubt that in the case of the European Communities in particular the adopted structures function within a framework very different from that of the World Organization. There can be no question of transposing institutions conceived for a regional context with the aim of integrating the economies of countries which have reached a very similar level of development — and incidentally few in number — into a world context where conditions are very different. But there is no reason why one should not be able to take over certain technical formulas or why, in examining the problems to be solved and the goals to be sought, such attempts at transposition should not help to throw light on the specific technical problems of the World Organization and find appropriate structural solutions for them.

Any reflection on the type of structure which can be envisaged must inevitably bear in mind the goals to be sought by a World Organization by the end of the twentieth century or the beginning of the twenty-first century . . .

'Regional development agencies or enterprises'

Development is the area in which the reconversion of the present structures should be most systematic and most thorough-going. I think I have demonstrated sufficiently clearly in the above pages that:

the sectoral approach is altogether inappropriate for a problem which calls for an integrated approach and organic cooperation by all the parties concerned;

any action in respect of development at world level means ignoring regional or national peculiarities and makes for a superficial view of the problem, generalities and ultimately to mere talk.

This being so, the only possible structural response lies in the organization of integrated systems of cooperation at regional level.

The alternative to the present decentralization of the System is not to be found in a type of centralization which would produce a bureaucractic monster and would in no way represent a response to the present shortcomings. What must be got rid of is the approach to the problem of development at world level and 'remote control' over concrete problems arising in the poorer parts of the earth by staff members living in the great capitals of the developed world. What is needed is a comprehensive view and a precise programme on a reasonable geographic scale, and the handling of problems must be done on the spot, in close collaboration with the peoples concerned. This is why the solution can only be regional or subregional and integrated, which means that all those having to do with development must be sent 'into the field'; in other words, the head-quarters of the bodies concerned must be located in the regional or subregional capitals, and all the organizations decentralized today by sectors (whether situated at headquarters or in the regions) must be centralized and transferred to each region, as part of a single, interdisciplinary development agency or enterprise responsible at once for health, agriculture, industry, education, etc. . . .

At the level of the United Nations System, this can only mean a total reconversion of all the operational structures, that is the structures of all the main programmes such as UNDP, WFP, UNFPA, UNICEF, etc., and most of the technical cooperation services of the main agencies such as the regional economic commissions of the United Nations (with the exception of the Economic Commission for Europe) and the regional services of the other main agencies, with a view to constituting, by region or subregion, 'regional development agencies or enterprises'.

The creation of 'regional development agencies or enterprises' should amount to a concentration of the means available on clearly identified problems: concentration of finances, manpower, fusion and restructuring of existing organs wherever possible. The structures to be envisaged to make this large-scale reconversion possible cannot be looked at in a stereotyped way; but while bearing in mind the need for adapting them to specific situations, it can also be argued that in a general way they should include an organ representing the governments of the countries of the region, another body on which outside countries contributing to the development of the region would be represented, and finally a joint council or commission to carry out the plan negotiated and adopted.

The intergovernmental regional organizations

A complete reconversion at regional level of all the development activities of the United Nations System could also provide an opportunity for examining region by region the existing 'intergovernmental regional organizations'. . .

Finally, the World Bank and its two affiliates — the International Finance Corporation and the International Development Association — should be associated with reflections on the problem and be able to consider whether they themselves could be concerned by reforms of this type. The projects launched by these three great organizations are different in kind and in size from those referred to in the present report. But any critical reflections on the need for a programme approach affects them too. Their participation in the regional development agencies or enterprises could have a decisive impact and help to facilitate joint action with other aid systems, multilateral (e.g. the European Development Fund) or bilateral.

In any event, the development aspect of reform of the United Nations System should be situated at regional level. It calls for in-depth studies on diagnosis; on structures; on budgets; on the methods most likely to bring about over the long term the financing of development of the countries of the region (or subregion); on public and private types of investment which should be encouraged as a priority measure; on formulas for association between aid donor countries and countries of the region concerned; and on many other administrative and technical problems . . . development at regional level can only be envisaged in close relationship with that of the negotiation system at world level.

The structures for identifying problems and for negotiation: the problem of representation

. . . It will take time to come to realize fully that the establishment of a better system of negotiations at world level is an indispensable prerequisite to the solution of many world problems. But the moment we begin to raise the question, it would be worthwhile exploring the theoretical solutions that might be found. The discussion of a 'blueprint' might speed up reflection. A clear-cut theoretical definition is all the more indispensable in that the problem is in actual fact already stated, but badly stated. More and more, the industrialized countries are beginning to raise the question of the decision-making powers within the international organizations. Thus the idea that the absolute sovereignty of states requires that each one, whatever its importance, shall have one vote is countered by the notion of weighting the votes on the basis of various criteria such as economic power or population . . . These signs are important in so far as they indicate an awakening of one basic question. But this discussion has nothing to do with the problem which ought really to be asked, namely that of the establishment of a visible system of negotiations at world level.

The present discussions are the outcome of the erroneous notion that a World Organization is, can be or should be an organ where Member States take decisions in common. Thus the discussion goes on as to how a decision-making organ should function, for example, in voting on budgets or adopting changes in programmes. In the framework of such reasoning, the problem of weighted voting has some significance. But if the question is to define a negotiating body, the problem arises in a different way. We then have to determine how 160 countries could be really represented by twenty persons, or at most twenty-four, certainly not more, each participant representing either one large country or a group of countries sufficiently coherent and important to be taken seriously by the rest.

If the question is put in this way, it is then no paradox to say that it no longer arises for the industrialized countries, but for the developing countries. The problem is indeed the following:

that the majority enjoyed in the United Nations by the countries of the Group of 77 has no real importance inasmuch as it affects only the adoption resolutions which have no practical consequences;
that, on the contrary, access to a table for discussion and negotiation where their problems would be taken into account and where they could influence really important decisions affecting their economies and their future has up to the present been denied them.

The developing countries have never yet stated the problem in those terms. On the contrary, they have tried to increase the number of members of all the United Nations bodies so as to increase the opportunities for direct representation by each individual country and to obtain a majority. This inflationary movement has thus become propagated among all the executive boards of organizations of programmes and in a great many subsidiary organs . . . While it is easy to understand the reasons for the pressure thus exerted, the results are well known: the forums where it would have been possible to negotiate on important problems have been drained of all content, the industrialized countries refusing to use them to deal with any question likely to have any follow-up.

In the context of reform, the consideration of technical problems becomes really important. 'Technology' can indeed play an essential role by helping to bring about a solution taking into account all the elements of a complex problem: the number of parties involved; their inequality in importance and power; their regional coherence or lack of coherence in the economic or ideological field; methods of identifying the problems to be studied and negotiated; the possible structures of intergovernmental organs; the structure of secretariats; the types of relationship between national and administrations and the 'world forum'. The questions to be examined are:

the system for identifying problems that can be negotiated;
the structure of political negotiating bodies;
the structure of the delegations of Member States.

An 'economic United Nations'

Sectoralization and fragmentation, inimical as they are to the integrated approach to development, today prevent the United Nations and its System from identifying world problems properly. The present forum, exaggeratedly ideological, seldom makes it possible to organize genuine negotiations — the only noteworthy exception being the law of the sea — and only makes for exchanges of views and the convergence of policies in relation to questions which do not have a direct bearing on fundamental issues — the only noteworthy exception being population . . .

The new World Organization would have to be essentially what we shall call, in the interests of simplicity, a genuine 'economic United Nations', i.e. a World

Organization in which purely political problems would certainly not be ruled out
but where economic problems would take first place.

The secretariat needed should have a structure almost the exact opposite of
those we have today: instead of sectoral secretariats dispersed over the United
Nations and the main agencies, what would be needed would be:

an interdisciplinary central secretariat with a large team of economists,
sociologists and specialists in various disciplines, with very high qualification;
smaller sectoral secretariats at the level of each of the agencies.

The central secretariat would be equipped to deal with economic information
at world level and to draw up diagnoses (possibly with arguments pro and con)
on national economic strategies; it should possess all the most up-to-date ways
and means of defining future trends; and it should study specific problems
thoroughly. Its statutes should enable it to work in a critical spirit and with
acknowledged independence. It should be specified that the studies it produced
would not hide differences in views or analyses, so that the negotiators would
be given a clear picture of the problems they would be faced with. The sectoral
secretariat in the agencies would work in direct contact with the central
secretariat.

The 'Council–Commission' formula transposed to world level — the 'Economic Security Council'

In any event, the definition of the structure of secretariats is inseparable from
the structure of the main intergovernmental organ. Thus a transposition to world
level, *mutatis mutandis*, of the 'Council–Commission' structure referred to . . .
above could usefully supply inspiration for the reformer. The combination of a
negotiating table where Governments were represented and a group of independent persons chosen by the international community for their competence would
be highly appropriate for the proper functioning of a world forum. This would
mean that sitting at the negotiating table as such (Council) would be the competent ministers according to the problems to be dealt with, and the secretariat
would be directed by a group of independent personalities . . .

The number of members an international negotiating body could have in order
to function properly would obviously have to be as small as possible if the more
important Member States were to agree to participate. The data concerning the
problem of representation in a Council or Commission of this type can be
outlined as follows:

There are ten countries whose gross national product (GNP) is more than 2.5
per cent of the gross world product. These ten countries together represent 72
per cent of this gross world product.
There are seven countries whose population is more than 100 million inhabitants
(and the seven of them together represent not much less than half the world
population). Two of them have a gross national product under 2.5 per cent of
the gross world product.

If we combine these two criteria, we get a list of twelve countries. If we reduce the GNP to 0.8 per cent of the gross world product, we have to add ten countries to the original list, and if we reduce the population criterion to 80 million inhabitants, four countries will be added to the previous list. Combining the criteria at this second level, we obtain twenty-six countries. Of the 159 countries Members of the United Nations, 133 countries do not meet either of these two criteria, although this does not prevent a large number of them from playing an important part on the world scene.

Bearing in mind the population figures and the GNP levels of the countries of various regions in the world not included in the list of twelve countries resulting from the application of the first two criteria, it can be envisaged that they ought to be able to be represented by the allotment of about eleven additional places at the negotiating table, e.g. two for Latin America, one for the Caribbean, one for the Arab countries, two for Africa south of the Sahara, one for Eastern Europe, two for South East Asia, one for Oceania, and one for the small and medium Western countries. This would give a figure of twenty-three. If we envisaged a larger body and wished to include the fourteen countries resulting from the application of less rigorous criteria, we would get a figure of thirty-seven.

These calculations give a clearer picture of the problem of the number of members possible for the two types of body to be set up. The main question in regard to the intergovernmental organ proper (Council) is to maintain the number of its members with the utmost rigour. It might be called 'Economic Security Council' so as to endow it with at least as much prestige as the Security Council. On the other hand, with regard to the independent persons who would be placed in charge of the various branches of the secretariat and would deliberate together, greater flexibility might possibly be achieved by setting up either two or even three Commissions (e.g. one for short-term, one for long-term measures, and possibly one for launching joint ventures), or specialist working groups to deal with specific problems.

Finally, if an 'economic United Nations' of this type were to be set up, the make-up of the delegations of Member States to it would have to include, side-by-side with a political representative of ambassador status, an economist of similar status representing the Ministry of Finance and Economic Affairs of each country. A direct link between the new World Organization and the national economic and financial services would in fact seem to be an essential precondition of its credibility.

Transition towards a third-generation World Organization

Reform implies setting up new institutions but also transforming and suppressing. The focus of reform of the World Organization will only be clear if it includes a means of transition between what exists today and what we would like to see. More precisely, the problem is to determine what we propose to keep, what should be transformed, what should be suppressed, and to establish a transformation plan complete with deadlines and details relating to transfers of resources and personnel. It is only when a reform plan has reached this degree of precision that there will be any change or chance of overcoming the resistance that would inevitably be applied by all those who have an interest in preserving the status quo. [The reform plan is then discussed: eds.]

Producing a 'transition plan' is without doubt the most complex exercise and the one most subject to controversy, since the power of resistance of the existing institutions is a well-known phenomenon. The general slant of the transformation required should therefore be clearly established. The approach proposed in this report would mean that there would be no attempt to modify the sector concerned with the direct search for peace, but there would be a profound transformation of the entire concept of operational aid and hence of its structures, and a wholesale reorganization of the system of identification of world problems and negotiations. The most important transformations to be studied would therefore be:

transfer of the resources, duties and staff of the present operational aid structures — in other words of all programmes such as UNDP, UNFPA, UNICEF, etc. and most of the technical cooperation services of the main agencies — to the 'regional development agencies'. This is the most substantial reconversion operation, but it would make it possible to endow the new regional development agencies from the outset with substantial resources, since the reconversion would apply to nearly three quarters of the activities of the United Nations System, or about $4 billion a year;

reorganization of the secretariats of the United Nations and the larger agencies (UNESCO, FAO, ILO, WHO) so as to concentrate and develop the economic and interdisciplinary services in the United Nations and to organize the relations of the central service with the sectoral secretariats;

reorganization of the intergovernmental machinery, the most important questions to be resolved here being the decisions to be taken in regard to the Economic and Social Council, UNCTAD and the intergovernmental organs of the main agencies, if an economic negotiation table of the type advanced . . . above were to be established;

reorganization of the interagency machinery, since the present mechanisms of ACC, which deals only with administrative problems, would no longer make sense in the framework of the reform envisaged here;

finally, reorganization of the relations with the non-governmental organizations and the committees and commissions which support the various organizations.

The measures listed above would in no way affect either the General Assembly or the Secretary-General or the machinery of the Security Council of the smaller functional agencies of the System. They would leave all the main agencies in being, but with a very considerable reduction of their activities and staff numbers, thus taking them back as it were to their original status as centres for reflection and coordination . . .

Conclusions

This report is not an admission of defeat. The author hopes he has shown that the United Nations and its System have succeeded, by fashioning for the first time in history the beginnings of a 'world political space' in demonstrating that a World Organization was indispensable. It is no contradiction to state in the same breath that the institution as it is today must be modernized, and indeed radically reformed, so as to make it more responsive to the hopes which a large proportion of the peoples of the United Nations continue to place in it.

The thesis propounded here can be summed up as follows:

1. A reform of the United Nations and its System is urgent, and in spite of deep-seated prejudice existing on the subject, it is feasible to envisage this seriously.

2. The time has come to begin to reflect in a serious and ambitious way on the definition of a third-generation World Organization. The introduction of reforms will be a lengthy process and will call for difficult searchings and negotiations.

3. The structures of the present System rest on three fallacious notions, false from the outset or gradually distorted — to the effect that the 'maintenance of peace' can be achieved through an institution, that the development of the poor countries can be achieved through a sectoral approach, and that negotiations among 159 States are possible without a prior definition of agreed negotiation structures.

4. In the present political context it is unrealistic to believe that sovereign states can deal in common with activities outside the limited sphere where a broad consensus exists. The basic role of a World Organization can only be the determined search for a better or a different type of consensus which will lead towards the far-off ideals set forth in the Charter.

5. In the present political context, reform cannot be focused on modifying the structures for the maintenance of peace or more generally the structures of a political United Nations. The successes achieved using an instrument ill suited for the purpose already constitute a paradox. We must continue, as the Secretary-General did in a recent report, to encourage the Member States to make the most of it. But it is impossible today to propose other structures which would be an improvement on the Security Council.

6. On the contrary, the reform should focus on the transformation of the structures that support development and on the institution of a genuine world economic forum. The aim would be to build up an 'economic United Nations' side by side with the political United Nations.

7. On one front, the reform should be a total recasting at System level of all structures concerned with development in order to constitute regional or subregional development agencies or enterprises. It might be hoped that the drive resulting from so radical a transformation of this part of the System would lead to a re-examination of the other regional or subregional intergovernmental structures. It would obviously be desirable for the World Bank to consider the possibility of taking a hand in the thinking and in the reform, and for joint efforts to be developed in this connection between the other aid systems, multilateral or bilateral.

8. On the other front, the reform should be to set up a genuine world forum to deal essentially with economic problems. The developing countries should not continue to be left out of the discussion at the negotiation tables where economic

and financial problems are concretely discussed. This situation does harm to the international community as a whole. Hence we must give some thought to the replacement of the present dual forum: Economic and Social Council UNCTAD, by a more restricted Council of the type envisaged in the original Charter, which set at eighteen the membership of the Economic and Social Council . . .

The seriousness and the urgency of the problems justify focusing the search in directions little explored up to now. A proposal to devise and install entirely new structures at least in the development area and in that of the system of negotiation at world level may strike some people as rash or utopian and others as mealy-mouthed. The author has been anxious here to confine himself to the universal United Nations Systems, without including the Bretton Woods organizations. It is obvious, however, that the construction of an economic United Nations is not conceivable without them, and it is desirable that the thinking on the subject should be broadened to include them.

The search should be able to be carried on and developed both inside and outside the System. The extraordinary difficulty of such an undertaking must not be underestimated. A certain political climate is a *sine qua non* before even a start can be made. But the political environment of a problem is conditioned by the way in which the problem is conceived. The deep-seated longing for peace which led to the creation of the United Nations has not abated today; but it is now possible to explore other paths than those followed forty years ago.

Note

1. The term 'United Nations System' generally has two different meanings: the first designating all the organizations, including the 'financial' organizations represented in the Administrative Committee on Coordination (ACC), which brings together the heads of the agencies under the chairmanship of the Secretary-General of the United Nations; the second designating only the non-financial organizations. In actual fact the System in the broad sense includes three types of global or near-global organizations, with very different functions and types of activities, namely:

(a) The organizations with overall competence, the United Nations itself and some major agencies, which, although theoretically in charge of a particular economic or social sector, have in fact a tendency to deal with all aspects of economic and social problems. It is possible to include in this group:

— the United Nations, which alone constitutes a complex system including the United Nations Industrial Development Organization (UNIDO, now being turned into a specialized agency), the United Nations Conference on Trade and Development (UNCTAD), the major operational and humanitarian Programmes like the United Nations Development Programme (UNDP), the United Nations Childrens Fund (UNICEF), the Office of the United Nations High Commissioner for Refugees (UNHCR), the United Nations Relief and Works Agency for Palestine Refugees (UNRWA), the World Food Programme (WFP), and some thirty juridically

independent funds, institutes, centres or councils;
— the United Nations Educational, Scientific and Cultural Organization (UNESCO), the Food and Agriculture Organization of the United Nations (FAO), the International Labour Organization (ILO), the World Health Organization (WHO).

(b) The 'functional' or 'technical' organizations, intended essentially to establish rules and ensure cooperation among the national services in the fields of common interest such as postal services, telecommunications or transport. In this category are the Universal Postal Union (UPU), the International Telecommunication Union (ITU), the International Maritime Organization (IMO), the World Meteorological Organization (WMO), the World Intellectual Property Organization (WIPO) and the International Atomic Energy Agency (IAEA). With few exceptions, all countries, including the USSR and the socialist countries, are members of these organizations.
(c) The 'financial' organizations, also called the Bretton Woods Organizations (indicating the place of the negotiations which led to the establishment of most of them). The USSR is not a member. They use a weighted voting system, do not accept the common rules adopted by all the other agencies for staff management and salaries, and their object is essentially to provide a framework for monetary and trade relations, and also for granting development loans. They are the International Monetary Fund (IMF), the General Agreement on Tariffs and Trade (GATT), the International Bank for Reconstruction and Development (IBRD), or World Bank, and its affiliates: the International Development Association (IDA) and the International Finance Corporation (IFC).

Lastly, IFAD, the International Fund for Agricultural Development, established in 1974, has functions comparable to those of the financial organizations.

In this report, the term 'United Nations System' (and sometimes 'World Organization') is used to designate the organizations described in (a) and (b) above.

Recommended reading

Maurice Bertrand, 1986, *Refaire l'ONU*, Geneva, Zoe.
Pierre Gerbet, Victor-Yves Ghebani and A. Mouton, 1973, *Société des Nations et Organisation des Nations Unies*, Paris, Richelieu.
Harold K. Jacobson, 1984, *Networks of Interdependence*, New York, Alfred Knopf.
Fred Lister, 1984, *Decision Making Strategies for International Organizations*, Denver, University of Denver.
Edgard Pisani, 1977, *La Main et l'Outil*, Paris, Robert Laffont.
Douglas Williams, 1987, *The Specialised Agencies and the United Nations*, London, Hurst.

13 Reforming the system: getting the money to talk

Paul Taylor

In this chapter two major developments concerning the reform of the United Nations system are brought together and their interrelationships explored. On the one hand is the process of attempting to reform the organisation from within, an effort which has been punctuated by a number of incisive, and often brilliant, reports, such as the Jackson Report of 1969, the Report of the Secretary-General's Experts in 1975, and more recently, 1985, the Bertrand Report.[1] This internal reform process also included a number of ambitious, but largely ineffective responses from the General Assembly, of which the most significant was resolution 32/197 of 1977.[2] This was the main legal basis of the reform process in subsequent years. There have certainly been some changes as a result of the expenditure of all this energy, such as the creation of the 'over-seer' post under the Secretary-General of a Director General for Development and International Economic Cooperation, but the net impact upon the system before 1986–7 was negligible.[3]

On the other hand there were attempts by the governments of the states which contributed most to the finances of the United Nations system to exert their authority, and, conversely, to resist the attempts by the minor and negligible contributors to use their voting strength to get their way. This dispute was a manifestation of an older quarrel between those — usually from the developed world — who preferred the bigger states to lead and manage the system, as in the Security Council, and those who believed that international organisation should be representative, and governed according to a version of democratic principle, with each state being equal to every other in having one vote.[4] The latter view was naturally strongly upheld by the newer and, usually, poorer states, which had been created since the 1950s, and led to attempts to expand the role of institutions such as the General Assembly, or UNCTAD, where they had a majority.

In the 1970s and 1980s the United States government, which, according to an agreed formula, contributed 25 per cent of the funds allocated by majority decision in the General Assembly to the United Nations system, expressed increasing dissatisfaction about a situation in which it could be outvoted by coalitions of states which each contributed less than 0.01 per cent. It is worth noting, though, that even this US contribution is less than that which would have resulted from the application of the formula agreed by the General Assembly in 1946, which required that the Committee on Contributions should take into account national income, per capita income, economic dislocations resulting from the war, and the ability of states to obtain foreign currencies. Decisions had been taken, however, to limit the total liability of any one member, in part because it was thought unwise to allow the organisation to become too dependent upon the financial contribution of any one state.

The fifteen contributors between them contributed 84.4 per cent of the resources and, out of 159 members, seventy-eight contributed less than 0.01 per cent.[5] A number of other major contributors, particularly the British, and the Soviet Union, itself a major contributor, also, however, supported efforts to reduce expenditure. The major contributing states' complaints were reinforced by what they saw as gross inefficiency in the use of resources, and by related failings such as politicisation, and even corruption. The first victims of their increasing dissatisfaction were the International Labour Organisation, from which the Americans withdrew in 1978 — to return in 1980 — and later, of course, UNESCO, from which both the Americans and the British withdrew in the early 1980s. The urge to seek a better use of resources was undoubtedly stimulated by the coming to power in both the United States and Britain of right-wing governments with monetarist inclinations, and by an increasing suspicion of international organisation in general, particularly in Reagan's America.[6]

But it must also be admitted that their complaints often had a clear basis in the facts, and that the difficulties of meeting them either within the particular organisation or within the system were formidable. Their only resort appeared increasingly to be either withdrawal, or the holding back of financial contributions.

Students of international organisation, even those who were strongly supportive of its development, had increasingly been brought to admit that the budgetary process, particularly in the central United Nations system, had serious flaws. In 1972 a number of reforms were undertaken which were intended to provide a way of reconciling claims for money put forward by the various 'proposing' or 'policy-creating' organs, such as the General Assembly itself, and its committees, with a longer-term plan for the work of the organisation. A two-year budgetary cycle was introduced which began when the Secretariat, represented, in particular, by the Controller and his office, collected the various claims for money and transferred them to the Fifth Committee of the General Assembly, which in turn forwarded them to the General Assembly itself for final decision.[7] In preparing the budget the Secretary-General would seek the advice, first, of a small and highly praised committee of experts, somewhat analogous with the Public Accounts Committee in Britain, called the Advisory Committee on Administrative and Budgetary Questions (ACABQ), which would give advice on the financial and administrative aspects of the proposals. (The role and status of this Committee is discussed in greater detail below.) In preparing the Budget, the Secretary-General would also seek the advice of the intergovernmental Committee on Programme and Coordination (CPC), which had the task of evaluating the programmes on which the money was to be spent in the light of the longer-term, six-year Medium Term Plan. The CPC was peculiar in that it served and acted as a committee of both the Economic and Social Council (ECOSOC) and the General Assembly. This procedure did not, however, work as intended: writing in 1977–8, Luard concluded that 'what is wholly lacking, and what exists in most national systems, is a central decision-making body, which makes the final overall decisions about the policies and programmes to be implemented'.[8] The reasons for this failure are discussed later.

One of its consequences, however, was that, rightly or wrongly, it was seen as one of the causes of a steady expansion of the United Nations budget; in the political circumstances of the early 1980s, especially in the United States, this made the organisation vulnerable to attack from hostile groups such as the right-wing Heritage Foundation. In the two years 1976–7 the assessed budget was around $800 million, whilst in the biennium 1986–7 it stood at $1.663 billion, an increase of around 100 per cent.[9] Since the early 1950s, the pattern was for the budget to double about every seven years. This sum was that spent through the central system: voluntary funding of the Funds and Programmes, and the budgets of the Specialised Agencies, were additional. The figure should, however, be put into perspective: $1.6 billion was only a little more than the amount spent on the development of one torpedo by the British government in the 1970s and early 1980s, and equalled the gross contribution — before the Rebate — by Britain to the EEC in the mid-1980s. The proportion of the assessed budget payable by the United States was around $200 million.

Despite the relative modesty of these sums, the US Congress approved, in August 1985, an amendment to the Foreign Relations Act instigated by Senator Nancy Kassebaum, which ruled that the United States' share should be reduced to no more than 20 per cent of the assessed budget until the system was reformed: later developments in Congress, in particular the Gramm-Rudman Balanced Budget Act of December 1985, which required the US government to balance its budget by 1991, further reduced Congressional appropriations for international organisation.[10] In May 1987 the sum indicated by Congress for the following financial year was reported as being only around 50 per cent of the assessed sum. Although the central system was the primary target the Specialised Agencies were also being squeezed to varying degrees: the World Health Organisation was owed $19 million by the United States out of a liability of $62 million; the International Labour Organisation was owed $7 million out of an assessed liability of $31 million. The Food and Agricultural Organisation had also been placed in financial difficulties.

The precise strategy behind these varying allocations, which was being pursued by the responsible agency in the United States, an office in the State Department, was hard to fathom. The general goal could, however, be fairly summed up as reform of the system, though this laudable ambition was open to various interpretation from a United States perspective. The specific reform mentioned in the Kassebaum amendment was the introduction of weighted voting, on the model of the controlling bodies of the International Monetary Fund and the World Bank, into the key organs of the United Nations and the other agencies. As the possibility of this being approved by the Security Council and accepted by a two-thirds majority of members, both being required to modify the Charter, was remote, it must be assumed either that Kassebaum and her supporters had little grasp of the practicalities of the issue, or that the demand was deliberately made unrealistic so that a reduction of US funding would be assured, or that there was a 'hidden agenda' of other more easily attainable reforms. The demand for weighted voting was in the latter approach to be seen as part of a strategy for getting the others to make more modest concessions. The balance of the evidence suggests that this came to be seen as the correct approach by the United States administration, whatever the views of Kassebaum and her supporters. Certainly there was no question of United States withdrawal from the United Nations, and even the views of the Heritage Foundation were described by senior bureaucrats as hard-hitting, but not 'off-the-wall', and not in favour of withdrawal.[11]

There was also strong evidence to suggest that the obvious explanation, that the United States simply wanted to pay less, was also incorrect. On a number of occasions the suggestion was put forward both within the United Nations, for instance, in a speech by the Colombian delegate to the General Assembly in 1985, and outside, that it would be a good idea if the maximum assessment for all states were to be reduced to 10 per cent of the budget, and the budgetary burden redistributed among the better-off members. The Secretary-General had also urged a reduction in the maximum assessment to 15 per cent of the total budget. After all, the sums were fairly small. The response of the United States administration to such suggestions was, however, generally one of hostility and embarrassment, a response which was not surprising in view of Reagan's general stance in international relations of attempting to make 'America great again'. The hidden agenda must be interpreted as including a strategy, not for reducing payments, but rather for getting a proportionate, or greater, weight of influence in the system in exchange for the 25 per cent assessment. The United States did not want to contribute less, but did very much want to get the money it contributed to talk more.

But these rather shorter-term US views and intentions about financing the system, which were characteristic of the attitudes of the developed states in the 1980s, should not be divorced from a much longer-term effort to adjust and reform the economic and social arrangements of the United Nations. The American hidden agenda also came to include the goal of contributing to this longer-term reform process, in which a large number of individuals and governments had been involved, although it used the levers which had been created by political and economic circumstances of the time: the budgetary ones. It is indeed probable that the prospects for stimulating *general* reform by using the financial weapon were not fully realised at the time of the Kassebaum amendment. As so often happened the opportunity was created before it was recognised, and was related to purposes which were not quite the same as those which were later stressed. The nature of the general reforms which were being sought by the Americans in 1986–7 will be discussed later. It is necessary, however, to outline first the various stages of the general reform process, as this was an essential part of the context of the later reform efforts.

Three stages in the process may be identified, each associated with the particular primary purpose then sought through reform. In each stage the range of reforms which were sought remained largely the same, but they differed with regard to the purpose which was dominant. The first phase was associated with the goal of adjusting the United Nations to the more effective pursuit of a new purpose which had not been clearly visible at the time that the central system and main agencies had been created, namely, the economic development of the less prosperous newer states. The adjustment of the organisation in order to facilitate the attainment of new goals was to become a persistent theme, associated with the creation of new organisations, especially the Funds and Programmes, and with the holding of Special Conferences, both in the form of *ad hoc* conferences, such as the 1972 Environment Conference in Stockholm and special sessions of the General Assembly, such as the 1974 Sixth Special Session on the New International Economic Order.[12]

But the primary purpose of the reforms sought in the late 1960s was arguably that of facilitating the goal of development, above others, and the outstanding report then, the Jackson Report of 1969, was primarily concerned with that end. Accordingly, although other associated changes were sought, the dominating proposal was for the strengthening of the United Nations Development Programme (UNDP), and for establishing it as the manager and coordinator of the development process through the control of technical assistance programmes. Other organisations, including the agencies, were to have their efforts with regard to developments fitted into schemes decided by the UNDP. The primary purpose of the first phase was, therefore, to adjust to the emergence of a particularly important new goal, though attempts at such adjustment in the light of other new goals were to become a permanent feature of the reform process.

In the 1970s, however, reform was aimed primarily at the more effective pursuit of existing goals in the economic and social areas. In the 1975 Report of the Secretary-General's Group of Experts[13] and in Resolution 32/197 of 1977, the dominating image was of a polycentric system which lacked effective central direction, and rational planning. Now there was need for a central 'brain', a more unified research and initiation process, more focus and better-adjusted programmes, and improved monitoring of operations. Hence there were lengthy proposals about reforming the Economic and Social Council, for ensuring that conferences and meetings were better managed, and for adjusting the Secretariat's arrangements to promote a greater efficiency. As has already been mentioned, the setting up of a new post of Director General for Development and International Economic Cooperation was one consequence of this effort; the Secretariat was also enjoined to monitor operations more closely, and there were various rearrangements, such as the introduction of facilities for generating the Cross Operational Programme Analyses (COPAS). In effect, however, though there had been considerable success in identifying problems, the reform effort led to few real achievements, partly because of the resistance of bureaucrats, and partly because of the failure of governments, which had achieved a reasonable degree of agreement about the nature of the problems, but could not agree to specific steps to put them right. In particular the Economic and Social Council remained unreformed, and the system still lacked any central manager.

The efforts of the 1970s, therefore, led to the adding of further items to the agenda of reform rather than to useful improvement: the goal of achieving more effective management was added to that of adjustment to new tasks. The

Bertrand Reports of 1984 on the supply of information in the system and of December 1985 on institutional arrangements, essentially added new dimensions to these themes. The main contribution was the incisive criticism of an approach which was seen to have become too narrowly focused on particular sectors, at the expense of integrated programmes, and the corresponding need to deal with operations within subregions where they could be more effectively coordinated and managed. The 1970s proposals tried to strengthen the role of the centre: Bertrand's 1985 Report argued that this was inpracticable and that, although there should be a central economic United Nations which dealt with research and provided a general overview of the problems, the practical work on the ground should be done through common arrangements by groups of contiguous states.[14] It is difficult and, indeed, unnecessary to convey here the admirable range and depth of critical insight found in the Bertrand and earlier reports; but, again, the resulting practical achievement was minimal. A further subheading was added to the agenda for reform.

It was in this context, however, that a third phase of the reform process was instigated as a result of the United States pressures on the budgetary process. In February 1986 a group of High-Level Intergovernmental Experts was set up by the General Assembly to be appointed by the President of the General Assembly.[15] The eighteen experts were selected from the world's major regions and subregions, and were chaired by Tom Vraalsen of Norway. Maurice Bertrand was also one of its members. In August 1986 this group, which became known as the Committee of Eighteen, produced a report in the form of a 'Review of the efficiency of the Administrative and Financial Functioning of the United Nations'.[16] This added a new dimension to the agenda of reform: that of achieving greater efficiency in the use of resources. This time, unlike on previous occasions, the budgetary imperative was paramount. It did not supplant the other items on the agenda but rather led to their being approached from this new perspective.

At the time of writing it seemed that this report had given a new impetus to the reform process and it is, therefore, now necessary to look in greater detail at the diagnoses and prescriptions which it contained with regard, first, to the budgetary process and, then, to the institutional and administrative arrangements. The central argument, however, is that the Americans, with the possible but unadmitted collusion of other major contributing states, saw the reform process in 1987 as an opportunity not only for reforming the budget and rationalising the procedures in the economic and social areas, but also for strengthening their own control. It involved a strategy for countering the voting strength in the General Assembly of the newer, smaller states. The latter had in the eyes of the major contributors too often pushed through decisions in policies and arrangements for which they did not pay.

The Committee concluded that the budgetary arrangements, as they had emerged since the major reforms of the early 1970s, contained two major inter-related weaknesses: first, the various claims for money were not being closely scrutinised in the context of any overall plan which included goals and priorities, in this case the Medium Term Plan — intended to cover a six-year period;

second, the Medium Term Plan was itself not being drawn up by the governments in such detail as would have allowed them a full appreciation of what
needed to be done, and encouraged their greater commitment to the stated and
implicit goals. 'The 6-year medium term plan should reflect the consolidated
objectives and goals of member states, and should constitute the principal policy
directive of the United Nations' (Paragraph 58). But the 'text of the medium
term plan, like the programme budget, is prepared by the Secretariat in a form
which is almost final, and member states have neither the means nor the time
to undertake major changes in the draft medium term plan' (Paragraph 66).

The Budget statement itself 'in fact . . . is merely the financial compilation
of a number of decisions and recommendations taken by a large number of intergovernmental bodies and interpreted in the various departments and divisions in
the Secretariat' (Paragraph 67). Its relationship with the plan was admirably
captured in the following comments, which though expressed in discreet and
measured tones, were a savage indictment of the budgetary process:

priority setting in the medium term plan takes place at the sub-programme level, while
resource estimates are provided at the major programme level . . . consequently there
is no clear linkage between priority setting and resource requirements, either in the
medium term plan or in the programme budget. [Paragraph 63]

Budget decisions were, of course, eventually ratified by the General Assembly,
and recommendations made by the Fifth Committee; at various stages, as
already indicated, there was ample opportunity for comment. But 'no central
organ really monitors the overall conception of the plan on such occasions'
(Paragraph 67(b)). Indeed, the opposite tended to happen: claims for expenditure at the subprogramme level tended in effect to lead to modifications every
two years of the medium term plan.

It was as if a tailor were to alter his measuring tape if he found the suit of
clothes were too small! Claims for additional expenditure, from the Secretary-
General and elsewhere, were also hard to resist, and this led to frequent
supplementary budgets. The budgetary process was, therefore, vulnerable to the
accusation that it allowed the poorer 'spending' states to exert continuing
pressure in favour of the uncontrolled expansion of the budget. This was another
feature of the system which the major contributing states resented.

The Committee was prepared to accept that 'over the past 15 years, the
General Assembly had established principles, methods and instruments which
should have made it possible to reach satisfactory results in this area' (Paragraph
58). Nevertheless, the budgetary procedures had caused major problems. In the
words of the Committee:

the Secretariat prepares the programme budget itself: the budget division sends the
budgetary directives around June of the year preceding the year in which the General
Assembly votes on the budget. Preparations last about 11 months; in May of the following year, the Committee for Programme and Coordination, on the one hand, and the
Advisory Committee on Administrative and Budgetary Questions on the other, begin
reviewing the programme budget: the former examines the programme content while the
latter examines the administrative and financial aspects of the programme budget, after
which the two committees submit their reports so that the Assembly can begin its

consideration of the programme budget in September and complete it by the end of the year. The opportunities which the two above-mentioned committees have for recommending modifications in the content of the programme budget are very slight and relate almost entirely to details, because the Secretariat tends to consider the submission of budget fascicles [*sic*] to be practically definitive. [Paragraph 67(c)]

Three problems may be found in the budgetary procedure as described above, one of which was made explicit in the Report, a second which was implicit in it, and one which was only indirectly considered there, but which has been widely discussed in other reports and studies on the coordination procedures in the United Nations. The first was the obvious point that the Secretariat dominated the early stages of the process, and took the determination of the budget to a point at which it was difficult to unravel it for close examination by the monitoring groups and committees. In addition there was naturally a certain hesitation about returning to ground already covered, especially as this could be at the risk of offending colleagues in the Secretariat. The powers of socialisation processes in bureaucracies should not be underestimated!

Secondly, however, the dividing line between the responsibilities of the ACABQ and the CPC was not entirely clear. The former was made up of experts and its mandate was of a technical nature with regard to finance and administration. There is a line to be drawn between judgements of a political nature, concerning the kinds of goals to be pursued, and those of a technical kind, concerning appropriate mechanisms and judgements about the best use of available resources. But the frontier between the two is hard to draw precisely: knowing the extent of its mandate was made more difficult for the ACABQ by the fact that its monitoring partner, the CPC, was an intergovernmental committee and, therefore, nominally with greater authority. Conversely, the CPC, though its role was monitoring the coordination of programmes and shaping the Medium Term Plan, was somewhat uncertain of its mandate. The net result was a kind of 'after you, Cecil' problem. This was, however, reflected in the judgements of the Committee of Eighteen when it came to its recommendations: members were divided about how far the role of either should be expanded or protected.

The third problem concerned the respective status of the ACABQ and the CPC, a question not addressed directly in the Committee of Eighteen's report. In reality the ACABQ had greater authority and a much superior reputation compared with the CPC, despite the difficulties which undoubtedly existed in the way of its increasing the effectiveness of its supervision. One indication of these was the increasing tendency for the Fifth Committee of the General Assembly to restore items which had not been recommended; another was the Secretary-General's habit of insisting upon budgetary supplements which it opposed. Its work was certainly facilitated by the fact that it was not intended closely to examine and comment upon — critically or otherwise — the declared objectives and policies of the member governments. Rather it was to check the financial aspects of the pursuit of those policies: in the central system this amounted to evaluating 'the Secretary-General's financial and administrative proposals for giving effect to those decisions'.[17]

The authority of the ACABQ was enhanced by a number of other considerations.

Its sixteen members were elected by the General Assembly in their individual capacity. Though each of the groups of states was to be represented, candidates were normally chosen by consensus on the basis of their individual expertise, and it was rare for the General Assembly to be asked to choose between rivals. The one exception to this was the Western European group within which there was sometimes disagreement about whose name to put forward, in recent years mainly between the British and the French. In 1987 the French were represented but not the British; the United States, the Soviet Union and the Japanese were invariably present, and accordingly its composition gave particular weight to the major contributors.[18]

Experts are, of course, not necessarily non-political. In this case, however, they were encouraged to be less so by the convention that their meetings, unlike those of the CPC, were held in camera. The chairmen of the Committee were also individually distinguished and in office for an unusually long period: there had been only four chairmen since the Committee was created in 1946, and the incumbent in 1987, M. Msele from Tanzania, had been in office for ten years. The Committee was in fact the oldest such committee created by the General Assembly. In addition its secretariat, though drawn from the main UN Secretariat, was independent from it in the sense that its head was not under the instructions of the Secretary-General. He was responsible solely to the Committee and through that to the General Assembly. It was for these various reasons that the ACABQ acquired a considerable reputation and its forty or so reports a year had, with a few exceptions, been treated with respect. This explains the preference of a number of governments and commentators for attempting to solve the problems of the budgetary process by extending and reinforcing the role of the ACABQ rather than by reforming the CPC.

In contrast the history of the CPC was somewhat chequered, though it is essential to be aware of the details of the make-up of the Committee as they are crucial for understanding and interpreting the later US strategy. The Committee was established in 1962, but its current role was not made specific until 1969: legislation then provided that the Committee should function as the main subsidiary organ of ECOSOC and the Assembly for planning programming and coordination.

In particular the Committee is charged with reviewing the programme of the United Nations as defined in the medium term plan, recommending an order of priorities among programmes, giving guidance to the Secretariat on translating legislation into programmes, developing evaluation procedures, making recommendations on work programmes . . . in the light of the need to avoid overlapping and duplication . . .[19]

After 1970 it consisted of twenty-one members, elected by the General Assembly on the nomination of ECOSOC, on the basis of equitable geographical distribution, namely five African, four Asian, four Latin American, three East European, and five West European and other members. The latter group naturally included the United States and the British. It was to meet for six weeks in 'plan' years and four weeks in 'budget' years. The practice was for its decisions to be taken on the basis of consensus, a point which should be carefully noted in view of later developments.

The CPC suffered, however, from several weaknesses and as a result failed to carry out its assigned functions satisfactorily. It suffered from insufficient and inappropriate information; hence the earlier rearrangement of the Secretariat to provide COPAS, which, however, only partially solved the problem. There remained a lack of substantial comprehensive evaluative materials. The CPC also failed to establish its status in relations with other institutions: the ACC also played a supervisory role and dealt with the CPC with such reluctance that mutual relations were described as a 'dialogue of the deaf'.[20] As already mentioned, the limits of its competence in comparison with the ACABQ were also unclear, though this was a case of uncertainty rather than hostility. But perhaps the central problem was that its staff were never of a sufficient calibre, or from sufficiently senior positions in member governments, to allow it to develop any degree of independent muscle. It usually met at the level of second-secretary; it also had a reputation for being overconcerned with minutiae, as in early 1987 when it allegedly spent two days deciding whether it would in future meet for two weeks or three. In its joint meetings with ACC it, therefore, suffered a serious 'status deficit'. This explains 32/197's recommendations that the supporting committees of ECOSOC should be abolished and their functions taken over by the Council itself, where, possibly, more senior people could be persuaded to participate.[21] At least this would avoid the repetition of discussions in the CPC and the full Council, which was characteristic of the existing arrangements. In the budgetary process as it had evolved by the late 1980s, the failure of governments to play an effective role in shaping the Medium Term Plan and the lack of a rational reconciliation of resources and programmes were, therefore, also attributable to the fact that these crucial functions had been entrusted to a weak reed.

The Committee of Eighteen also pointed to weaknesses in two other areas, though it is not necessary to go into great detail here about these. The personnel policies of the organisation were severely criticised. Problems included a lack of training, a disillusionment about promotion prospects, and especially excessive numbers at more senior levels. The point was made that there had been too many appointments at the level of Under-Secretary-General, and it was implied that member governments did not necessarily regard administrative talent as a condition of emplacement. The Committee also did not point out that much of this expansion had taken place during the tenure of Kurt Waldheim as Secretary-General! There were twenty-eight posts at this level: 'today's structure is both too top heavy and too complex' (Paragraph 32). Many of these personnel criticisms had been made before. Indeed, Shirley Hazzard produced a pungent attack on staffing policies in the early 1970s.[22] The point was also made by the Committee that 'the present organisational structure is too fragmented with 9 political and 11 economic and social departments' leading to a 'duplication of work' and a 'diffusion of responsibility'. Another area where problems were detected, though it was essentially a similar weakness to the previous one, though on a larger scale, was in the structure of the United Nations economic and social organisation: '. . . expansion in the agenda has led to a parallel growth in the intergovernmental machinery, which had in some cases resulted in duplication of agendas and work, particularly in the economic and social fields' (Paragraph 16).

The earlier discussion has shown that the personnel and structural problems were recognised in a number of earlier reports and studies. An element which was new in 1986–7, and which added a new dynamic to the reform process, was that the pressure for reform now derived primarily from the need to save money and not other pressures, such as the need to adjust to new tasks or to be more effective. The Americans had made this the case. Another new element was that in the process of seeking reforms to the perceived problems the Americans found an opportunity for pressing for changes which they thought would give power to the payer. This strategy will now be considered in the context of the specific reforms which were proposed and initiated.

The Committee put forward three sets of proposals on the reform of the budgetary process and the drawing up of the medium term plan. The first two sets were fairly detailed and in most respects were rather similar. They both sought to strengthen the role of the CPC, though the second saw this more as a matter of fully implementing its existing terms of reference, whilst the first reckoned that these might also need to be 'adjusted'. Both were concerned to persuade the governments to recognise the importance of the CPC's work by appointing people on the basis of their 'technical competence and professional experience' (Paragraphs 34 and 31). Both proposals also held that the CPC should 'take part in the planning and budget procedures from the very beginning and throughout the process' (Paragraphs 29 and 32). It should 'consider and make recommendations to the General Assembly on priorities among the programmes' and a 'calendar of procedures' in these consultations was to be drawn up by the Secretary-General after consultation with governments and the institutions involved. The key role of the CPC with regard to the medium term plan was to be recognised.

The first two sets of proposals were also in agreement about the need for a new timetable for making the programme budget. An outline budget was to be prepared by the Secretary-General in the spring of the non-budget year, with an indication of the resources which the Secretary-General expected to be available, and advice and recommendations then tended to the General Assembly through the Fifth Committee. Decisions taken then would guide the Secretary-General in initiating a second stage of the process in the budget year. This time round the draft budget would again be subject to examination, recommendations, formulations, and then the whole referred back to the Assembly for decision. The first two sets of proposals did, however, differ in the respective roles which were to be allowed to the CPC and the ACABQ in the process of giving advice and making recommendations in the budget. The first clearly implied that the CPC would have the lead role in advising the Assembly, though it would take into account the advice of the ACABQ: this was the measure of the expected 'adjustments'. With regard to the budget process, the second set of proposals saw the two bodies as having responsibility in particular fields — in federalist fashion, 'independent' but 'coordinate' — each advising the Assembly separately in those fields. The Secretary-General was to send the outline budget and the draft budget to both the CPC and the ACABQ: in the first set of proposals the budgets were to be addressed to the CPC alone. The second set reflected an anxiety about not downgrading the ACABQ, which had acquired a considerable reputation over the years, though this was at the risk of losing effective leadership by one or other institution in the budget process.

The third set of proposals seemed to reflect this fear in a somewhat exaggerated way though it also showed evidence of United States views. It asserted bluntly that the distinction between the functions of the ACABQ and the CPC were unreal, and that the new CPC should perform both. It also held that decisions about the resources which would be available for the coming biennium should be taken by the CPC in its new form *before* the Secretary-General began work on the outline budget: he would be informed about 'the amount of resources that member states can and are prepared to make available to the organisation' (Paragraph 35). One implication of this, of course, was that the established policies and programmes of the United Nations, which the Secretary-General could be expected to wish to support, and which would form a basis for his budgetary calculations, could in this arrangement be altered in the light of quite unrelated national financial considerations. In other words, the Medium Term Plan would, in the system resulting from these proposals, be no better a guide for budgetary planning than in the older, inefficient one. All three sets of proposals agreed, however, that once the budget had been approved it should no longer be exceeded by special, supplementary budgets: within a biennium 'additional expenditures resulting from legislative decisions . . . must be accommodated within the budget level decided upon by the General Assembly' (Paragraph 34). The size of a contingency fund — called a financial envelope — was placed at 2 per cent of the total budget, but clearly the Committee recognised that the adding of extra items to the agreed budget in an uncontrolled way, a habit about which the ACABQ had long complained, would have to be stopped. By implication the third set of proposals also accepted the new timetable outlined in the other two.

Up to the time of writing, May 1987, two sets of decisions had been taken to implement the recommendations of the Committee of Eighteen. First, the General Assembly, after a debate which was described as tense, even cliffhanging, adopted a Resolution on the 18 December 1986, which introduced a new budgetary procedure, requested that the Secretary-General should reduce the number of his staff and that the Administrative and Financial functioning of the United Nations should be reviewed.[23] Second, in February 1987 the Economic and Social Council decided to conduct an 'in-depth study of the United Nations inter-governmental structures and functions in the economic and social fields',[24] with a view to implementing, in particular, Recommendation 8 of the Report of the Committee of Eighteen. This suggested that the arrangements of, *inter alia*, UNCTAD, UNDP, UNFPA, UNEP and UNICEF be examined with a view to their 'rationalisation'. Recommendation 8(3) even referred to the possibility of 'merging existing bodies in order to improve their work'! But all existing organisations were enjoined to submit 'within 30 days' their proposals for internal restructuring.[25] Such an approach seemed unusually energetic and ambitious by the standards of the United Nations: the final report resulting from the in-depth study was to be available for the Economic and Social Council to consider at its second regular session for 1988. It remained to be seen what the net outcome of these efforts would be, but the United Nations had probably never been closer to closing down some of its offices. There was now an unusual head of steam behind the reform process and a considerable effort would be required to resist it.

It might be mentioned also, that the Secretary-General had acted upon the Committee of Eighteen's proposals on staffing: the cut of 15 per cent within three years recommended in Recommendation 15 (2a) was very much in view, as was the proposed reduction of 25 per cent in the number of posts at the level of Under-Secretary and Assistant Secretary-General, requested in Recommendation 15 (2b). No doubt the Secretary-General was not entirely averse to the latter. Reductions were, however, more the result of 'wastage' than planning, and there were reports that staffing problems had arisen as a result. The budgetary process agreed on 18 December 1986 could be seen as a compromise between the Committee of Eighteen's first and second sets of proposals. It rejected the proposal in the third set that the CPC should determine in advance the resources available, but accepted the CPC's primary role in considering the Secretary-General's outline budget and proffering advice on it to the General Assembly in the 'off-budget' years. In the budget years, however, after the budget had been reconsidered by the Assembly, and turned into firm proposals by the Secretary-General, it would be forwarded to both the CPC and the ACABQ which were to advise the Fifth Committee 'in accordance with their respective mandates'. The Resolution also accepted the various proposals concerning the upgrading of the CPC and it looked as though it would now be a more formidable institution, expected to play a key role in relating the budgetary proposals to the Medium Term Plan, and in shaping the latter. It was to be involved from the beginning in the process of shaping the budget. In other words it was accepted that the CPC would be the principal 'advisory' and 'intergovernmental' committee on these matters.

In view of this, one particular decision in the resolution attracted particular attention, and was regarded as a break-through by United States officials. This was the agreement in Paragraph 6 that the CPC should 'continue its existing practice of reaching decisions by consensus'.[26] Paragraph 7 took this further with the stipulation that 'all possible efforts' should be made in the Fifth Committee 'with a view to establishing the broadest possible agreement'. The argument seemed to be that though consensus had been the established way of reaching agreement before the reforms, this was not significant as long as the CPC's role was modest. With the development of that role, however, there was a greater risk that voting would take place, and lines drawn between the larger number of smaller contributors, and the smaller number of larger contributors. Conversely, the requirement of consensus would greatly increase the leverage which could be exercised by the major contributing states over the others. The client states would be more frequently placed in a situation in which either they concurred with the contributing states, or they risked losing the latter's funds. The consensus approach, in other words, was viewed as a weapon in the hands of the rich which could be used to get the poor states to accept the discipline of the Medium Term Plan. The rich states would also, however, have been able to play a decisive role in shaping the Medium Term Plan in the CPC: decisions in that process would also be taken on the basis of consensus. There is evidence to suggest that the US administration, or at least, officials within it, regarded these arrangements as largely satisfying the demands made at the time of the Kassebaum amendment, and that they were now prepared to make approaches to Congress, with a view to restoring full funding to the UN system.[27]

It is not, of course, that the CPC could be sure that its budgetary proposals would be accepted by the Fifth Committee or the General Assembly. But the richer states could be expected to exercise greater authority in the smaller CPC. The question of whether insisting upon consensus voting was compatible with the Charter — that it was legal — also remained to be examined. The appeal for consensus in the Fifth Committee would only marginally reduce the chances of adverse votes. A more important disincentive, however, would be that it would be more difficult and, from the point of view of the poor states, even dangerous to unravel a carefully structured budget, relating resources to priorities, monetary commitments to programmes and intentions, which had already been agreed in the CPC. It was, therefore, more a question of tipping the balance of probabilities in favour of the richer states, of making it easier for them to lead and more difficult for the poorer states not to follow, rather than one of eliminating opposition. It would be a matter of management, not of control.

It is, however, arguable that the financial weapon, as used by the United States, was likely to prove a powerful incentive for the more general reform of the United Nations system. The report of the Committee of Eighteen itself exemplified this. The proposed changes in the budgetary process may be seen as attempts at institutionalising in the United Nations arrangements the ability of the rich to use the financial weapon to press on a continuing basis for reforms which they preferred. In other words, they were aimed at in effect incorporating the Kassebaum amendment informally into the United Nations Charter. The discrepancy between voting power and financial power, which had long irritated the United States, was to be reduced. That this prospect was in the minds of US officials was revealed by their view that improving the budgetary process in the central system was only the beginning of the reform effort. The agenda, no longer hidden, was for similar reforms to be introduced into all the Specialised Agencies: they were all to be required to accept consensus voting in their key budgetary committees as a condition of full funding. Even the International Labour Organisation, which was regarded as having reformed its budgetary arrangements after the 1978 US withdrawal, was nevertheless to be deprived of funds unless and until the consensus procedure had been introduced. This was the position taken by US officials in the summer of 1987. Consensus became the practical alternative in US eyes to weighted voting.

There are obviously a number of distinctive features about the reform process in the United Nations in the period 1986–7. The reduction of funding, and the threat to cut further, stimulated a more energetic effort to change than had been seen before. But, as the crisis developed, opportunities for going beyond the list of potential reforms, which had emerged over the years seemed to be recognised, though these took forms that were not apparent in the Kassebaum amendment. It remained to be seen whether consensus could be a functional alternative to weighted voting and, indeed, whether the planned reforms would be achieved. There certainly emerged, however, a US strategy for change. The cynic might be forgiven for wondering how far a concerted strategy for change had emerged which involved not only the Americans but also the other major contributing states, such as the British, the Japanese or the West Germans. After all, the contributing governments consult each other fairly closely, and on a routine basis, about the level of their funding of the various international arrangements, in particular through the so-called Geneva Group which exists in the various UN capitals with the exception of New York. By the time of writing, no specific evidence that these other states were involved had, however, emerged.

Postscript

By November 1987 the picture described above had changed only in a few details. It had become evident that the process of staff reduction had been carried out on the basis of 'attrition', i.e. not filling vacancies resulting from retirement, rather than in the light of a rational management strategy. This was in flat contradiction of the stipulation in A/41/L.49, that staff reductions should be carried out 'with flexibility in order to avoid, *inter alia*, negative impact on programmes'.

Furthermore, the meetings of CPC in September–October 1987 did not employ the consensus principle. Members disagreed about a number of matters including the level of the contingency fund. It was pointed out, however, that the period 1987–8 was essentially transitional, and that the new arrangements were to be introduced in the autumn of 1988.

There was, however, the view that the acceptance of the new arrangements had been part of the bargain, the other side of which was a return by the Americans to full funding. The administration in Washington now seemed to favour this, but Congress was divided on the issue and not disposed to treat it with any sense of urgency. The Senate was in favour of a higher level of funding than the House, but for both the matter was small-been compared with the budgetary crisis in the United States. It looked unlikely, in view of the current strains upon the United States finances, that any serious effort could be made for the time being to find more money for the United Nations.

Nevertheless, there was still a strong sense that this was a turning point in the history of the United Nations. Continuing funding shortfalls encouraged the various efforts to adjust and reform.

Notes

1. 'Jackson Report': R.G.A. Jackson, 1969, *A Study of the Capacity of the United Nations Development System*, Geneva, UN Doc. DP/5 1969; Joint Inspection Unit, 1985, *Some Reflections on Reform of the United Nations*, prepared by Maurice Bertrand, JIU/REP/85/9, Geneva.
2. 32/197 Section 11; contained in UNGA Official Records, Thirty-Second Session,

Supplement No. 45 (A./32/45) Sept.–Dec. 1977 at pp. 121–7.

3. For an assessment of the impact, see Douglas Williams, 1987, *The Specialized Agencies and the United Nations: the System in Crisis*, London, Hurst.

4. For an account of reactions to developing states' claims regarding development, see Craig N. Murphy, 1983, 'What the Third World want', *International Studies Quarterly*, vol. 27, pp. 55–76.

5. Figures from an internal US administration document marked IRM: 6 November 1986.

6. See the critical evaluations of the United Nations produced by the Heritage Foundation, such as *Africa is Starving and the United Nations is to Blame*, written by Roger A. Brooks, for *Backgrounder: A United Nations Assessment Project Study*, Washington, DC, the Heritage Foundation, 14 January 1986.

7. See Evan Luard, 1979, *The United Nations: How It Works and What It Does*, London, Macmillan, pp. 130–1.

8. Evan Luard, ibid., p. 133.

9. Latter figure from *Report of the Group of High-Level Intergovernmental Experts to Review the Efficiency of the Administrative and Financial Functioning of the United Nations*, G.A. Official Records; Forty-first Session, Supplement No. 49 (A/41/49), New York 1986 (henceforth called *Report of Committee of Eighteen*); former figures from Luard, op.cit., p. 113.

10. See the excellent account of these developments in Arthur Kilgore, 1986, 'Cut down in the crossfire', *International Relations*, vol. VIII, no. 6, November, pp. 592–610.

11. Interview with officials, US Mission to the UN, April 1987.

12. For a close examination of the role of *ad hoc* conferences and G.A. Special Sessions, see Paul Taylor and A.J. Groom, 1988, *Global Issues in the United Nations Framework*, London, Macmillan, forthcoming.

13. *Report of Group of Experts*, E/AC 62/9, United Nations, New York, 1975.

14. See Note 1.

15. In G.A. Res. 40/237, 18 December 1985.

16. See Note 9: *Report of Committee of Eighteen*.

17. Martin Hill, 1978, *The United Nations System: Coordinating Its Economic and Social Work*, Cambridge, Cambridge University Press, p. 66.

18. Information about ACABQ was obtained in interviews with officials from its Secretariat, October and November 1987.

19. New Zealand Ministry of Foreign Affairs, *United Nations Handbook, 1986*, Wellington, New Zealand, p. 66.

20. Joint Inspection Unit, *Reporting to the Economic and Social Council*, JIU/REP/84/7, Geneva, 1984, p. 16, para. 35.

21. A/32/197, loc. cit., Section II, see Note 2.

22. Shirley Hazzard, 1973, *Defeat of an Ideal: A Study of the Self-Destruction of the United Nations*, Boston, Atlantic Monthly Press.

23. General Assembly, A/41/L.49, 18 December 1986, Section I, Para. I.

24. ECOSOC, E/1987/INF/2, Para. I.

25. ibid., sub-paragraph i.

26. A/41/L.49, Section I.

27. Interviews with US Officials, Geneva, April 1987.

Recommended reading

Houshang Ameri, 1982, *Politics and Process in the Specialized Agencies of the United Nations*, Aldershot, Gower.
Douglas Williams, 1987, *The Specialized Agencies and the United Nations: the System in Crisis*, London, Hurst.

List of contributors

Maurice Bertrand was a Member of the French Cour des Comptes from 1945 to 1982, and a Member of the Joint Inspection Unit of the UN System from 1968 to 1985. In 1986 he was a Member of the Group of Experts to review the efficiency of the functioning of the UN. He has written numerous articles and reports on the UN system.

George A. Codding, Jr is a Professor of Political Science at the University of Colorado. He is on the Board of Directors of the Master of Science in Telecommunications, the Center for International Relations and the Center for Space and Geosciences Policy at that institution. Professor Codding is the author of *The International Telecommunication Union* and co-author with Anthony M. Rutkowski of *The International Telecommunication Union in a Changing World*.

George Foggon CMG, OBE, joined the British Ministry of Labour in the 1930s. After war service he was seconded to the Military Government of Berlin with responsibilities for labour and trade-union affairs. In 1949 he transferred to the Colonial Office and served six years in West Africa on loan from Whitehall, including four years as Federal Commissioner of Labour, Nigeria. He was appointed Labour Advisor to the Secretary of State for the Colonies in 1958, later to the Foreign and Commonwealth Office. From 1976 to 1982 he was Director of the London Office of the ILO.

A.J.R. Groom is Professor of International Relations at the University of Kent at Canterbury and Co-Director of the Centre for the Analysis of Conflict. He has written widely in the area of international organisation with Paul Taylor. He has also published books and articles in the fields of strategic studies, conflict research and international relations theory.

Mark Imber is a lecturer in International Relations at the University of St Andrews. He received his first degree from the University of London, and from Southampton. He has published several articles in the fields of international organisation and nuclear proliferation, and is currently engaged on a study of the United States' relations with the UN specialised agencies.

Randolph C. Kent is a Visiting Research Fellow at the Refugee Studies Programme, Queen Elizabeth House, University of Oxford, and Director of the School of International Relations (United Kingdom Graduate Program),

University of South California. From 1982 to 1985, he led a project on 'Disasters, Disaster Relief and the International System', funded by the Economic and Social Research Council, and in 1986 was awarded a Nuffield Foundation grant to evaluate the performance of the UN Office for Emergency Operations in Africa. He compiles the annual 'Disaster Monitor' for *Third World Affairs*, and is the Review Editor for the *Journal of Refugee Studies*.

Anthony Mango O.B.E. spent twenty-seven years working for the United Nations Secretariat. From 1970 to 1983 he was the head of the secretariat of the Advisory Committee on Administrative and Budgetary Questions, the financial watch-dog committee of the United Nations General Assembly. From 1983 until his retirement at the end of February 1987 he was head of the United Nations Joint Staff Pension Fund.

James Mayall is Reader in International Relations at the London School of Economics. He has written extensively on the politics of international economic relations, on the theory of international relations and on Africa. He edited and contributed to *The Community of States* (Allen and Unwin, 1982).

Paul Taylor is Senior Lecturer in International Relations at the London School of Economics and Political Science. He has written about the European Communities, and about general international organisation, in the latter field editing a number of books with A.J.R. Groom.

Peter Willetts is a Lecturer in International Relations at City University, London, specialising in the Third World and international organisations. His publications include *The Non-Aligned Movement, The Non-Aligned in Havana, Pressure Groups in the Global System* and (with Barry Jones) *Interdependence on Trial*.

Andrew Williams received his first degree from the University of Keele in Staffordshire and a doctorate from the University of Geneva in Switzerland. While in Geneva he worked for the Graduate Institute of International Studies and the Centre for Applied Studies in International Negotiations. At the latter he worked on issues related to the United Nations. He is currently a lecturer in international relations at the University of Kent. He has written on various aspects of the history of East–West relations, revolutionary foreign policy and international organisation.

Index